Predicates and Terms in Functional Grammar

A.M. Bolkestein
C. de Groot
J.L. Mackenzie (eds.)

1985
FORIS PUBLICATIONS
Dordrecht - Holland/Cinnaminson - U.S.A.

Published by:
Foris Publications Holland
P.O. Box 509
3300 AM Dordrecht, The Netherlands

Sole distributor for the U.S.A. and Canada:
Foris Publications U.S.A.
P.O. Box C-50
Cinnaminson N.J. 08077
U.S.A.

CIP-data

ISBN 90 6765 104 4 (Paper)

Printed in the Netherlands by ICG Printing, Dordrecht.

Foreword

Functional Grammar (FG) was first presented as an overall theory of the system-
aticity of language use in Dik (1978). Since the publication of that book, Simon
Dik and a growing number of collaborators, not only in The Netherlands but
throughout the world, have been working on the extension and refinement of the
theory. The present volume offers thirteen contributions to this effort, all of
which have arisen from papers given to the Colloquium on Functional Grammar held
in Amsterdam, 4-8 June 1984. The thirteen chapters share a concern with the
major constituent elements of predications, namely predicates and terms.

   In Functional Grammar, the lexicon of each language is held to consist of a
list of predicates (contentive lexemes), stored in the form of predicate-frames
which contain all requisite information on the phonological and morphological
properties of the predicate, its syntactic category, its semantic valency and
the selection restrictions it imposes on its arguments. Each predicate designates
a set of states of affairs (Actions, Positions, Processes, States) in such a way
that the total lexicon indicates much of how its users (the speakers of the
relevant language) conceptualize ambient reality. This virtual relation between
predicate and designatum achieves greater concreteness in the assemblage of
actual utterances by means of the creation of a predication, i.e. the attribution
of predicate operators indicating tense, aspect, mood, etc. and the insertion of
terms into the argument slots opened by the predicate. These terms are themselves
formed from predicates and invite the Addressee to identify one or more referents
that satisfy the description offered by those predicates. Information relevant to
this task, concerning definiteness, proximateness, number, genericness, etc., is
made available in the form of term operators. Each term bears a semantic function
(Agent, Goal, Recipient, ...) and may, through the assignment of syntactic
functions (Subject, Object) and pragmatic functions (Topic, Focus, ...), come to
play further roles within the predication: these functions are expressed in
various ways, notably by means of relators (adpositions, subordinators, ...).
For a full treatment of the organization of a Functional Grammar, the reader
should consult Dik (1978, 1980a); for further reading on syntactic and pragmatic
functions, see Bolkestein et al. eds. *Syntax and Pragmatics in Functional Grammar*
(1985), the companion to this volume.

The lexicon contains only those predicates which cannot be formed by productive rules from other predicates. Thus, in English, child$_N$ is found in the lexicon,
but childlike$_A$, created by the regular suffixing of *-like* to the noun *child*, is
said to be a derived predicate, and the rule whereby it is formed is called a
predicate formation rule. The chapters by Dik, Mackenzie, Vet and De Groot deal
with various aspects of predicate formation rules. Dik considers two such rules,
First Argument Reduction and Causative Predicate Formation, as well as the
phenomenon of nominalization, with especial reference to the expression of the
derived predications that result. He shows that derived constructions will tend
to model their formal expression on non-derived constructions, proposing
'prototypical expression models' for each type of predication; he further demonstrates that a derived construction will tend to adopt the semantic properties
of the relevant non-derived construction. In the case of argument reduction,
this leads to a deactualization of the meaning of the input. Dik contrasts the
consequences of his approach for the analysis of causativization with Comrie's
'relational theory' and Cole's 'semantic theory'. As for nominalizations, Dik
provides expression rules (for Dutch) which account for the tendency for embedded
predicates, if non-finite, to model their expression on that of nominal terms. A
somewhat different view is taken by Mackenzie, who suggests that nominalization
should be analysed as involving a predicate formation rule, specifically a
category-changing form of valency reduction. Supporting his analysis with data
from Aguacatec and Labrador Inuttut, he shows that his approach provides an
account of productive nominalizations in English, and in particular of the form
taken by such constructions in actual discourse. Vet argues that the passive in
French, rather than merely resulting from the assignment of the Subject function
to the Goal argument, is also the result of a valency-reducing predicate formation rule. He goes on to consider the formation of reflexive predicates, which,
he claims, can best be regarded as involving a form of argument incorporation.
Vet's analysis of causative predicates is like Dik's in assuming predicate formation, but differs in taking causativization to bring about a shift in the
semantic function of the causee. De Groot's chapter seeks to inhibit any tendency
to overuse the powerful mechanism of predicate formation rules by establishing
criteria for distinguishing between instances of the same predicate having more
than one representation and instances of truly different predicates. Having
considered the nature of the set of states of affairs designated by the predi-
cate(s) in question with respect to the features Dynamism, Momentaneousness,
Control and Telicity, De Groot proposes criteria for distinguishing predicates.
These are then applie to various instances of *meg*-prefixation in Hungarian: it

is shown that predicate formation is involved in only some of the cases. De Groot thus also makes a contribution to delimiting the domain of derivational morphology.

The distinction between derivational and inflectional morphology is central to Watters' chapter. The major claim is that the distinction, which has proved problematic in many grammatical models, follows naturally from the organization of a Functional Grammar: derivational morphology reflects processes in the fund, i.e. the aggregate of all predicate-frames and terms, basic or derived, while inflectional morphology results from the application of expression rules. Inasmuch as the fund and the expression rules stand at 'opposite ends' of the FG model, the two types of morphology are rigorously demarcated. Watters illustrates his approach with reference to the Western Ejagham language, devoting detailed attention to the matter of rule ordering in inflectional morphology. In the next chapter, Fortescue takes issue with the need for unidirectional rule ordering in his investigation of 'anaphoric agreement' in Aleut. He demonstrates that the agreement phenomena in that language can be accounted for only in a model that permits reference to pragmatic functions, specifically Theme and Topic. Fortescue recurrently compares Aleut with Eskimo, claiming that the ergativity of the latter is historically derived not from an earlier 'nominative' system, as has been posited for many ergative languages, but from a system akin to that manifested by present-day Aleut. His chapter furthermore provides support for the anaphoric term operator 'A' that has been tentatively added to the repertoire originally proposed in Dik (1978).

A radical extension of the repertoire of term operators is proposed by Brown in a defence of Functional Grammar as a theory of reference. His proposals are based on the assumption that the Speaker, in using a term, is making reference to a set or members thereof. He shows that the class of term operators required to give an account of all the possibilities offered by the English language is definable, with only minimal additions, in terms of set theory. In this way, Brown puts forward criteria for the identification of term operators across languages. The chapters by Limburg and Kahrel are concerned with another language-universal aspect of the grammar of terms, namely the expression, by means of 'relators', of their relation to the predicate with which they are associated. Limburg considers Dik's definition of relator, and argues for a stricter understanding in terms of head-dependent relations. An examination of genitival constructions from a representative sample of thirty languages offers support for the principles governing the placement of relators, provided, that is, that relators are, in accordance with the new definition that is proposed,

analysed as marking dependents rather than heads. Limburg concludes by considering the possibility that relators may never be referential and that the original
definition should be modified to incorporate this. Kahrel also addresses the
typological adequacy of the notion 'relator', with reference to the marking of
embedded questions. He concludes, again on the basis of a cross-linguistic
sample, that the word-order principles governing relator placement are borne out
if they are extended to cover not only syntactic but also secondary relators.
The former are ordinary relators that occupy the position predicted for them by
Dik's word-order principles, while the latter are elements that occupy a relator
slot left open as a result of the position of syntactic relators being determined
by other principles.

The four remaining chapters, by Shiratsuki, Goossens, Van der Auwera and
Junger, offer language-specific investigations of predicates and predicate formation. Shiratsuki examines two related constructions in Basque, which she iden-
tifies as expressing resultative aspect. The distinction between the two constructions is shown to reside in the valency of the predicate, and explanations
are given for the interpretations that can be assigned to each construction.
Goossens presents a first analysis of modality, a subject that has hitherto
received little attention in FG, with special reference to the modals of English.
He suggests that a scale of grammaticalization is involved such that three forms
of analysis are possible according to the point on the scale: modals as basic
predicates with full predicate-frames, modals as input to a predicate formation
rule yielding a complex derived predicate, and modals as predicate operators.
Van der Auwera discusses the French construction exemplified by *J'ai vu Paul qui
fumait* 'I saw Paul smoking', which contains a relative clause that functions as
a 'complement clause'. He argues that such constructions must be accounted for
by assuming a special predicate-frame for *voir* 'see' and other French perception
verbs which, in his words, 'is neither simply two-place nor three-place, but
something in between'. In this way, he seeks to account for the possibility of a
clause being at once predicative and relative. Junger's chapter is devoted to
causative constructions in Modern Hebrew, specifically those which involve either
of the derivational patterns HIFIL and PIEL in verbal morphology. A predicate
formation rule is shown to be responsible for HIFIL (although not for PIEL) and
conditions on the input-predicate and the 'caused state of affairs' are given
precise formulation. Junger argues that the causee, in both constructions, is
typically to be analysed as a Goal (this is also Vet's conclusion for French),
but that other analyses are called for with a limited number of predicates.

It remains for us to offer our thanks to those who have contributed, in one way or another, to the production of *Predicates and Terms in Functional Grammar*. Firstly, we wish to express our indebtedness to the Faculty of Letters of the University of Amsterdam for financial undertakings concerning this volume. We are also very grateful to Caroline Kroon, Michel van de Grift and Angeliek van Hout for help with proof-reading and with preparing the indexes of languages and authors. Annemieke de Winter and Janneke Timmermans have done invaluable work typing and retyping manuscripts. And finally we wish to thank our typist, who prepared the camera-ready copy with precision, speed and critical acumen.

A. Machtelt Bolkestein   Amsterdam

Casper de Groot   Tilburg

J. Lachlan Mackenzie   Amsterdam

Table of Contents

List of abbreviations and symbols

Semantic functions:

Ag   = Agent
Go   = Goal
Rec   = Recipient
Ben   = Beneficiary
Instr = Instrument
Loc   = Location
Temp = Temporal
Dir   = Direction
Proc = Processed
Fo   = Force
Po   = Positioner
Exp   = Experiencer
∅   = Zero function
SF   = Semantic function

Syntactic functions:

Subj = Subject
Obj = Object
DO   = Direct Object
IO   = Indirect Object

Pragmatic functions:

Top = Topic
Foc = Focus
Th = Theme

Categories:

A   = Adjectival
N   = Nominal
V   = Verbal
Vf = finite Verb
Vi = non-finite Verb
mv = modal Verb
PRO = Pronoun
NP = Noun Phrase
PP = Pre-/Postpositional Phrase
Po = Postposition
Pr = Preposition
Dem = Demonstrative

Predicate operators:

π   = arbitrary predicate operator

Term operators:

ω   = arbitrary term operator
d   = definite; maximal, exhaustive
i   = indefinite; partitive
1, sg = singular
m, pl = plural
+p   = proximate
-p   = non-proximate
A   = anaphoric
f   = rational term operator
each   = distributive operator
corp   = corporate operator
every = universal operator
cert   = specific operator
any   = random operator

Morpho-syntactic categories:

p1, p2,
p3   = first, second, third person
Neg   = negation
pres   = present
fut   = future
t_1 = starting point
t_2 = terminal point
IA   = Inner Aspect
OA   = Outer Aspect
pf   = perfective
impf   = imperfective
R   = realised aspect
dur   = durative
hab   = habitual
hort   = hortative
cond(it) = conditional
dub   = dubitative
ign   = ignorative
IndYN   = indirect yes-no question
IndQW   = indirect Q-word question

Positions:

S	=	Subject position
O	=	Object position
V	=	Verb position
X	=	neutral position
PØ	=	special position
P1	=	Clause-initial position
P2	=	Theme position
P3	=	Tail position

Cases:

nom	=	nominative
acc	=	accusative
gen	=	genitive
dat	=	dative
rel	=	relative
abs	=	absolutive
erg	=	ergative
ter	=	terminalis
mod	=	modalis

Constructions and markers:

anaph	=	anaphoric
GM	=	Goal marker
-M	=	marker of nominalization
-R	=	reduction marker
R	=	Relator
Rc	=	relative clause
REFL	=	reflexive
S	=	standard
SFX	=	suffix

Theories of grammar:

FG	=	Functional Grammar
RG	=	Relational Grammar
GB	=	Government and Binding Theory
TG	=	Transformational Grammar
EWP	=	Extended Word-and-Paradigm Model
ATN	=	Augmented Transition Network

General:

ϕ	=	predicate
ϕ_m	=	mass predicate
ϕ_c	=	count predicate
t_i	=	term
$x_i, \ldots, x_n$	=	argument variable
$y_i, \ldots, y_n$	=	satellite variable
=	=	identity
$\subseteq$	=	inclusion
$\subset$	=	proper inclusion
X	=	variable over set
$\in$	=	set membership
m	=	measure function; size of domain (mass set)
card	=	cardinal number function
G	=	semantic function plus rest of predication
F	=	all restrictors of a term
U	=	universe of sets in Speaker's pragmatic information
D	=	domain
R	=	referential set
n	=	positive integer numerator
c	=	size of domain (discrete set)
<	=	fewer than
<<	=	far fewer than
>	=	more than
$\approx$	=	is approx. equal to
$\underset{\approx}{<}$	=	is less than and approx. equal to
$\leq$	=	is equal to no more than
/	=	proportion
{Rn}	=	distributive referent set
SoA	=	state of affairs
Co	=	Control
Tel	=	Telicity
Dyn	=	Dynamism
Mom	=	Momentaneousness
C	=	Consonant
V	=	Vowel
S	=	Speaker
H	=	Hearer
PFA	=	Principle of formal adjustment
PSA	=	Principle of semantic adjustment
PEM	=	Prototypical expression model
LIPOC	=	Language-Independent Preferred Order of Constituents
MH	=	Modern Hebrew

Chapter 1

Formal and semantic adjustment of derived constructions

Simon C. Dik
Institute for General Linguistics, University of Amsterdam

0. Introduction

Derived constructions in natural languages often have properties which are difficult to explain in terms of the usual expression rules of the language involved.
Consider the following examples:

(i)   *Derived intransitives*

Compare the following constructions:

(1) a.   Mary is washing the clothes
    b.   These clothes wash easily

In (1a) the predicate *wash* is used in its basic value of a two-place Action predicate taking an Agent and a Goal argument. In (1b) the same predicate appears
with only one of these arguments, corresponding to the original Goal term. But
this argument acts as if it were the first argument of the derived construction.
There is also a semantic shift involved in the relation between (1a) and (1b):
whereas (1a) designatés an Action, (1b) rather designates a property which can be
predicated of *these clothes*. Thus, what is a clear Goal term in (1a) returns as
the first argument of the same verb *wash* in (1b), and the element of agency which
is present in (1a) has disappeared in (1b).

(ii)   *Causative constructions*

The Causee argument in causative constructions often surfaces in unexpected forms.
Consider French, where an Agent term is normally marked by *par*, as in (2a),
whereas the CauseeAgent in certain cases appears with *à*, as in (2b), which is the
normal expression for the Recipient, as in (2c):

(2) a. Ce   livre a   été acheté *par Jean* (Agent)
        this book has been bought by   John

   b. Pierre a   fait acheter ce   livre *à Jean* (CauseeAgent)
       Peter has made buy   this book to John
       'Peter has made John buy this book'

   c. Pierre a   donné ce   livre *à Jean* (Recipient)
       Peter has given this book to John

The appearance of the Causee in the guise of a Recipient or Indirect Object constitutes a notoriously difficult problem for grammatical theory.[1]

(iii)   *Nominalizations*

Compare the following constructions:

(3) a. John recklessly drives the new car

   b. I disapprove of John's reckless driving of the new car

In (3a) we have a regular Action predication involving an Agent, a Goal, and a
Manner satellite realized in adverbial form. In (3b) we have, in a sense, an embedded version of that same predication. However, the Agent appears in the form
of a Possessor, the Manner satellite in the form of an adjective, and the Goal,
again, in the form appropriate for a Possessor. Again, the question poses itself
of how these unexpected formal properties of the derived construction can be explained.

In this paper I will approach these and similar phenomena in terms of some general
principles concerning the formation and expression of derived constructions in
natural languages. These principles are rather simple in themselves, but I will
try to show that their explanatory power is considerable. I will first formulate
the principles (section 1), and then show how they work with respect to the three
construction types mentioned above: (i) constructions involving 'valency reduction'
(section 2), (ii) constructions involving 'valency extension' (section 3) and (iii)
nominalizations (section 4).

1. Some general principles

I will assume that the following general principles govern the formal expression
and the semantic properties of derived constructions:

(4)   *Principle of formal adjustment* (PFA)

Derived constructions of type X are under pressure to adjust
their formal expression to the prototypical expression model
provided by non-derived constructions of type X.

(5)   *Principle of semantic adjustment* (PSA)

To the extent that a derived construction yields to the pressure of the PFA, it will also tend to adjust to the semantic
properties of the prototypical expression model.

If these principles are to have any empirical content, we must of course have
some independent definition of the notion 'prototypical expression model' for
non-derived constructions of type X. And if the principles are to have any general typological validity, they must be defined in a language-independent way.[2]
Such a language-independent definition can be given as follows:

(6)   *Prototypical expression models* (PEMs)

(a) zero-place predicates have no PEM.

(b) one-place predicates: the PEM is the expression model for
    one-place predicates with a specified first argument.

(c) two place predicates: the PEM is the expression model for
    a two-place predicate with an Agent and a Goal argument.

(d) three-place predicates: the PEM is the expression model
    for a three-place predicate with an Agent, a Goal, and a
    Recipient argument.

(e) four-place predicates have no PEM.

(f) terms: the PEM is the expression model for a term with a
    non-derived nominal as its head, possibly modified by
    attributive adjectives and possessor phrases, and deter-
    mined by one or more term operators.

In English, the following construction types exemplify these different prototypical expression models:

(7)   PEMs for English:

    (a) zero-place predicates: ---

    (b) one-place predicates: John walks

    (c) two-place predicates: John bought the book

    (d) three-place predicates: John gave the book to Peter

    (e) four-place predicates: ---

    (f) terms: the old house of my friend

The two principles PFA and PSA, together with the different PEMs as defined in (6), constitute a theory of what is likely to happen to derived constructions of different types in particular languages. I shall now detail the implications of this theory for the different construction types mentioned in the introduction to this paper.

2. Valency reduction[3]

By the valency of a predicate I understand the number of arguments with which this predicate combines. Many languages have predicate formation rules by which the valency of a given input predicate is reduced by one or more argument positions. Various kinds of detransitivization belong here. I shall here first concentrate on valency reduction rules which reduce a given input predicate-frame by its first argument position. The processes involved in such rules can be described in terms of three elementary operations:

(8)   (i)   *argument reduction*: one argument position of the input predicate-frame is removed.

    (ii)   *argument shift*: a given argument shifts to another argument position.

    (iii)   *satellite absorption*: a constituent which would have the status of a satellite with respect to the input predicate-frame gets the status of an argument in the output predicate-frame.

Let us illustrate the nature of these operations with the following examples. Suppose we start out with a basic two-place predicate such as:

(9) a. John sells these houses

    b. $sell_V (x_1)_{Ag} (x_2)_{Go}$

Argument reduction, when applied to the first argument position of (9b), would
yield the following derived predicate-frame:

(10) $sell_V$-R   (∅) $(x_2)_{Go}$

In this predicate-frame, (∅) indicates that the first argument position has been
removed. 'R' is a 'reduction marker', symbolizing the reduced nature of the
predicate. In English there is no overt expression for R: the verbal predicate
in an argument-reduced construction such as (9b) does not differ in form from
the original input predicate (English has zero-derivation in this respect). In
other languages, R is spelled out in some way or another, either as a morphological marker on the verb (see Dik 1983a for some examples of this), or in some
separate particle. The so-called reflexive element which occurs both in the
Romance and in the Slavic languages will here be interpreted as the expression
of R.[4]

     A derived construction of the form of (10), in which argument reduction has
applied to the first argument position, could only be expressed in an impersonal
construction of a type which is not grammatical in English:

(11)   (It) sells houses
         'Houses are being sold'

Such constructions are grammatical in other languages, as we shall see below.

     In English, a derived structure such as (10) can only lead to a grammatical
expression if argument shift is also applied. Argument shift involves a derivation of the following form:

(12) $sell_V$-R   (∅) $(x_2)_{Go}$

         $sell_V$-R $(x_2)_{∅/Proc}$

Through argument shift, the original second argument of the predicate *sell* has
now usurped the first argument position. At the same time, there is a shift in
semantic function. This is necessary because it is assumed in FG that Goal is
not a possible first argument function. Therefore, when argument shift is applied,
the original Goal function must necessarily also undergo semantic function shift,
adopting one of the first argument semantic functions compatible with the nature

of the original second argument of the input predicate-frame. In this case, the only available options are the functions Ø (for States) and Processed (for Processes). A derived predicate-frame of type (12) would thus be expected to be realized as in (13), and to have either the meaning (a) or the meaning (b):

(13)   These houses sell
         (a) 'These houses are being sold' (Process)
         (b) 'These houses have the property of being 'sellers'' (State)

In English, constructions such as (13) are only marginally acceptable, with a pregnant interpretation of 'these houses sell very well'. Usually, there must be some kind of extension, which may either take the form of a Manner constituent of some kind, or of negation (cf. Kahrel 1984):

(14) a. These houses sell very well
     b. These houses sell like hot pancakes
     c. These houses don't sell

Where an extension by a Manner constituent is more or less obligatory, this can be described in terms of satellite absorption:

(15) $[sell_V \ (x_1)_{Ag} \ (x_2)_{Go}] \ (y_1)_{Manner}$

         $[sell_V\text{-R} \ (x_2)_{\emptyset/Proc} \ (x_3)_{Manner}]$

This representation is intended to signal that the Manner satellite, originally an optional extension to the input predicate-frame, has been drawn into the nuclear predicate-frame as an obligatory argument in the output. Note that in the representation (15) it is assumed that argument reduction, argument shift, and satellite absorption have all three applied.

Let us now see what the general principles sketched in section 1 imply for various types of first argument reduction. First argument reduction in general can be formulated as follows:

(16)   FIRST ARGUMENT REDUCTION

        input: $pred_V$ (x_1) (x_2) ... (x_n)

        output: $pred_V$-R $(\emptyset)$ (x_2) ... (x_n)

        meaning: 'the n-place predicate $pred_V$ is relevant only to

                        (x_2) ... (x_n)'

The output predicate will thus describe the state of affairs designated by the input predicate in such a way that the identity or even the presence of a first argument is completely irrelevant.

When the rule of first argument reduction is applied to a one-place input-predicate, the result is a zero-place construction:

(17) $walk_V$-R $(\emptyset)$
       '(it) walks' = 'there is walking going on'

Now the PFA says that such a derived construction will tend to adjust to the PEM of corresponding non-derived constructions, but according to (6), such a PEM does not exist. This means that there will be no non-derived construction which provides a model for the expression of (17). This 'problem' may be solved in either of the following two ways: (a) avoid an output of the form of (17): (b) apply satellite absorption, so that at least a one-place predicate is provided as output.

These predictions seem to be confirmed by the following facts: (a) it is rare to find derived constructions of type (17) in languages; (b) where they occur they often require some obligatory extension.

One language in which constructions of type (17) are possible is Czech (cf. Bubenik 1983, Van Dijkeren and De Jong 1984):

(18)   Tancuje   se
       dance-3sg R
       'There is dancing going on'

However, such constructions must be heavily contextualized in order to be used as such. Usually they require some form of satellite absorption, as in:

(19)   Tancuje   se do   rána
       dance-3sg R   until morning
       'There is dancing going on until the morning'

Satellite absorption in this case at least yields a one-place predicate, so that zero-place predicates are avoided. However, a construction of type (19) does not conform to the PEM for one-place predicates, since the term *do rána* does not play the role of a first argument. Thus, (19) is still predicted to be a marked construction type, although somewhat less marked than constructions of type (18).

When rule (16) is applied to a two-place predicate, the result is a one-place predicate with an empty first argument position:

(20) $sell_V$-R $(\emptyset)$ $(x_2)_{Go}$

Such a construction could be realized as an impersonal construction with a Goal argument, as in French:

(21)   Il se vend beaucoup de livres en Hollande
        it R sells many   of books in Holland
        'Many books are sold in Holland'

(cf. Afman 1983). However, according to PEM (6b), this is not a favoured model for the expression of one-place predicates. Therefore we may expect a strong pressure towards reorganizing the construction in such a way that the original second argument shifts to the first argument position:

(22) $sell_V$-R $(x_2)_{\emptyset/Proc}$

In French, this would deliver the alternative:

(23)   Beaucoup de livres se vendent en Hollande
        many   of books R sell   in Holland
        'Many books are sold in Holland'

Note that we assume that argument shift of this type also involves a shift in semantic function. This would imply that there is, between (21) and (23), a (possibly subtle) difference in meaning: (21) expresses the activity of 'selling many books' without the responsible Agent being specified (or specifiable). (23) indicates either that many books are in the process of being sold, or that many books are such that they are sold in Holland. Especially in the latter case, the difference between (21) and (23) is quite clear.

Note that there is no solid proof that *beaucoup de livres* has Goal function

in (21). An alternative analysis would assume that *beaucoup de livres* already
has the function of first argument in (21), but that it has not received Subject
function (as is evident from the lack of agreement). The construction would then
be similar to:

(24)   Il est arrivé trois bateaux
         it is arrived three boats
         'Three boats have arrived'

in which *trois bateaux* clearly is a first argument of *arriver*, but does not
trigger agreement on the verb. Vet (1981a, 1981b) has described such constructions as (24) as due to the absence of Subject assignment.

     In other languages, however, we find constructions corresponding to (21) in
which there are clear indications that the argument in question functions as a
Goal to the verb. Thus, Comrie (1977) gives the following example from Spanish:

(25)   En Europa no se nos conoce
         in Europe not R us knows
         'In Europe one does not know us'

where *nos* is the Object rather than the Subject form of the pronoun. Also in
Spanish, where specific animate Goals are marked with *a*, we find constructions
such as the following, discussed in Givón (1982):

(26)   Se curó   a las mujeres
         R cured-sg Go the women
         'The women were cured'

in which the argument *las mujeres* is clearly marked as a Goal term.

     Similar examples are given by Givón from Ute, where first argument reduction
can be applied quite freely to all kinds of predicate-frames, without affecting
the expression of the remaining part of the frame. Interestingly, this rule can
apply freely *unless* the output predicate-frame would then be without argument
at all, as in:

(27)   *wʉʉka-ta-x̂a
          work -R -Ant
          'There was working going on'

This again confirms the non-preferred status of zero-place predicates.[5]

Let us now look at the effect of rule (16) on three-place input predicates. In such a case, the output would be as follows:

(28) $\text{give}_V\text{-R} \; (\emptyset) \; (x_2)_{Go} \; (x_3)_{Rec}$

This would lead to such constructions as:

(29)   (It) gives a bonus to the winner
         'A bonus is given to the winner'

This construction would be non-favoured according to our principles, and I have no clear example of it in any language. Judging from the information Givón (1982) gives on Ute, this construction would probably be grammatical in that language.

On the other hand, if argument shift applies to (28), this will yield a derived predicate-frame of the following form:

(30) $\text{give}_V\text{-R} \; (x_2)_{\emptyset/Proc} \; (x_3)_{Rec}$

which could be realized as:

(31)   A bonus gives to the winner
         'A bonus is given to the winner'

Such a construction would again be non-preferred, because it does not conform to the PEM (6c) for two-place predicates. The construction does occur in French, however (Afman 1983):

(32)   Une telle récompense ne   se donne pas à n'importe qui
         a   such   reward   neg R gives neg to no-matter who
         'Such a reward is not given to just anybody'

Our principles predict that first argument reduction applied to three-place input predicates, whether followed by argument shift or not, will always result in non-favoured, marked construction types.

When we consider the combined effect of the PFA and the different PEMs on rules of first argument reduction, the net result is that the following construction type is predicted to be the most usual outcome of such rules:

(33)   These houses sell-R

    (a) 'these houses are in the process of being sold'

    (b) 'these houses are such that they sell'

This is of course the familiar 'pseudo-passive' or 'medio-passive' construction
which we find in many different languages. All the other variant outputs of first
argument reduction are predicted to be marked options, which will be less usual
and less favoured across languages.

    The principle of semantic adjustment (PSA, (5) above) is relevant to first
argument reduction in two ways. First, as has been argued in Dik (1983a), any
form of argument reduction easily leads to a 'deactualization' of the meaning of
the output predicate-frame, where deactualization means that the output predicate-
frame tends to get a generic, habitual, or potential reading rather than a reading
which directly designates some actual state of affairs. In the second place, as
has been suggested above, when argument shift applies, the semantic function of
the shifted argument will also be affected, so that Process or State expressions
are derived from original Action predicates. The general hypothesis is that where
argument shift has not applied, the meaning of the output predicate-frame will be
closer to that of the input predicate-frame than if argument shift has applied.

3. Valency extension

As a counterpart to valency reduction rules, many languages have predicate formation rules which extend the valency of the input predicate by one argument position. Causative predicate formation is the prime example of such valency extension rules. The causative predicate formation rule can be quite generally
formulated as follows:

(34)   *Causative predicate formation*

    input: pred (x_1) ... (x_n)

    output: caus-pred $(x_0)_{Causer}$ $(x_1)_{Causee}$ ... (x_n)

    meaning: 'x_0 brings it about that the state of affairs
                  designated by the input predicate-frame takes
                  place/obtains'

Thus, the causative predicate formation rule extends the valency of the input
predicate-frame by an extra Causer argument. This Causer argument generally

usurps all the rights of the 'first argument' of the construction. This implies that the original first argument, now Causee, loses some of its rights and privileges.[6] Cross-linguistically, the main 'problem' of the causative construction is the question of how the Causee argument is to be treated in the formal expression of the derived predicate-frame.

Several theories have been proposed to account for the cross-linguistic patterning of Causee expression.

Comrie's relational theory (Comrie 1975, 1976a) is formulated in terms of the hierarchy of grammatical relations (35), and the general principle (36):[7]

(35)   Subject > Direct Object > Indirect Object > Oblique

(36)   The Causee is demoted to the first available position in hierarchy (35).

This theory works fine for patterns such as the following in French:

(37)   Pierre fait marcher Jean   (Causee = Direct Object)
         Peter makes walk   John

(38)   Pierre fait ouvrir la porte à Jean   (Causee = Indirect Object)
         Peter makes open   the door to John

(39)   Pierre fait donner un cadeau à Marie par Jean (Causee = Oblique)
         Peter makes give   a present to Mary by John

There are various facts about causative constructions, however, which show that the relational theory embodied in (35) and (36) cannot be taken to tell the whole story. First, note that French also has the alternative construction:

(40)   Pierre fait ouvrir la porte par Jean   (Causee = Oblique)
         Peter makes open   the door by John

In this case we must assume that the Causee has skipped the IO position in hierarchy (35). This is a case of what Comrie called 'extended demotion'. The occurrence of extended demotion itself, however, is not predicted by the theory. Nor is the fact that, as we shall see later on, there is a semantic difference between (40) and (38).

Another not infrequent breach of the relational theory is the occurrence of 'doubling', where the Causee takes on a grammatical relation which is already represented in the construction, as in Dutch:

(41)   Jan liet Marie (DO) een auto (DO) kopen
         John let Mary   a   car   buy

Finally, a more general problem is the status of the Oblique relation in hierarchy (35). One fact which does not follow from the theory is that if the Causee
is demoted to Oblique position, the form of the Causee is typically that of an
Agent phrase, as in French constructions such as (39) and (40). A second fact is
that in certain languages the Causee can take different forms, where these forms
do not depend on the relational hierarchy, but rather on the underlying semantics
of the input predicate-frame. This can be illustrated with the following Dutch
constructions:

(42)   Marie kocht een auto
         Mary bought a   car

(43)   Piet liet een auto kopen door Marie (*aan Marie)
         Pete let a   car buy   by   Mary (to Mary)

(44)   Marie zag een auto
         Mary saw a   car

(45)   Piet liet een auto zien aan Marie (*door Marie)
         Pete let a   car see to Mary (by   Mary)

Usually, the Causee can be expressed in an Agent phrase, as in (43). But with a
limited number of verbs, the Causee is expressed in an *aan*-phrase, which is the
usual expression for a Recipient in Dutch. This expression of the Causee is
triggered by verbs of perception and some verbs of cognition and can thus not be
explained in terms of a more or less automatic demotion down the relational
hierarchy (see Dik 1980a: ch. 3 for details).

A more semantically oriented theory of Causee expression was proposed in Cole
(1983). According to this theory, the choice between alternative expression forms
for the Causee always have semantic import. Cole's theory is based on the following suppositions:

(46)   (i)   types of formal expression available to the Causee can be ordered
                 on a hierarchy of 'diminishing control' (in the sense of less and
                 less agency):

(47)   instrumental > dative > accusative

(ii)   if there is an opposition between an expression higher and an expression lower on this hierarchy, the Causee will retain more
control/agency in the higher than in the lower expression form.

(iii)   arguments of intransitive verbs have a lower degree of intrinsic
control than first arguments of transitive verbs. The former will
therefore more easily slip into accusative expression than the
latter which, if not expressed in the instrumental, will prefer
the dative.

Cole's semantic theory is an important complement to Comrie's relational theory,
and certainly goes some way towards explaining the *semantic* properties of causative constructions. Again, however, this semantic theory cannot be the whole
story, for the following reasons:

(a) there are languages which do have oppositions along the lines of hierarchy
(47), but without discernable semantic difference between the variants. In other
words: formal oppositions may, but need not carry a semantic opposition. Therefore, the semantic aspects cannot be explained in terms of properties of the
expression devices.

(b) there are quite a few 'agentive' intransitive verbs, and many 'non-agentive'
transitive ones (as Cole admits, 1983: 127). Thus the tendency for Causees of
intransitive verbs to slip into the accusative, and for Causees of transitive
predicates to slip into the dative, can only be motivated in terms of a rough
correlation between intransitive/transitive and non-agentive/agentive.

(c) it is not clear why certain languages should have a difference between
Causee arguments of transitive predicates (e.g. in the dative), and Causee arguments of ditransitive predicates (e.g. in the instrumental). For surely there is
no reason to assume that the Agent of a verb such as *give* is more 'agentive'
than the Agent of a verb such as *kiss*.

We may thus conclude that neither a purely formal, nor a purely semantic treatment of Causee expression provides a full account of the relevant facts. This
means that some sort of combination of formal and semantic principles has to be
assumed to be responsible for the expression of causative constructions.[8]

Let us now see how these facts would be accounted for in terms of the principles
proposed in section 1. We shall again discuss the various conditions in terms of
(pseudo-)English examples, and refer to other languages where this is particularly
relevant.

Where the input to the Causative predicate formation rule (34) is a one-place predicate, the output will be a two-place predicate:

(48) a. John$_{Ag}$ walks

    b. Peter$_{AgCauser}$ makes John$_{AgCausee}$ walk

If the Causee were to be expressed according to its underlying semantic function, we would expect an expression such as:

(49)   Peter makes walk by John

If, however, the underlying semantic function of the Causee is not Agent, then we expect a different expression of the Causee, according to the pattern (50):

(50) a. Mary$_{Exp}$ shivers

    b. Peter$_{AgCauser}$ makes Mary$_{ExpCausee}$ shiver

    c. Peter makes shiver to Mary

Thus, in the case of such realizations as (49) and (50c), we assume that the formal expression of the Causee is determined by its underlying semantic function in the input predicate-frame. This immediately accounts for different kinds of 'oblique' realization of the Causee: these are not the result of (extended) demotion, but simply represent the most faithful mapping of the underlying semantic function of the Causee.

However, constructions such as (49) and (50c) are two-place derived constructions, which will therefore be sensitive to the PFA, and be under pressure to model their expression on the PEM for two-place predicates. We thus expect that, if the pressure of the PFA is yielded to, the Causee will take on the formal guise of a Goal term. In other words, we expect such constructions as:

(51) a. Peter makes walk John

    b. Peter makes shiver Mary

This is the pattern which we actually find in a great many languages. It is almost standard that in a two-place causative construction, the Causee will behave as if it is the object of the derived verb. We may thus assume that the pressure of the PFA is quite strong in the case of two-place derived constructions.

When the input to rule (34) is a two-place predicate-frame, the output will be a three-place construction. When no formal adjustment takes place, we expect formal expression according to the following pattern:

(52) a. Mary$_{Ag}$ bought a car$_{Goal}$

   b. Peter$_{AgCauser}$ makes Mary$_{AgCausee}$ buy a car$_{Goal}$

   c. Peter makes buy a car by Mary

(53) a. Mary$_{Exp}$ saw a car$_{Goal}$

   b. Peter$_{AgCauser}$ makes Mary$_{ExpCausee}$ see a car$_{Goal}$

   c. Peter makes see a car to Mary

This is the pattern which we find in Dutch, witness the examples given in (43) and (45). Again, we regard these expression types as the most faithful mappings of the underlying structure rather than as due to some kind of demotion process.

(52c) and (53c) are three-place derived output predicate-frames. These will therefore be subject to the PFA, relative to the PEM for three-place predicates. We thus expect the following alternative expression forms:

(54) a. Peter makes buy a car to Mary

   b. Peter makes see a car to Mary

where in both cases *to Mary* is the standard expression form for Recipients in the language concerned.[9]

Finally, if a three-place predicate-frame is input to rule (34), the output will be a four-place predicate-frame, which, if not adjusted, will be expressed according to the following pattern:

(55)   Peter makes give a present to Mary by John

Note that it is difficult to find a three-place predicate in which the first argument is not Agent. We thus expect no other realizations of the Causee than in the form of an Agent phrase. A derived construction of type (55) will in principle be sensitive to the PFA, but there is no PEM for four-place predicates (according to (6e)). Therefore, we expect no formal adjustment of (55), at least not on the basis of the principles formulated so far.

Recapitulating, we can say that our principles predict the following expression forms for causative constructions:

(56) a. Peter makes walk by John

    b. Peter makes walk John

(57) a. Peter makes shiver to Mary

    b. Peter makes shiver Mary

(58) a. Peter makes buy a car by Mary

    b. Peter makes buy a car to Mary

(59) a. Peter makes see a car to Mary

    b. Peter makes see a car to Mary[9]

(60)   Peter makes give a present to Mary by John

These possibilities do indeed cover the majority of expression types of causative
constructions which are found across languages, with the exception of constructions involving 'doubling'. These I will discuss separately below.

Let us now turn to some semantic aspects of causative constructions. We have seen
that the Causee can be expressed according to its underlying semantic function
(non-adjusted), or according to the model provided by the relevant PEM (adjusted).
The principle of semantic adjustment now predicts that, if there is any semantic
difference between the non-adjusted and the adjusted form, the non-adjusted form
will retain more of the underlying semantics of the Causee argument. In order to
see this more clearly, consider the following opposition:

(61) a. Jean fait ouvrir la porte par Pierre (non-adjusted)

    b. Jean fait ouvrir la porte à Pierre   (adjusted)

The PSA now predicts that if there is a semantic difference between (61a-b) at
all, the expression *par Pierre* will retain more of the Causee's underlying Agent
function than the expression à *Pierre*.

    This prediction is correct in the case of (61): there is indeed a semantic
distinction between (61a) and (61b), although it is a subtle one. Zimmer (1976:
405) describes the difference in terms of the following pair:

(62) a. J'ai   fait nettoyer les toilettes par le   général

       I have made clean   the toilets   by the general

    b. J'ai   fait nettoyer les toilettes au   général

       I have made clean   the toilets   to-the general

(62a) expresses that in some way or other I have arranged for the toilets to be cleaned by the general, while the latter may have been quite unaware that this was my doing. The general's agency is not strongly diminished in (62a). In (62b), on the other hand, it is suggested that I have more or less directly forced the general to clean the toilets. Thus, (62b), but not (62a), describes a humiliating experience for the general.

This difference, which recurs in other languages, is often referred to as a distinction between *indirect* and *direct* causation. In indirect causation, the Causee retains more of his control or agency. Our PSA thus predicts that if such a difference exists at all, it will pattern as it does in French: indirect causation will be associated with non-adjusted expression of the Causee; direct causation will be associated with adjusted expression of the Causee.

This prediction is confirmed by facts from quite different languages. Thus, in each of the following pairs, the first construction has the non-adjusted Causee expression, the second the adjusted expression. And in each case the semantic opposition is along the lines of indirect vs. direct causation:

(63)   Japanese (Shibatani 1976, example from Comrie 1981: 174)

    a. Taroo ga   Ziroo ni ik-ase-ta
       Taro Subj Ziro Ag go-caus-past
       'Taro made Ziro go'

    b. Taroo ga   Ziroo o ik-ase-ta
       Taro Subj Ziro Go go-caus-past
       'Taro got Ziro to go'

Note: *ni* can be interpreted as a Recipient or as an Agent marker. It is clear that according to our theory it must be interpreted as an Agent marker in (63a): if it were a Recipient marker, it could only have arisen through adjustment, but this form of adjustment is not predicted by the theory: moreover, the semantic difference could on that interpretation not be explained in the same uniform way.

(64)   Hungarian (Hetzron 1976)

    a. köhögtettem a   gyerekkel
       I-caus-cough the boy-instr
       'I had the boy cough' (by asking him to do so)

    b. köhögtettem a   gyereket
       I-caus-cough the boy-acc
       'I induced the boy to cough' (e.g., by blowing cigarette smoke in his face)

(65)   Bolivian Quechua (Cole 1983: 117)

   a. nuqa Fan-wan   rumi-ta apa-ci-ni
      I   Juan-instr rock-acc carry-caus-1sg
      'I had Juan carry the rock'

   b. nuqa Fan-ta   rumi-ta apa-ci-ni
      I   Juan-acc rock-acc carry-caus-1sg
      'I made Juan carry the rock'

Note: Cole describes the difference as follows: (65a) would be used 'where
the causee retains control over his actions and submits voluntarily to the
speaker's wishes', whereas (65b) would be used '... in a situation in which
Juan is directly under the speaker's authority and has no control over
whether he will carry the rock.'

We may thus conclude that, at least in the languages cited, the PSA makes the
correct predictions concerning the semantic difference between the non-adjusted
and the adjusted expression forms of causative constructions.

A final note should be added on so-called 'doubling'. As Comrie (1976a) has shown,
a number of languages allow 'doubling' on the Direct Object or the Indirect Object
position. This means that the Causee is expressed as a DO, even if there already
is a DO in the construction, or that it is expressed as an IO, even though there
already is an IO in the construction. The former is very common in Dutch: in fact,
the general rule is that the Causee can always be expressed as an Object, no matter in what conditions (cf. Dik 1980a: ch. 3). Compare:

(66)   Jan liet zijn haar knippen door zijn vriendin
      John let his hair cut   by   his girl friend

(67)   Jan liet zijn vriendin   zijn haar knippen
      John let his girl friend his hair cut

Doubling on IO is illustrated in the following French example (Comrie 1976a: 277):

(68)   J'ai fait donner à Claude une pomme au   professeur
      I have made give to Claude an apple to-the teacher
      'I have made Claude give an apple to the teacher'

This type of construction, with two terms treated as Goals or Recipients, does
not follow from our theory, unless Comrie is right in his suggestion that it
tends to occur in languages which also have such doubling in simplex sentences.
At least in a number of languages it seems clear that this type of construction

is modelled on similar non-derived constructions. Such cases could be accounted for in terms of a more language-dependent extension of the PFA.

Another way of looking at doubling is to interpret it in terms of a process of analogy. Since with one-place input predicates the Causee will almost invariably be treated as a Goal of the derived construction (expressed, e.g., in the accusative), it is understandable that the idea that the Causee appears in the accusative is generalized to other constructions, even if this yields output for which there is no model available in the non-derived constructions of the language. In such a case one might say that the formal adjustment of the derived construction to the model provided by non-derived constructions 'overshoots' its target: through adjustment to existing models, constructions arise for which there is no model in the language. Below we shall see that exactly the same thing happens in the expression of nominalizations.

4. Nominalizations

I shall regard nominalizations as a particular type of embedded predication, where an embedded predication is a predication which fills the position of some term (argument or satellite) in some superordinate predication. Embedded predications can be realized in their full verbal form, as in:

(70)   I heard that *John recklessly drove the new car*

But they can also take on a varying number of nominal properties, as in:

(71)   I regret *John's reckless driving of the new car*

I shall only speak of nominalizations when an embedded predication has at least acquired some nominal properties.

The acquisition of nominal properties by basically verbal predications can be understood in terms of the PFA: an embedded predication is a predication acting as a term in some higher predication. Terms are usually nominal expressions. According to the PFA, then, we will expect embedded predications to be under pressure to model their expression after nominal terms.

The adjustments of embedded predications to the pattern of nominal terms are quite uniform across languages. They can be described in terms of the following schema:

(72)   *verbal predication*

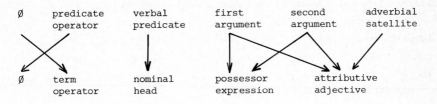

nominal term

In this schema, the most common adjustments of the embedded verbal predication
to the expression pattern of the nominal term have been indicated by arrows. It
is noted that within and across languages, varying numbers and combinations of
these adjustments may together characterize a 'nominalization'. This also means
that certain nominalizations will be more 'verbal', and others more 'nominal'.
In other words, there will be a scale of possibilities in between the purely
verbal and the purely nominal construction. This has been demonstrated in Comrie
(1976b) on a general typological basis, and by Mackenzie (1984) for English.
Mackenzie gives the following sequence of progressively more nominal embedded
predications:

(73) a. that my horse beat the favourite

      b. my horse beating the favourite

      c. my horse's beating the favourite

      d. my horse's beating of the favourite

      e. my horse's victory (over the favourite)

It is quite clear, then, that the PFA is quite forcibly at work in the expression
of embedded predications, pressing the basically verbal structure into the mold
of the nominal term, by some combination of the adjustments graphically displayed
in (72).

   I have no room here to discuss all these adjustments in detail. Therefore I
shall restrict myself to what is perhaps the most salient of these adjustments:
the adjustment of arguments to the expression of possessor phrases. With respect
to these adjustments, the following points are to be noted:

(i) *The target is the possessor phrase*
It is often said that within the domain of a nominalization arguments are expressed in the 'genitive'. Depending on the argument adjusted, these genitives are then
often referred to as the 'subjective genitive' and the 'objective genitive'.
Cross-linguistically speaking, however, it is much more appropriate to say that
certain arguments are expressed in the form appropriate for *possessors*. This is
better for the following two reasons:
(a) languages may have possessor expressions which are not correctly described as
'genitives' (the genitive being, after all, a specific case form). In such languages, whatever the possessor expression is, this expression constitutes the
model for the expression of arguments of nominalizations.
(b) even in languages which do have proper genitives for the expression of possessors, and where these may be targets for the expression of arguments of embedded predications, there may be alternative expression forms for possessors
which can also function as such targets. This is even the case in English, where
possessive pronouns, which cannot properly be labelled 'genitives', do provide a
possible target for the expression of arguments of nominalizations, as in:

(74) a. *my* rapid driving of the car
     b. *their* repeated asking for the number

(ii) *The adjusted arguments are typically the central arguments*
By the central arguments of a predication I understand the first argument and
the second argument, where the latter will typically have Goal function. It is
indeed rare to find any other argument adjusted to possessor expression.

(iii) *There is often a certain amount of competition between the central arguments*
When one-place predicates are embedded into term positions, adjustment is
straightforward: the single (central) argument of the embedded predication will be
expressed in possessor form if adjustment takes place at all. Two-place embedded
predications, however, meet with a problem: each of the two central arguments is
under pressure to be expressed according to the possessor model, but in the nominal target structure only one possessor position is available. What we then see is
a certain competition between the two central arguments, with the first argument
winning the match in certain languages (or conditions), and the second argument in
other languages (or conditions). In certain languages (or conditions), this may
lead to 'doubling' on the possessor position: the adjustment, in a sense, outdoes

its model in that both the first and the second argument are moulded into possessor expression.

I shall illustrate this competition with examples from Dutch, noting that in many
other languages we find similar phenomena, but often with the balance tipped in
favour of another solution to this problem.

In Dutch, the situation is as follows. There are two main ways of expressing
possessors: (i) by a prenominal possessor expression, which may be either a possessive pronoun or a noun in the genitive (the latter restricted to proper names
and some near-proper names such as *vader* 'father' and *moeder* 'mother'), (ii) by a
postnominal prepositional phrase with *van* 'of':

(75) a. Mijn boek
        my   book

     b. Jans   boek
        John's book

     c. Het boek van mijn vriend
        the book of my   friend

The prenominal and the postnominal possessor expression cannot be combined:

(76)   *Zijn boek van mijn vriend

In other words, there is only one possessor position available in nominal terms.

   Now, the rules for the expression of central arguments within a nominalization
can be formulated as follows:[10]

(77)   (i)   if there is a first argument that is compatible with the
               requirements imposed on prenominal possessors, then
                   (a) express the first argument as a prenominal pos-
                       sessor (optional)
        (ii)   if there is a Goal term, then
                   (b) express the Goal in a *van*-phrase (obligatory)
        (iii) if not (i) or (ii), then, if there is a first argument,
                   (c) express the first argument in a *van*-phrase
                       (optional, but preferred)
        (iv)   terms not treated as specified in (a)-(c) are expressed
               according to their own semantic function.

In order to see what the effect of these rules is, let us first consider one-place embedded predications such as:[11]

(78) $(x_i: [lopen_V (Jan)_{Ag}] (x_i))$

Condition (i) is fulfilled, since *Jan* can be expressed as a prenominal possessor. If option (a) is chosen, the result is:

(79)   Jans   lopen
        John's walking

If option (a) is not chosen, then, since condition (iii) is fulfilled, option (c) may yield:

(80)   het lopen   van Jan
        the walking of John

And if (c) is not chosen, then (iv) will yield:

(81)   het lopen   door Jan
        the walking by   John

which, at best, is a marginal construction in Dutch.
   Let us now consider a two-place input predicate, as in:

(82) $(x_i: [slaan_V (Jan)_{Ag} (de hond)_{Go}] (x_i))$

Again, condition (i) is fulfilled. If option (a) and the obligatory rule (b) are applied, the result is:

(83)   Jans   slaan   van de hond
        John's beating of   the dog

If (a) is not applied, then, since (c) can in this case not apply, the result of (iv) will be:

(84)   het slaan   van de hond door Jan
        the beating of   the dog by   John

Note the following characteristics of this system:

1. there is a strong preference for at least one central argument to take possessor expression.

2. if there is a Goal, the Goal must take possessor expression; this can only be done in postnominal possessor position.

3. the constellation of rules may yield a construction with two central arguments in possessor expression, but this is only possible when one of them is a prenominal possessor and the other a postnominal possessor, and when the prenominal possessor represents the first argument.

Thus, a construction of the following form is not grammatical:

(85)   *het slaan   van de   hond van Jan
         the beating of   the dog   of   John

I have described the expression of the central arguments of a nominalization in terms of a competition to model on the available possessor expressions. There is evidence, however, that in actual practice this competition may be less severe than it would seem to be at first sight.

In an arbitrary sample of 100 Dutch nominalizations culled from a newspaper, I found only one instance of a transitive predicate with both the Goal and the Agent expressed. This means that in most actual occurrences of nominalizations, these will be of one of the following forms:

(86)   Lopen   is gezond
         walking is healthy
(87)   Het stijgen van de prijzen is vervelend
         the rising of the prices is a nuisance
(88)   Het verhogen van de prijzen is onvermijdelijk
         the raising of the prices is inevitable

In other words, an actually occurring nominalization will almost invariably have at most one central argument, and the expression rule in such cases can simply be:

(89)   Express the central argument in a possessor phrase.

This pattern provides an interesting parallel with that of Dutch causative constructions. These start providing problems when not only the Causee, but also an underlying Goal argument is to be overtly expressed. Again, I found that in the

great majority of actual cases this situation is avoided. More than 80% of actually occurring causative constructions have one of the following forms:

(90) a. Piet liet de konijnen eten
        Pete let the rabbits eat

     b. Piet liet de konijnen vangen
        Pete let the rabbits catch

where either the Agent of an intransitive verb, or the Goal of a transitive verb
is the only term overtly expressed in the complement of the causative construction (see Dik 1980a: ch. 3).

We can thus say, in general, that in situations where adjustment is to take
place, the 'difficult' cases of adjustment are at least statistically avoided.

Another parallel between the expression of causative constructions and nominalizations concerns the occurrence of doubling. We saw that the adjustment of
causative constructions may overshoot its mark in leading to constructions with
two objects or two 'Recipients'; similarly, adjustment in the case of nominalizations may lead to constructions with two 'possessors'. Note that in the latter
case, there is no non-derived model available. The reasoning behind double possessor expression would appear to be something like the following: if first arguments can be expressed as possessors in condition A, and second arguments in
condition B, why should not both be expressed as possessors in condition C?

Interestingly, however, the parallel goes even a little bit further. Consider
the following examples of doubling in the French causative:

(91) a. J'ai   fait donner à Claude une pomme au   professeur
        I have made give   to Claude an apple to-the teacher

     b.*J'ai fait donner une pomme au professeur à Claude

As Comrie notes in passing (1976a: 280), French and some other languages only
allow doubling on the IO position if the two terms in question are non-contiguous.
This finds an exact parallel in double possessor expression in Dutch, as we saw
above: two arguments can only be expressed in the form of possessors if one of
them takes the form of a prenominal and the other the form of a postnominal possessor. The same is true for English:

(92) a. the enemy's destruction of the city

     b. the city's destruction by the enemy

(93) a.*the enemy's the city's destruction

     b.*the destruction of the city of the enemy

This parallelism, whatever its source may be, again suggests that in the expression of causative constructions and nominalizations similar processes are at work, similar problems are encountered, and similar solutions are found to these problems.

Finally, let us consider what the PSA would say about the semantic aspects of the different types of nominalization . Predications designate states of affairs; terms refer to entities. Embedded predications refer to entities which consist of states of affairs. The PSA predicts that, the more an embedded predication is adjusted to the formal expression of a basic nominal term, the more 'entity-like' will be its meaning. There are various indications that this prediction is correct.

First, reconsider schema (72) and the scale of embedded predications given in (73). In proceeding from the more verbal end to the more nominal end of the scale, predicate operators for Tense, Aspect, and Mood gradually disappear, and term operators for definiteness and number take their place. At the same time, as demonstrated in Mackenzie (1984), the number of specified arguments and satellites diminishes. Together, these adjustments lead to a more and more general referentiality of the nominalization, ending up in constructions such as:

(94)   Murder is a heinous crime

in which the Action-like character of the original predicate has been reduced to a minimum, the Agent and Goal arguments of that predicate have almost completely receded into the background, and the nominal term *murder* refers to an entity conceived of in an 'object'-like fashion, almost comparable to 'table' or 'tree'.

It appears, then, that the PSA again makes the correct predictions concerning the semantic aspects of formal adjustment of derived constructions.[12]

5. *Conclusion*

I believe it may be safely concluded that the two principles of formal adjustment (PFA) and semantic adjustment (PSA), together with the prototypical expression models (PEMs) defined in (6), have considerable explanatory power with respect to general typological properties of three at first sight quite different construction types: constructions involving valency reduction, constructions involving valency extension, and nominalizations. Further research will be required to see to what extent these principles can be refined in the light of further data, to what extent they can be applied to other construction types, and in what way the relevant facts can be integrated into the actual rule system of a functional grammar.

NOTES

[1] See Comrie (1975, 1976a, 1981) for discussion of this phenomenon.

[2] As we shall see below, the battery of PEMs might be extended with further models for particular languages.

[3] The view of valency reduction developed here is based on earlier analyses presented in Dik and Gvozdanović (1981) and Dik (1983a). I have further profited from several theses written on this subject as it manifests itself in different languages: Afman (1983) on French; Van Duijkeren and De Jong (1984) on Czech; De Groot (1982) on Russian; Heijn Papousek (1983) on Spanish; Kahrel (1984) on English and Dutch; and Van Schaaik (1984) on Turkish. The last-mentioned has also been suggestive with respect to the treatment of causative constructions to be presented in section 3 of this paper. Horn (1983) discusses the phenomenon of 'argument reduction' within the framework of Lexical Functional Grammar. Givón (1982) discusses similar phenomena in terms of 'Agent suppression'. Keenan (1984) recently suggested a rule of valency reduction within the framework of a theory of semantically interpreted categorial grammar. My account differs from that of Givón and Keenan in that I do not use 'valency reduction' in order to account for 'passive' constructions. In FG, passivization is treated in terms of alternative Subject assignment to the arguments of a predicate-frame which remains otherwise unchanged. In particular, the Agent position is not removed in the case of a passive construction. If the Agent is not specified in the passive (which is usually the case), this is interpreted in terms of a non-filled, but available Agent position rather than in terms of absence of the Agent position.

[4] In Dik (1983a) it has been demonstrated that this may lead to a unified account of all constructions containing the so-called 'reflexive' element.

[5] See note 3 for the difference between my interpretation of this rule and that of Givón.

[6] Compare Givón (1976a).

[7] Note that in Comrie (1981a) this theory is somewhat modified in the light of Cole's semantic theory (Cole 1983), to be discussed below.

[8] Such a combination is also advocated in Comrie (1981a).

[9] Where Experiencers have a different marking than Recipients, we expect a formal difference between (53c) and (54b).

[10] These rules apply to that type of nominalization in which the predicate is expressed in infinitival form. The rules for nominalizations with verbal nouns differ slightly, in that Goals can also be moulded into prenominal possessors (though marginally so).

[11] On the representation of embedded predications and nominalizations in FG, see Dik (1981) and Mackenzie (1983).

[12] For further discussion, see also Mackenzie's paper in the present volume.

Chapter 2

Nominalization and valency reduction

J. Lachlan Mackenzie
Department of English, Free University of Amsterdam

0. Introduction*

The analysis of nominalization in Functional Grammar (FG) remains uncertain. Two proposals have been made in the existing literature, one involving a predicate formation rule of nominalization, the other assigning to the expression-rule component the responsibility for the form taken by nominalizations. Neither proposal offers an explanation for the fact that the overwhelming majority of nominalizations, as compared with analogous finite predications, display a marked reduction in 'actual valency', i.e. the number of arguments that receive overt expression in attested discourse. The purpose of this paper is to present a new analysis of nominalization which does justice to the reduction in actual valency and account for the form of adnominal constituents, notably those with genitive case-marking or adpositions. This analysis involves treating nominalization as a variant of a predicate formation rule of valency reduction similar to the detransitivization rule proposed by Dik (1983a). Data will be presented from English, Aguacatec (Mayan) and Labrador Inuttut (Eskimo).

1. Functional Grammar analyses of nominalization

Terms, expressions with referential potential, are represented in FG by the schema (1):

(1) $(\omega x_i : \text{pred } (x_i)_\emptyset)$

There are three possibilities for the position 'pred': firstly, a predicate drawn from the lexicon; secondly, a derived predicate, i.e. a predicate resulting from the operation of a predicate formation rule; thirdly, as has been recognized since Bolkestein et al. (1981), a full predication. It is this third option, which takes account of one aspect of the recursivity of language structure, the possibility of embedding predications within predications, that will be discussed in this paper; that is, we will be concerned with terms that display the following structure:

(2) $(\omega x_i: [\text{pred } (x_m) \ldots (x_n) (y_m) \ldots (y_n)] (x_i)_{\emptyset})$

where $m \geq \emptyset$ and what is the predicate-slot in (1) is occupied by a (possibly
extended) predication. This schema will be called upon for the representation of
a range of hypotactic constructions, i.e. all embedded clauses that have
argument-status with respect to a predicate (roughly subject- and object-clauses
in traditional terminology), all embedded clauses that have satellite-status
with respect to a predication (approximately adverbial clauses), but also the
non-finite congeners of such clauses, covering various gerundial, absolute and
infinitive constructions, and, importantly for this paper, nominalizations of
diverse kinds. Hypotactic constructions that receive a different analysis in FG
include relative clauses and participial constructions, which are analysed as
restrictors rather than as predicates (see Dik 1978: 64ff).[1] All predications
occurring as predicates in representations conforming to (2) will be referred to
as subordinate predications.

Of particular interest in the present context are those subordinate predications which display one or more indications of nominalization, in the sense that
they manifest structural properties characteristic of terms the Head (i.e. the
first restrictor) of which is an underived nominal predicate. As recognized by
Dik (1978: 63), the primary use of a nominal predicate is as Head of a term
phrase; conversely, the unmarked Head of a term phrase is a nominal predicate
(cf. Dik 1978: 59). For a verbal predication to occupy the slot reserved in the
unmarked case for a nominal predicate may therefore already be regarded as an
instance of nominalization, and this is indeed Lehmann's (1982: 68) position, who
treats all cases of what is here called subordination as 'nominalization'.

The distinction between subordination and nominalization is, however, retained
by Dik (forthcoming), who defines nominalization, with respect to Dutch, as 'any
non-finite form of *expression* [my emphasis, JLM] of an embedded predication',
whereby an embedded predication is a 'predication functioning as a term ... within a higher predication' (i.e. = our subordinate predication), and 'non-finite'
means 'not specified for the category Tense' (all translations mine, JLM). This
definition permits a clear demarcation in Dutch between nominalized and non-
nominalized subordinate predications. Similarly, Dik (this volume) analyses
nominalizations as being subject to the Principle of Formal Adjustment, a principle which is intended to pertain to the expression rules. However, alongside
this approach to nominalization as a non-finite form of *expression*, there are
also hints in the FG literature that nominalization may involve predicate form-

ation. Thus, Dik (1978: 64) considers the term *the frequent mowing of the lawn*
and *the killing of the tiger* to result from a predicate formation rule 'nominalization'; in Dik (1980a), nominalization is mentioned as one of the predicate
formation rules that brings about a change in category; and in Mackenzie (1983),
the shooting of the hunters is regarded as being derived by a predicate formation
rule.

Accordingly, two analyses of *the killing of the tiger* may be derived from the
existing proposals:

(3) $(d1x_i: [kill_V\text{-}ing_N (x_j: \text{animate} (x_j))_{Ag} (d1x_k: tiger_N (x_k))_{Go}] (x_i)_\emptyset)$

(4) $(d1x_i: [kill_V (x_j: \text{animate} (x_j))_{Ag} (d1x_k: tiger_N (x_k))_{Go}] (x_i)_\emptyset)$

In (3), the predicate $kill_V\text{-}ing_N$ is derived by a predicate formation rule taking
a verbal predicate frame as input and yielding a nominal predicate frame. In (4),
the predicate $kill_V$ is drawn directly from the lexicon, and receives its form
killing through the operation of the expression rules.

Given FG as currently constituted, (3) and (4) are the only plausible alternatives, since predicates must be unambiguously assigned to one of the three
categories N, V and (irrelevantly for the present issue) A. Introduction of a new
lexical category (say, VN) for predicates that have partly verbal and partly
nominal characteristics would make it possible to recognize $killing_{VN}$ as a lexical predicate and thereby to obviate having to choose between the rivalling
representations (3) and (4). One major drawback of such a 'lexicalist' solution
would be that the productivity of the relationship between $kill_V$ and $killing_{VN}$
could no longer be stated in that component of the organization of a FG which is
designed to capture productive relationships between predicates, i.e. the set of
predicate formation rules. Another problem is that in many languages, as Dik
(forthcoming) has shown for Dutch and Mackenzie (1984a) for English, there are
several forms that may plausibly be regarded as nominalizations each of which has
its own set of properties such that a scale can be recognized ranging from relatively 'verby' to relatively 'nouny' constructions.[2] Thus, Mackenzie (1984a:
77-79) points out that the range of constructions exemplified by *that my horse
beat the favourite, my horse beating the favourite, my horse's beating the favourite, my horse's beating of the favourite* and *my horse's victory over the favourite* displays gradual loss of the properties typical of verbal predicates/
predications (assignment of syntactic functions, morphological marking of voice,

aspect and tense distinctions, auxiliary-verb marking of mood distinctions) and gradual gain of typically nominal properties (restrictors rather than arguments and satellites, adnominal adpositional phrases, term operators). On the assumption that the predicate *beat* may be assigned to the category V and the predicate *victory* to the category N, it would be necessary to postulate three intermediate categories, say VN_1, VN_2 and VN_3, to cover the range of data. Rather than accept this proliferation of categories, however, we may provisionally agree that (3) and (4) do indeed present the possible analyses hitherto available in FG.

2. Nominalizations in use: valency reduction

The bulk of the recent literature on nominalizations has concentrated on the parallelism between the internal structure of the terms in question and the structure of corresponding sentences. Indeed, much of the original motivation for X' Syntax was drawn from observations of such parallelisms (cf. Chomsky 1970, Jackendoff 1977). The assumption that nominalization, whether as a predicate formation rule or as an expression rule (-cluster), results in a structure parallel to that of the non-nominalized equivalent is also inherent in the motivation for representations (3) and (4). However, observation of the actual occurrence of nominalizations in texts shows that there is an overwhelming tendency for nominalizations of all types *not* to be structurally parallel to their non-nominalized counterparts. The difference resides in the fact that the terms associated with a nominalized verbal predicate are much more likely not to be expressed than is the case with non-nominalized verbal predicates. Nominalization, then, is typically associated with a reduction in *actual valency*, by which I mean the number of arguments that receive overt expression (for numerical data supporting this assertion, see Hopper and Thompson (1980: 285) and Mackenzie (1984a: 80) for English; and Dik (forthcoming) and Mackenzie (1984b) for Dutch). Thus, a textually typical sequence is the following, taken from *The Observer*, 26.2.84, p. 2:

(5)   A pilot usually requires a horizon so that he can orient himself. He should still scan his instruments from time to time, but if he cannot see a horizon, then *this scanning* becomes much more important.

These observations of actual valency reduction are not, of themselves, damaging for X' Syntax, conceived as it is within the formal paradigm in which the absence of constituents can be accounted for by means of deletion rules whose frequency of application is immaterial; but they are of importance for FG, which assumes

that 'the study of the language system must from the very start take place within
the framework of the system of language use' and 'that the description of linguistic expressions must provide points of contact for the description of their
functioning in given settings' (Dik 1978: 5). How can the analysis of nominalizations be improved in such a way as to take account of the observations of actual
valency reduction and to link them to an understanding of the function of nominalizations in context?

2.1. Three factors favouring nominalization

As observed above, to subordinate a predication is, in FG terms, to present it as
the Head of a term. In employing a term of any kind, a speaker is issuing an in-
vitation to his addressee to attend to some entity (or set of entities), i.e. to
the *referent*. In the case of structure (2), the referent cannot be a person,
animal or other tangible object. Rather, in Lyons' (1977, 1979) terms, it must be
an entity of a higher order: either a second-order entity (in FG, this is the
state of affairs designated by the embedded predication); or a third-order entity
(in FG, the proposition represented by the embedded predication, i.e. its intensional correlate). Now, whether the speaker is referring to a first-, second- or
third-order entity, he will strive to provide just enough information, in the
form of the predicates (the major information-bearing elements) that he incorpo-
rates in the term, for his addressee to make the intended identification. This
is, I would propose, relevant to one of the factors determining the options
available to a speaker of a language with a range of expression possibilities
for subordinate predications. If the speaker assesses that naming the predicate
will be a sufficient clue to the predication as a whole, this will induce the
choice of a form of expression that does not require the specification of all
arguments, and this will be most readily offered by the relatively nouny variants.
But the desire to observe the Maxim of Quantity (Grice 1975) in this way is certainly not the only factor determining the occurrence of nominalizations.

A second reason why a speaker may elect to nominalize is in order to achieve
greater syntactic versatility. In English, for instance, a finite subordinate
clause may appear only in P1 position, or else, under the influence of LIPOC, is
strongly constrained to adopt predication-final position. A nominalized subordinate predication is, however, of lesser categorial complexity and can therefore
also show up in S position, in O position, after prepositions, etc.:

(6) a. *Is that Mary has been sacked common knowledge?

    b.   Is Mary's sacking common knowledge?

(7) a. ?I mentioned that Mary had been sacked to Pete

    b.   I mentioned to Pete that Mary had been sacked

    c.   I mentioned Mary's sacking to Pete

(8) a. *I hadn't reckoned with that Mary had been sacked

    b.   I hadn't reckoned with Mary's sacking

A third factor favouring the choice of a nominalized predication is the desire to signal the introduction of a new discourse referent in a particularly explicit fashion. Nominalization permits the speaker to give a name to the higher-order entity that is being hypostatized, a name that enjoys a versatility of use that complements the syntactic versatility mentioned above (note, for example, the use of nominalizations in titles, definitions, etc.). Just as a combination of operator and first-order noun may not, in specific pragmatic circumstances, offer enough information for purposes of identification, and additional restrictors may be required, so the naming of higher-order entities may involve recourse to restrictors, notably restrictive relative clauses; non-nominalized subordination does not permit such restriction.

These three factors, the avoidance of redundancy, the achievement of syntactic versatility, and the introduction of discourse referents, need not always work together. If, for example, a two-place subordinate predication is to be used in S-position, on the double assumption that neither argument is communicatively redundant and that the speaker wishes to introduce a discourse referent, then, on the strength of the second and third factors, a nominalization will be chosen, but one in which both arguments of the embedded predication are specified:

(9)   They tell me that Pete's sacking of Mary has caused quite a stir.
        It was the talking point at lunch, since it had been leaked pre-
        maturely despite the board's express wish that it be kept secret ...

The structure that results, *X's N of Y*, is testimony to the compromise of which it is born. This structure is not found where N designates a first-order entity: *Pete's ball of Mary*.

2.2. Problems of expression

To nominalize a predication is to give it a structure which approximates to the prototypical structure of terms whose head designates a first-order entity. This

is clearly problematic, especially in the case of many-place predicates, since
the prototypical nominal predicate, in most languages at least,[3] is avalent, i.e.
opens no argument-positions. There are indeed languages which do not display
nominalization of subordinate predications (Chinese, Lahu, ...). And there are
others in which the head of the subordinate predication may manifest nominal
properties, but without any effect on the form of the accompanying arguments
(Hua, Tamil, ...), or allow this as one possibility (Quechua, Niuean, ...).
Future discourse studies of such languages will indicate whether nominalization,
here too, is typically associated with a reduction in actual valency. In many
languages, however, use is made of the fact that nominal predicates, although
typically not opening up any argument-positions, may be accompanied by satellites,
as argued for English in Mackenzie (1983): *the house on the hill, a cathedral by
Wren, John's office*. If the speaker of such a language wishes both to nominalize
and yet to specify the arguments of the input predication, one important strategy
involves adding satellites that refer to the referents of the input arguments.
It is this strategy that will be examined in this paper. The advantage of the
'conversion-to-satellite' strategy is that the nominal predicate displays the
appropriate lack of valency, yet the potential of referential specificity is
retained.

3. Nominalization as valency reduction

How may this be formalized in FG? The treatment of detransitivization in Dik
(1983a) is suggestive. Here a predicate formation rule is proposed which takes as
input a two-place predicate frame and yields a one-place frame:

(10)   DETRANSITIVIZATION (= VALENCY REDUCTION ONE)

       Input: $pred_V$ (x_1) (x_2)

       Output: $pred_V$-R (x_1)

       Meaning: the relation expressed by $pred_V$ applies to x_1

Dik argues that it is the operation of this rule, which I shall rename Valency
Reduction One, that is indicated by the alleged 'verbal reflexives' of such
languages as Serbo-Croatian, Dyirbal, Yavapai and Hixkaryana. His claim is that
the derived predicate (pred-R) presents a riddle to the interpreter, since its
meaning appears paradoxical: 'how can a two-place relation be relevant to only
a single entity?' (Dik 1983a: 234). The riddle is solved by constructing an

interpretation in which it is possible for a two-place relation to be applied to a single entity. This may involve (i) an unspecified second argument interpretation as in (11a) from Yavapai; (ii) a reflexive interpretation, as in (11b) from Serbo-Croatian; (iii) an unspecified first argument interpretation, as in (11c) from Yavapai; or (iv) a reciprocal interpretation, as in (11d) from Serbo-Croatian:

(11) a. ?ña-c ?-cθul-v-km   (= Dik's (44))
        1-Subj 1-wash-R-incompl
        'I am washing (something)'

     b. Ivan se je ubio   (= Dik's (24))
        Ivan R   aux killed
        'Ivan killed himself'

     c. hlo-v-c   si:l-v-kñ   (= Dik's (45b))
        rabbit-dem-Subj fry-R-compl
        'The rabbit (was) fried'

     d. Djeca   su se vidjela   (= Dik's (25))
        children aux R   seen
        'The children saw each other'

Dik also points out that the riddle may be solved in more than one way for any one sentence: thus (11a) and (11d) may also receive a reflexive interpretation.

The same rule may well also be involved in an FG account of 'anti-passivization' in languages like Dyirbal and Eskimo (cf. Dik 1978: 167ff), and possibly also in the representation of passivization in certain languages (cf. Vet, this volume, on French). Rather than dwell on this possibility, however, I should wish to suggest that this same rule has a role to play in an account of nominalization in those languages in which there is a preponderance of actual valency reduction and in which the conversion-to-satellite strategy is adopted. Note that the semantic functions of the arguments are not specified in rule (10), so that (x_1) may be either Ag/Fo/Po or Go, although, in a particular language, specification may be possible (cf. sections 4 and 5). Furthermore, there is nothing preventing the addition of a satellite to a predication formed from the output frame with the same reference as (x_2), provided that it is clearly marked as such. In anti-passivization, for example, (x_2) may be optionally specified as satellites in the modalis-instrumental (Eskimo) or dative (Dyirbal) or ergative-instrumental (Dyirbal).

In case of nominalization, assimilation to nominal structure, another form of valency reduction is required. There is considerable evidence to suggest that, alongside (10), FG must also recognize a rule reducing the valency of one-place predicates to zero: this predicate formation rule may, for instance, be involved

in an account of the passivization of one-place predicates in Dutch, Latin,
Turkish, etc. Consider the following sentences from Dutch, Latin and Turkish
respectively:

(12) a. Er   werd gevochten
        there was fought
        'There was fighting (going on)'

     b. Pugnabatur
        fight-imperf-passive
        'There was fighting (going on)'

     c. İstasyon-a   bu   yol-dan gid-il- ir
        station- Dir this way-Abl go- Pass-Aorist
        'This is the way to the station'

In none of these sentences can the passive morphology be ascribed to the assignment of Subj to a non-Agent; rather, the passive voice indicates that a particular
state of affairs obtains without there being any specification of the agentive
participant(s) in that state of affairs. A general formulation of the rule would
appear as in (13):

(13)   VALENCY REDUCTION TWO

        Input: pred (x_1)

        Output: pred

        Meaning: the state of affairs designated by pred obtains

In principle, any one-place predicate, derived or not, could be input to this
rule. Thus, even a predicate derived by (10) could be subject to further valency
reduction by virtue of (13): the so-called 'iterated passive' of Turkish may be
analysed as giving evidence for a double application of valency reduction, i.e.
of (10) and then (13). The following example was given by Keenan (1984):

(14)   Bu   şato- da boğ-   ul- un- ur
        this chateau-Loc strangle-Pass-Pass-Aorist
        'Strangling takes place in this chateau'

        (Note that -ul- and -un- are phonologically conditioned allomorphs)

   My suggestion is that nominalization - if syntacticized as a predicate formation rule - is a version of (13) such that the input predicate is marked as
verbal and the output as nominal. Nominalization is thus a category-changing
form of Valency Reduction Two:

(15)   NOMINALIZATION

Input: $pred_V (x_1)$

Output: $pred-M_N$

Meaning: the state of affairs designated by $pred_V$ or its intensional correlate (where M = marker of nominalization (possibly $\emptyset$))

Specifically, the 'nominalization' of a two-place predicate involves two steps: firstly, reduction of the valency to one, as a result of (10), and then Nominalization proper, as a result of (15); the 'nominalization' of a one-place predicate involves only the application of (15). Thus, *scanning* in (5) above results, in this analysis, from the successive application of (10) and (15) with respect to a two-place input predicate frame $scan_V (x_i)_{Ag} (x_j)_{Go}$; the marker of nominalization, M in (15), is in English *-ing*. Now, if the speaker, having selected a predicate derived by Valency Reduction One and Nominalization, wishes to specify one or both of the arguments of the input predicate, he may do so by appending satellites, just as satellites may be appended to a finite verbal predication to indicate Time, Place, etc. The form given to these satellites, in very many languages of widely differing typological characteristics, is that of a Possessor. It is as though the higher-order entity designated by the subordinate predication, by virtue of its nominalization, its assimilation to nominal structure, is conceptualized as an entity that is capable of having a Possessor, i.e. is treated as if it were a first-order entity. Such satellites will therefore be shown in the representation of the predication as Possessors.

The major motivation for this analysis of nominalization is that the reduction in actual valency reported above is reflected directly in the structure of the underlying predication rather than being the result of arbitrary deletion rules. Whereas this analysis seems appropriate for cases of nominalization in which 'nouny' properties heavily predominate over 'verby' ones, it does not seem adequate to account for such hybrids as the English gerund, which retains many 'verby' properties while also manifesting some 'nouny' attributes. For such constructions, the analysis proposed in Mackenzie (1983) still appears to me to be the most appropriate, whereby the gerund in English is analysed as a non-nominalized form of subordination, and the case-marking regularities are handled by the expression rules. In the sense of Watters (this volume), the gerund is a matter of inflectional morphology while nominalization is a matter of derivational morphology.

In English, there is no clear evidence for valency reduction in the form
taken by predications (unless - under an analysis of passivization as detransitivization (cf. Vet, this volume) - the Goal argument in the output is chosen as
Subj of a finite predication, in which case passive morphology is evident). In
sections 4 and 5 we will briefly consider two languages in which valency reduction *is* given regular morphological expression and in which the form of the
nominalization betrays the operation of Valency Reduction prior to the operation
of Nominalization proper.

4. Nominalization in Aguacatec

Aguacatec, a Mayan language spoken in NW Guatemala, is described by McArthur and
McArthur (1966) and Larsen (1981). In this (ergative) language, both one-place
and two-place predicates may be nominalized by means of the suffix -*e7n*. The following examples from Larsen (1981) show nominalizations of one-place predicates:

(16)   t- ook- e7n
         its-enter-nom
         'its entering'

(17)   ky- opoon- e7n
         their-arrive-nom
         'their arriving there'

Two-place predicates appear to occur in nominalizations only if they include
the suffix -*l* (with allomorphs -*ch* and -*w*), which, according to McArthur &
McArthur (1966: 157), is used 'with certain transitive verb stems to form derived
intransitive stems', i.e. for detransitivization (valency reduction). This suffix
is not confined to nominalizations: thus, from *al* 'say' may be formed *al-ch-ij*
'be said', where the 'second-order suffix' -*ij* has 'a passive sense' (McArthur &
McArthur 1966: 158). Thus, from Larsen:

(18)   x- e7t- e7n tzun-tz   tan x- txum- l-   e7n juun
         his-start-nom then-'same topic' to its-think-detrans-nom one
         tajtzaa7ql
         idea
         'So, starting to have an idea, ...'

Or, from McArthur & McArthur, with slightly different spelling conventions:

(19)   ma   jalchan na chi- b'en cob' chakum   tan b'iy-l-   e'n
        then early   asp they-go two messengers to kill-detrans-nom

        cne'r Xchimal
        sheep Xchimal
        'Two messengers go early in the morning to kill a sheep in Xchimal'

(20)   ten   Ø- cu   tzaj yaj tan t- il- w-   e7n
        long:ago he-comes:down hither man to its-see-detrans-nom
        'The man came down to see it a long time ago'

From these and similar data it would appear that in Aguacatec there is evidence
for the application of Valency Reduction One in the formation of nominalizations
from two-place predicates. I would suggest that the suffix -*l* is an indication
of the operation of Valency Reduction One as a predicate formation rule (cf.
(10)), which, it will be recalled, also forms one-place predicates from two-place
predicates for purposes other than nominalization. The fact that nominalization
can be (and in this language often is) extended by a Possessor satellite suggests
that in Aguacatec nominalization results in an avalent predicate:

(21)   TWO-PLACE   ONE-PLACE

                                $pred_V$ Ag Go $pred_V$ Arg

         VAL RED 1 $pred_V$-l Go   ---------

         NOMLZN $pred_V$-l-e7n$_N$ $pred_V$-e7n$_N$

In Aguacatec, as in English, it will be necessary to specify that Valency Reduction One deprives the predicate of its first argument (represented in (21) as Ag).

5. Nominalization in Labrador Inuttut

In the next language to be discussed, Labrador Inuttut, a dialect of Inupik
Eskimo spoken in Eastern Canada, this restriction does not apply. In this language, which is like Aguacatec in displaying ergative structure (data from Smith
1981; the morpheme-analysis has been modified in accordance with M. Fortescue,
p.c.), two-place predicates may have their valency reduced either by relegating
the ergative subject to the status of an optional satellite (with the terminalis
case) - the so-called 'passive' - or by relegating the absolutive object to
optional satellite status, marking it as modalis and the remaining argument, the
Ag, as absolutive, the case required for the sole argument of a one-place predicate - the so-called 'antipassive'. Thus, given a two-place input, Valency
Reduction One can have either of two effects:

(22)   VALENCY REDUCTION ONE

    a. Input: pred Ag Go
       Output: pred-pass Go_{abs}

    b. Input: pred Ag Go
       Output: pred-antipass Ag_{abs}

There is evidence to suggest that both predicate formation rules (22a) and (22b),
either of which can be captured by the general schema for valency reduction given
in (10) above, can apply prior to nominalization, and indeed always do so if the
input predicate is two-place. Nominalizations in Labrador Inuttut are recogniz-
able by the suffix -*giak* or -*nik* (and their various allomorphs): according to
M. Fortescue, p.c., -*giak* is used typically for designating second-order entities
and -*nik* for designating third-order entities in the sense of Lyons (1977, 1979).
Consider the following example from Smith (1981):

(23)   pisun-nik Naini-mut ippasak ...
     walk- nom Nain- ter yesterday
     'Walking to Nain yesterday ...'

     (ter = terminalis case, expressing the semantic function Direction)

Note that the argument of the input predicate need not be specified and that the
addition of satellites (in this case with the semantic function Dir and Temp) is
regularly possible. Although *pisunnik* is here avalent, a possessive suffix and
possibly also a possessive-marked noun phrase may be added if the argument of
the one-place input is to be specified: *pisun-ni-nga* 'his walking'. The following
example involves a two-place predicate:

(24)   Anguti-up   tuqut-si-   ni- nga tigigannia-mik tatamitit-si-
     man-   poss kill- antipass-nom-his fox-   mod surprise- antipass-
     vuk iluunnangin-nik
     3ps everyone-   mod
     'The man's killing of the fox surprised everyone'

     (mod = modalis case, probably expressing semantic function Instrument)

The derived nominal *tuqutsinik* is here accompanied by two satellites, one marked
as Possessor (the input Ag) and one as modalis (the input Go). The nominal further
includes an antipassive suffix -*si*: it will be recalled that Go's under antipassive are reduced to satellites marked as modalis (note that (24) also shows the

operation of antipassive on the finite predicate). I therefore suggest that the following sequence of predicate formation rules are involved in the formation of the nominal predicate tuqutsinik$_N$:

(25)   VALENCY REDUCTION ONE (ANTIPASSIVE)

	ARGS	SATS
Input:	tuqut$_V$ Ag Go	
Output:	tuqut-si$_V$ Ag	Mod

NOMINALIZATION

	ARGS	SATS
Input:	tuqut-si$_V$ Ag	
Output:	tuqut-si-nik$_N$	Poss Mod

In Labrador Inuttut, it is not necessary for the suffix -si to be present with all predicates, as is clear from Smith's examples tusaan$_V$-nik$_N$ 'hearing', but the conversion to satellites is identical to the case outlined above, cf. (26):

(26)   qimmi-up   tusaan-ni- nga sivanim-mik ...
        dog- poss hear- nom- its bell-   mod
        'The dog's hearing of the bell ...'

With such verbs, antipassive valency reduction merely fails to append a suffix. The other possibility alluded to above, passive valency reduction, is illustrated by (27):

(27)   tigigannia-p   tuqu-tau- gia-nga anguti-mut ...
        fox-   poss kill-pass-nom-his man-   ter
        'The fox's being killed by the man ...'

Again, the derived nominal tuqutaugiak is accompanied by two satellites, one marked as Possessor (the input Go) and one as terminalis (the input Ag). The nominal includes the passive suffix -tau: it will be recalled that Ag's under passive are reduced to satellites marked as terminalis. I therefore suggest that the following sequence of predicate formation rules is involved in the formation of the nominal predicate tuqutaugiak$_N$:

(28)   VALENCY REDUCTION ONE (PASSIVE)

		ARGS	SATS
Input:	tuqut_V	Ag Go	
Output:	tuqu-tau_V^4	Go	Ter

NOMINALIZATION

Input:	tuqu-tau_V Go	
Output:	tuqu-tau-giak_N	Poss Ter

It would appear that the operation of passive valency reduction is always sig-
nalled by the presence of the suffix *tau*.

6. *Unitary nominalization*

Aguacatec and Labrador Inuttut have been presented as two particularly clear
cases of languages in which nominalization is a predicate formation rule operating
upon an input predicate that is either lexically one-place or one-place by virtue
of valency reduction. In both languages, the output of Valency Reduction One may function as a predicate without nominalization taking place; in other languages, e.g.
English, the output of Valency Reduction One, cf. (10), has less independent
justification in FG as currently conceived, although it may well turn out to be
relevant to the analysis of 'middle' or 'ergative' verbs and, possibly, in con-
junction with syntactic function assignment, to the analysis of passive. Be that
as it may, I will here present the hypothesis that Valency Reduction One and
Nominalization work together in languages like English as a unit, as one rule
combining the detransitivization and nominalizing effects as follows:

(29)   UNITARY NOMINALIZATION

> Input: pred_V Ag Go
>
> Output: pred_N -R-M
>
> Meaning: the state of affairs designated by pred_V

   If this analysis is adopted, it will be apparent that neither of the representations (3) or (4) is an adequate representation of a nominalized subordinate predication in English. (3) is better in presupposing a predicate formation rule of
nominalization, but, in retaining the argument-structure of the input verbal
predicate, it does not do justice to the valency reduction phenomena associated

with nominalization. Much is also left to the expression rules: in Mackenzie
(1983) it was noted as a problem that *of*, according to this analysis, marks
either Go or Subj in the nominal domain without any explanation of why the same
formative should mark a syntactic function and a semantic function and why specifically these. In the proposal embodied in the present paper, *of*, and its Prefield alternant *'s*, are merely markers of a Possessor, albeit a possessor in a
somewhat metaphorical sense of an entity associated with a higher-order entity
(Seiler 1983: 51 calls this 'POSSESSION in a relatively weak sense'). The ambiguity of *the shooting of the hunters* results from the vagueness of this associa-
tion (indeed, in a technical sense, such a phrase is no longer regarded as ambiguous). It has been pointed out, however, that nominalization involves a structural *approximation* to nominal form: as in the case of *Peter's sacking of Mary*
in (9), combinations are possible for which there is no parallel where the possessum is a first-order entity. This structure is textually very infrequent, but
it is difficult to represent in the analysis proposed here, where *sacking* is
avalent and *Peter's* and *of Mary* are represented indiscriminately as Possessor
satellites. This would appear to be a case in which the argument structure of
the input predicate, in some way, lives on in the nominalization: *Peter's* can
only be interpreted as the Agent and *of Mary* only as the Goal.

It was noted earlier that (unitary) nominalization is problematic in that it
attempts to squeeze a polyvalent peg into an avalent hole. It is therefore to be
expected that the conversion to nominal structure will be less than perfect and
that aspects of the transitivity of the input predication may linger on. In those
languages in which more than one Possessor function may be recognized, e.g.
Kresh, in which there is a distinction between alienable and inalienable possession (R.D. Brown, p.c.) or Samoan, which distinguishes between 'dominant' and
'subordinate' possession (cf. Chung 1973: 643), one of these may be specialized
to indicate the Agent of the input predicate frame (in Kresh, the alienable; in
Samoan, the dominant) and the other to indicate the Goal. Where there is only
one Possessor function (as in English, where the opposition between *'s* and *of*
does not reside in the nature of the possession but rather is conditioned by a
range of factors including definiteness, Topic-Focus distribution, an animacy/
empathy hierarchy and syntactic length/complexity; cf. Mackenzie 1983), relatively arbitrary rules determine the interpretation (or conversely expression)
of double-possessor constructions (X's p_V-ing$_N$ of Y - where p_V is the input
verbal predicate). The rules of English appear to be a syntactic codification of
an analogy with the formally very similar active gerund construction
(X's p_V-ing$_V$ Y), according to which, in the double-possessor construction, X is

interpreted as an Agent and Y as Goal. This applies less rigorously to the textually less frequent cases of nominalization with one Possessor satellite. Where
no reference is made to the Agent (a/the p_V-ing_N of Y), Y is predominantly
interpreted as Go (cf. the corresponding gerund p_V-ing_V Y), although in suitable
contexts Y may be interpreted as Ag: *the sackings of the new boss have reached
alarming proportions.* Similarly, where no reference is made to the Goal
(X's p_V-ing_N), X will preferentially be regarded as Agent (cf. the formally
identical corresponding gerund X's p_V-ing_V), although, here too, a Go interpretation is possible, provided the predicate is of very high transitivity (cf.
Mary's sacking in (6b), (7c) and (8b), as against the impossibility of interpreting the Possessor as Go in *Peter's seeing* or *Mary's loving*). The explanation
for this may be that only predicates of very high transitivity (here interpreted
as a scalar property, cf. Hopper and Thompson 1980: 252) retain enough transitivity through the process of (unitary) nominalization to permit a Go to occupy a
slot preferentially destined for Ag, i.e. to undergo the further valency reduction that goes with such usurpation (cf. passive).

What is true of nominalizations of the form p_V-ing is also applicable, but in
lesser measure, to those lexical nouns that designate second- or third-order
entities (cf. *promotion, nominalization, appraisal, removal, ...*). Since such
nouns cannot be formed by productive rule (for the same reasons as preclude a
transformational analysis in the view of Chomsky 1970), they are listed in the
lexicon, the link to any etymologically related verbal predicate being stated,
if at all, in the meaning definition. The representation of such nouns as polyvalent nominal predicates, as given in Mackenzie (1983), suffers from essentially
the same defects as (3): the patent fact that such nouns typically occur either
without any accompanying terms or with a Possessor phrase does not receive any
natural representation. I therefore now propose that such nouns be shown in the
lexicon as avalent; just like first-order nominal predicates, they remain capable
of being supplemented by satellites. They resemble nominalizations in that, on
occasion, they may be accompanied by two Possessors: thus *Pete's sacking of Mary*
in (9) could be replaced - under parallel pragmatic conditions - by *Pete's dismissal of Mary.* As with the productively formed *Pete's dismissing of Mary*, the
Prefield Possessor is necessarily interpreted as Ag and the Postfield Possessor
as Go. Likewise, a sole Postfield Possessor will be preferentially interpreted
as Go, and a sole Prefield Possessor as Ag, although a Go interpretation is again
possible where the predicate designates a state of affairs in which the Go is
strongly affected by the Action (cf. Fiengo 1980), a property characteristic of
highly transitive verbal predicates (cf. *Pete's dismissal* in which *Pete* may be

interpreted as Go). Again, it would appear that syntactically codified analogy with the very similar nominalization construction may be brought forward as permitting an understanding of the interpretation of the Possessors that accompany nominal predicates referring to higher-order entities.

7. *Conclusion*

Although the discussion of the interpretation of Possessor phrases in the preceding paragraphs partially concerns the expression rules, it does not vitiate the main conclusion of this paper, that nominalization is, in English and - I would hypothesize - all the many languages characterized by a conversion-to-satellite strategy, intimately bound up with predicate formation, *in casu* the formation of avalent nominal predicates. The major advantage of this approach is that it accounts in a natural way for the textually evident fact that nominalized predications are, relative to their non-nominalized counterparts, characterized by a marked lack of actual valency. By representing nominalization as a form of valency reduction, we also give formal acknowledgement to the link, discussed by Hopper and Thompson (1980) and Mackenzie (1984a), between nominalization and other techniques for presenting backgrounded information in which valency reduction is also involved (passivization, antipassivization, reflexivization, etc.). As a result, the analysis of nominalization put forward here will not only account for observed syntactic tendencies towards valency reduction but also play its part in the desired integration of FG and discourse analysis.

NOTES

*   The research for this paper was conducted in the framework of the conditionally financed research project 'Functional Language Research: Grammar and Pragmatics' of the Free University of Amsterdam. The paper was written during the author's fellowship at the Netherlands Institute for Advanced Studies in Wassenaar, in the context of the project 'Explanation of Linguistic Universals'. The paper owes much to the FG Work Group on nominalizations organized by Simon Dik at the University of Amsterdam in 1983-84 and especially to preliminary discussions of the Aguacatec and Labrador Inuttut data. The final version of this paper has also benefited considerably from the reactions of Michael Fortescue and Paul Schachter to the oral presentation.

[1]   It is not clear to me whether the 'headless' relative clauses of Mohave, Usan, etc. should be analysed as restrictors or as subordinate predications.

[2]   Ross (1973a), in a somewhat different framework, provides an extremely well documented analysis of this scale in English; the terms 'nouny' and 'verby' are also his.

[3]   See, however, Seiler's (1977) discussion of the extensive set of relational
       (two-place) nouns in Cahuilla.

[4]   Note that *tuqut* 'kill' is truncated to *tuqu-* before *-tau*. *Tuqut* is itself
       subject to further analysis into *tuqu-* 'die' + *-t* 'causative', cf. also
       tatamitit in (21), analysable as *tatami-* 'be surprised' + *-tit* 'causative'
       (M. Fortescue, p.c.). The input to detransitivization may therefore be a
       predicate formed by means of a valency-increasing predicate formation rule
       of causativization.

Passive, reflexive, and causative predicate formation in French

Co Vet
Department of French, University of Groningen

0. Introduction*

Sentences generally do not give an exhaustive description of the states of
affairs they refer to. The time and the location of a state of affairs are very
often not mentioned. In the same way the instrument and the beneficiary are fre-
quently not relevant enough to be mentioned. At any rate their absence does not
affect the well-formedness of the sentence:

(1)   John opened the door (with a key) (at nine o'clock) (for his neighbour)

The absence of other constituents does make the sentence unacceptable:

(2)   *Opened the door with a key for his neighbour

In this paper the syntactic criterion of necessary presence versus optional presence in the sentence will be used to distinguish between arguments and satellites
(see Dik 1978: ch. 3 for further discussion). This means that both *John* and *the
door* in (1) are arguments, and the other constituents are satellites. However,
the arguments of a predicate are not always sufficient to predict all its conceptual possibilities. It will be shown that passive predicates and a certain
type of reflexive predicate can only be distinguished by the presence or absence
respectively of an agentive satellite in the predicate-frames of these predicates.
According to the syntactic criterion adopted here this Agent cannot be regarded
as an argument since its presence in the passive predicate is optional.

The distinction between arguments and satellites plays an important role in
the treatment of the passive I will propose in the first section of this paper.
It will be argued there that passive predicates in French have to be regarded as
the result of a detransitivization process, which within the framework of Functional Grammar can be formulated as a predicate formation rule. The main function
of this rule, which takes an active predicate as its input, is to change the
status of the Agent (from an argument to a satellite).

The second section of this paper deals with different types of reflexive pred-

icates in French. It will be shown that reflexive predicate formation results in
a different conceptualization of the state of affairs such a predicate can refer
to (different with respect to the corresponding active and passive predicates).
It is also shown that reflexives of the *se laver*-class have not become entirely
intransitive, as has been claimed by Aissen (1982), but, rather, that they behave
in some contexts as intransitive predicates and in others as transitive predicates.
In my view this paradox can be solved if reflexive predicate formation is regarded
as a form of argument incorporation as described by Dik (1980a).

In the third section of this paper the causative constructions of French will
be examined. With Dik (1980a) we regard causative predicates as the result of a
predicate formation rule, but I will not adopt his view with respect to the presence of two Agents in the derived predicate. It will be shown that French has developed two different strategies to avoid this kind of predicates. In this section
the difference between arguments and satellites as well as Semantic Function Shift
will play an important role.

1. Passive predicates

The main *raison d'être* of the passive voice in French (as in other languages) is
that it enables a Goal constituent to occupy the Subject/Topic position of the
sentence. An interesting question is, in this respect, whether this has any consequences for the Agent which normally occupies that position. Consider the examples (3) and (4):

(3) a. Pierre a réparé cette bicyclette
     'Pierre repaired this bike'

   b. *Pierre a réparé hier soir
     'Pierre repaired yesterday evening'

(4) a. Cette bicyclette a été réparée par Pierre
     'This bike was repaired by Pierre'

   b. Cette bicyclette a été réparée hier soir
     'This bike was repaired yesterday evening'

These examples show that, from a syntactic point of view, the Agent of the passive
sentence has become an optional constituent (a satellite), while in both the active and passive constructions the Goal (*cette bicyclette*) is an argument. From
the fact that the active predicate and its corresponding passive counterpart allow
the same configuration of semantic functions (Agent and Goal) it may be concluded
that they are equivalent, from a conceptual point of view.

A decisive argument for the assumption that passive predicates have only one argument seems to me the following. In French the impersonal construction is possible only with one-place verbal predicates. Compare:

(5) a. Deux trains arrivèrent
        two   trains arrived
        'Two trains arrived'

   b.   Il arriva   deux trains
        it arrived-3sg two trains
        'There arrived two trains'

(6) a. Patrick fume   des cigarettes
        Patrick smokes some cigarettes
        'Patrick smokes/is smoking cigarettes'

   b. *Il fume   Patrick des cigarettes
        it smokes Patrick some cigarettes

But (7b) is perfectly acceptable:

(7) a. Des centaines en   ont été vendues
        Some hundreds of-them have been sold
        'Hundreds of them have been sold'

   b.   Il en   a   été vendu des centaines
        it of-them has been sold some hundreds
        'There have been hundreds of them sold'

It should be noted that it is not possible to form an active impersonal equivalent of (7b). The reason for this is, evidently, that according to the criterion adopted here the active predicate *vendre* 'sell' is a predicate with two arguments, of the same class as *fumer* 'smoke' (see (6a, b)). From the acceptability of *être vendu* 'be sold' in the impersonal sentence (7b) I conclude that passive predicates have only one argument. For this reason I do not adopt for the French passive Dik's proposal for the formation of passive sentences (Dik 1978: 18), since in his approach the passive and the active construction only differ with respect to the argument to which the Subject is assigned, but in both cases the predicate preserves at least two arguments. Instead I propose to account for the difference between passive and active predicates by means of a predicate formation rule, which is also compatible with the framework of Functional Grammar. This rule takes as its input an active predicate with as its arguments an Agent and a Goal. The predicate formation rule Passive changes the syntactic status of the Agent: it becomes a satellite. The rule also changes the morphological form of the predicate. In (8) *réparer* is used as an illustration:

(8)   PASSIVE (French)

     Input: réparer_V $(x_1)_{Ag}$ $(x_2)_{Go}$

     Output: $[\hat{e}tre_V \text{ réparé}]_V$ $(x_2)_{Go}$ $(y_1)_{Ag}$ (x: argument; y: satellite)

(Throughout this paper I will not change the subscripts of the constituents of the input so that it is clear which element has become what in the output.)

2. Reflexives

2.1. General remarks

In French there are several types of reflexives. For my purpose the following categories may be distinguished:

I. *The inherently reflexive predicates* (example *s'évanouir* 'faint')
The predicates of this class can only have the form of a reflexive predicate. They do not have a non-reflexive counterpart. Sometimes there is a predicate of the same form, but then the meaning of the reflexive and non-reflexive predicates is quite different. For example *rendre* 'give back', *se rendre (à)* 'go (to)'. Consider also:

(9)   Pierre s'évanouit
     Pierre REFL-faints
     'Pierre is fainting'
(10)   *Marie-Cécile évanouit Pierre
     'Marie-Cécile is fainting Pierre'

It may be concluded that the reflexives of this class are certainly not derived by some predicate formation rule but have to be regarded as basic predicates which are listed as such in the lexicon. The reflexive pronoun (*se*) has completely lost its argument status (see also 2.2 below) and can best be regarded as a kind of pronominal prefix which agrees in person and number with the subject of the sentence. I propose for *s'évanouir* the following predicate-frame:

(11) REFL-évanouir_V $(x_1:$ animate $(x_1))_{Proc}$

   For the four other types of reflexives I will discuss here there is always a non-reflexive counterpart (with the same meaning).

II A   *The Agent-oriented* se laver *class*

The members of this class are 'real' reflexives in that they express a relationship between some entity and itself (Dik 1983a: 231). Consider the following
examples:

(12)   Pierre se   lave
        Pierre REFL washes
        'Pierre washes/is washing himself'
(13)   Pierre lave   Paul
        Pierre washes Paul
        'Pierre washes/is washing Paul'

I have used the term 'Agent-oriented' for this class because it is the Agent in
this kind of construction that has the function of Subject. In section 2.2 I will
discuss Aissen's claim that the predicates of this class are real intransitive
verbs, just like those in class I.

II B   *Goal-oriented reflexives*

The predicates of this class do not express a relationship between some entity
and itself, but rather express the involvement of the Subject of the sentence in
a process; the difference between this type of predicate and the passives is that
they do not allow the presence of an Agent in the sentence. This can be illustrated by the following examples:

(14)   Le verre s'est   cassé (*par Jean)
        the glass REFL-is broken (by Jean)
        'The glass has broken'
(15)   Jean a cassé le verre
        'Jean has broken the glass'
(16)   Le verre a été cassé (par Jean)
        'The glass has been broken (by Jean)'

These examples clearly show that there is a conceptual difference between *se
casser* 'REFL break' and *être cassé* 'be broken'. This is confirmed by the following examples (from Ruwet 1972: 119):

(17)   Cette branche a   été cassée { *sous son propre poids }
                                        { d'une seule main   }
        this branch has been broken
        'This branch was broken under its own weight/with one hand'

(18)   Cette branche s'est   cassée   { sous son propre poids }
        this   branch REFL-is broken   { *d'une seule main   }
        'This branch broke under its own weight/with one hand'

The possibility of having an Instrument (*d'une seule main*) in the passive predication (17) but not in the reflexive construction (18) is interesting for it
shows that an Instrument is possible in predications where the Agent is absent
in the sentence. Apparently the fact that an Agent is conceptually present in
the predicate-frame of a predicate is a sufficient condition for using an Instrument in the sentence. From the impossibility of adding an Agent or an Instrument
to predication (18) I conclude that this sentence refers to a process.

II C   *Reflexives implying inalienable possession*

This class can be illustrated by the following example:

(19)   Jean s'est   cassé la jambe
        Jean REFL-is broken the leg
        'Jean broke/has broken his leg'

Note that in a sentence such as (20):

(20)   Jean a   cassé sa jambe
        Jean has broken his leg
        'Jean has broken his leg'

the interpretation in which *Jean* and *sa* 'his' are coreferential is excluded. In
(20) it is the leg of someone else. From this observation it is clear that the
use of the reflexives from this class involves inalienable possession with
respect to the Goal of the predication. Some grammars therefore regard the reflexive pronoun as the expression of this possessive relationship. In my view
this kind of construction has to be related to that of sentences such as:

(21)   Le coup lui   a   cassé la jambe
        the blow to-him has broken the leg
        'The blow broke his leg'

where *le coup* has the function of Force, *lui* the function of Experiencer and *la
jambe* that of Goal. In (19) *Jean* clearly has the same function as *lui* in (21) so
that this kind of reflexives may be called 'Experiencer-oriented'

II D   *Habitual or generic reflexives*

An example of this last type is (22):

(22)   Ces   lunettes se   nettoient facilement
        these glasses REFL clean   easily
        'These glasses are easy to clean'

Like the predicates of class IIB the reflexives of this class are Goal-oriented,
but here the predicate expresses a property of the Subject rather than a process
which can be located in time and space; compare:

(23)   *Ces   lunettes se   sont nettoyées hier   à   huit   heures et   quart
        these glasses REFL are   cleaned   yesterday at eight hours and quarter
        'These glasses were cleaned yesterday at a quarter past eight'

        (The example is from Ruwet 1972.)

One feature all the reflexive predicates have in common is that, in the perfect
tenses, they take the auxiliary *être* 'be', whereas the non-reflexive counterparts
(if they exist) take the auxiliary *avoir* 'have' (see (19) and (20), for example).
The reflexives share this property with a relatively small class of intransitive
verbs such as *aller* 'go', *venir* 'come', etc. It is not possible to conclude from
this that reflexives are also intransitive nor can *être* be regarded as the exclusive intransitivity marker since many intransitive predicates take the auxiliary *avoir* 'have'. Nevertheless the use of *être* with the reflexive predicates
may be regarded as an indication that the transitivity of these predicates is
somehow involved. Another point is that no reflexive predicate can constitute
the input for Passive (see section 1). This is another property they share with
intransitive predicates. In section 2.2 I will discuss a proposal by Aissen
(1982) that the reflexive predicates of class IIA are real intransitives. It
will be shown, however, that this claim is too strong and that the predicates of
this class display rather paradoxical behaviour in this respect. In order to
solve this paradox I will propose in section 2.3 that the reflexives should be
seen as the product of a process of argument incorporation. At the end of this
section predicate formation rules will be proposed for the different types of
reflexive predicates distinguished here.

2.2. Are reflexive predicates intransitive?

In this section I will first summarize Aissen's (1982) arguments in favour of the intransitivity hypothesis and then discuss some counter-examples.

According to Aissen (1982: 13-14) the intransitivity hypothesis can explain the behaviour of reflexive predicates in causative constructions. The argumentation is as follows. It has long been observed that the 'deep subject' of an intransitive verb appears as a direct object in the causative construction:

(24)   Il a   fait partir son amie
          he has made leave his friend
          'He made his friend leave'

If the verb *faire* 'make/do' is followed by a transitive verb its deep subject turns up as an indirect object in the causative:

(25)   Il fera   boire un peu   de vin à son enfant
          he make-FUT drink a little of wine to his child
          'He will have his child drink a little wine'

If *se laver* 'REFL wash' is indeed a detransitivized (one-place) predicate one would expect it to show the behaviour of *partir* 'leave' in (24). If it has remained a two-place predicate, its deep subject will take the form of an indirect object as in (25). The following examples show that predicates of the *se laver*-class behave like intransitive verbs:

(26) a. La crainte du   scandale a   fait se tuer le frère du   juge
        the fear   of-the scandal has made REFL kill the brother of-the judge
        'Fear of scandal made the judge's brother kill himself'

    b.*La crainte du   scandale a   fait se tuer au   frère du   juge
        the fear   of-the scandal has made REFL kill to-the brother of-the judge

There are, however, some puzzling facts which make Aissen's conclusion somewhat less obvious. The first counter-example to the intransitive hypothesis is the behaviour of the *se laver*-type reflexives in impersonal constructions. We have seen in section 1 that these can only be constructed with intransitive verbs. The inherently reflexive predicates of class I behave in this respect like intransitives, witness the grammaticality of the following example:

(27)   Il s'est   présenté plusieurs candidats
          it REFL-has gone-in several   candidats
          'Several candidates have gone in (for the examination)'

But as soon as we have a reflexive of class IIA the sentence becomes ungrammatical:

(28)   *Depuis le commencement de la crise il s'est   tué   plusieurs personnes
         since the beginning   of the crisis it REFL-has killed several   persons
         'Since the crisis began, many people have killed themselves'

A second fact which cannot be explained in Aissen's analysis is that inherently
reflexive predicates (class I) show a very strong tendency to show up in a non-
reflexive form in causative constructions, for example:

(29)   Il se   tait
        he REFL be-silent
        'He is silent'
(30)   Je le ferai   taire
        I him make-FUT be-silent
        'I will impose silence upon him'
(31)   ?*Je le ferai   se   taire
        I him make-FUT REFL be-silent

But if the reflexive pronoun is omitted in (32) the predicate loses its reflexive
meaning (the * concerns this meaning only):

(32)   *La crainte du   scandale a   fait Ø tuer le frère du   juge
         the fear   of-the scandal has made   kill the brother of-the judge

A third difference between inherent and derived reflexives is that the latter
allow Focus assignment to their Goal (se). For example:

(33)   Jean s'est   regardé   lui-même dans la glace
        Jean REFL-is looked-at himself in   the mirror
        'Jean looked at himself in the mirror'

In (33) the dominant reading implies that Jean did not look at someone else.[1]
If it were the case that, as Aissen claims, the reflexive verb has become intransitive, it would be a very serious problem that the pronoun lui-même in (33)
can refer to a non-existent Goal and not to the only argument of the sentence.
Moreover it is impossible to explain why type I reflexives never allow this em-
phatic use of lui-même.

These observations indicate that a rule that completely detransitivizes the
predicate of the input is too strong. However, the reflexives of the se laver-type
do not behave like normal transitives either, witness the unacceptability of (34):

(34)   *D'abord il a   jeté   la table par la   fenêtre, puis lui-même
         first   he has thrown the table by   the window   then himself
         'First he threw the table out of the window, then himself'

(35)   D'abord il a   jeté   la table par la   fenêtre, puis il s'est
         first   he has thrown the table by   the window   then he REFL-is

         jeté   lui-même par la   fenêtre
         thrown himself   by   the window
         'First he threw the table out of the window, then he threw himself
         out of the window'

This shows that we are dealing here with two different predicates (*jeter* and the reflexive *se jeter*) since the Goals of these predicates cannot be coordinated. In the next section I will try to explain the behaviour of the reflexives of the *se laver*-class.

2.3. Reflexivization as a form of argument incorporation

In this section I will try to solve the intransitive-transitive paradox of the reflexives of the *se laver*-class by describing them as the result of a process of argument incorporation. Usually this process produces constructions which in pseudo-English would have the following form:

(36)   John bird-catches

Dik (1980a: 39f) rejects any possibility of relating this type of construction to their non-incorporated counterpart by means of a transformation since this would not account for some of the properties of the incorporating constructions. One important difference between (36) and (37):

(37)   John catches a bird

is that in (36) *bird* is not a fully developed term. That is why Dik proposes to form constructions of type (36) by means of a predicate formation rule which takes as its input a verbal predicate and a nominal predicate and combines them into a derived verbal predicate. The form of the rule is as in (38) in which the hypothetical case of (36) is used as illustration:

(38)   ARGUMENT INCORPORATION

        Input: a. $\text{catch}_V (x_1)_{Ag} (x_2)_{Go}$

                  b. $\text{bird}_N (x_1)_{\emptyset}$

        Output: $[\text{bird catch}]_V (x_1)_{Ag}$

Discussing a number of cases of argument incorporation Dik establishes the following list of features as characteristic of this phenomenon (1980a: 42f):

A. the incorporated nominal is typically an uninflected, unmodified nominal stem;

B. incorporation typically reduces the number of arguments of the input predicate;

C. constructions with incorporation typically have a more 'generic' or 'habitual' meaning than their non-incorporating counterparts;

D. the incorporated nominal typically does not refer independently;

E. incorporating constructions tend to develop idiomatic meanings;

F. incorporated nominals may become insulated in the predicate formation component or in the lexicon, and thus lose their relation with freely occurring nominal predicates.

With the exception of the last point the properties listed here seem to apply, at least partially, to the reflexive constructions examined in this paper. Point A applies to all classes in so far as the reflexive pronoun cannot be regarded as a term. More generally, the reflexive pronouns belong to the same rhythmic group as the verb and in common with the verbal suffixes they agree in person and number with the subject of the sentence. Thus they are inflections rather than inflected.

Point B applies to the reflexives of the classes IIA, B, C, D. Compared with the corresponding non-reflexive predicates the reflexives have *se*, etc. instead of a fully developed argument. Consequently *se* may be regarded as a sign that argument reduction has taken place. The different subclasses of II differ with respect to the argument which has been reduced: in IIA it is the Goal, in IIB, C, D it is the Agent, while in IIB, D there is also a Semantic Function Shift: the Goal becomes a Processed.

Point C clearly applies to class IID. Point D applies to all the classes and E applies to class I. As we have seen above, the members of class I either do not have a non-reflexive counterpart or they differ considerably from it in meaning so that they cannot be formed by a productive rule. This is what distinguished class I from the classes of II (although with some hesitation with respect to class IIB).

I will now return to the differences between the reflexives of class I and class IIA. We have seen that in the reflexives of class I the reflexive pronoun has entirely lost its argument status whereas in the reflexives of IIA this process is not (yet) completed. This explains why, in the case of *se laver*, *se* can be 'reinforced' by means of *lui-même* (see (33)) while this is not possible with the predicates of class I. It also explains why members of class I can be used in the impersonal construction while reflexives of class IIA cannot (see (27) and

(28) respectively). Finally the behaviour of predicates of class IIA in causative constructions can be explained by the fact that the reflexive pronoun forms a unity with the verb yielding a group that is treated in the same way as a non-complex verb (this point will be dealt with in more detail in section 3 below; the absence of the pronoun in the predicates of class I in causative constructions will be explained there too). For these reasons I will maintain my analysis of the class I reflexives. Their reflexive character is a lexical property and has to be accounted for in their predicate-frames (see (11) above).

For the reflexives of IIA it is possible to formulate a predicate formation rule which takes as its input a verbal predicate with two argument positions: Agent and Goal. The output of this rule is a verbal predicate with one independently referring argument and one incorporated argument with strongly limited syntactic and referential possibilities. The rule is as in (39) (*laver* 'wash' is used as an example):

(39)   REFLEXIVE (type IIA)

Input: $laver_V$ $(x_1)_{Ag}$ $(x_2)_{Go}$

Output: $[laver_V$ REFL $(x_1)]_V$ $(x_1)_{Ag}$

In the output of this rule the same subscript is used for both the incorporated and the non-incorporated argument in order to indicate that they cannot refer to different entities. I will further assume that the incorporated argument has undergone neutralization of its semantic function since this kind of information does not seem to play any role with respect to the form nor with respect to the semantic behaviour of the derived predicate. Note too that it has to be stipulated that the presence of REFL blocks term insertion in the incorporated argument position. The structure underlying a sentence such as *Jean se lave* ('Jean washes/is washing himself') can serve as an illustration of these points. It is given in (40); it is obtained by inserting a term into the derived predicate-frame of (39) and introducing a tense marker:

(40)   PRES $[laver_V$ REFL $(x_i)]_V$ $(d1x_i: Jean_N$ $(x_i))_{Ag}$

In this predication the syntactic function Subject and the pragmatic function Topic are automatically assigned to the Agent:

(41)   PRES $[laver_V$ REFL $(x_i)]_V$ $(d1x_i: Jean_N$ $(x_i))_{AgSubjTop}$

REFL agrees with the non-incorporated argument which has the same subscript
(here x_i) and so does PRES. Expression rules copy the features [singular] and
[third person] on to REFL and PRES. It is also the task of the expression rules
to give them their final linguistic form:

(42)   Expression rules:

     REFL [3 person] [sing] (x_i) → *se*
     PRES [3 person] [sing] laver$_V$ → *lav+e*

The rules for the reflexives of IIB, C, D are comparable to the rule proposed
in (39) for the reflexives of class IIA. For the IIB-class I take as an example
se casser 'REFL break'. The input for the predicate formation rule which forms
this type of predicate has to be a verbal predicate with an Agent and a Goal:

(43)   REFLEXIVE (type II B)

    Input: casser$_V$ $(x_1)_{Ag}$ $(x_2)_{Go}$

    Output: [casser$_V$ REFL (x_2)]$_V$ $(x_2)_{Proc}$

As I noted above the rule brings about a Semantic Function Shift: the Goal of the
input becomes a Processed. This corresponds with the fact that from a conceptual
point of view there is no Agent (see (14)).

    The rule for reflexives of class IIC takes as input a predicate with three
argument positions: Agent, Goal and Experiencer. The verb *casser* 'break' from
examples (19) and (21) is used as an illustration. It may be regarded as a variant of the verb *casser* in rule (43) above. It has the same meaning, but a different predicate frame. (It is, by the way, quite common for the same verb to
have more than one reflexive use.) The rule for class IIC can be formulated as
follows:

(44)   REFLEXIVE (type IIC)

    Input: casser$_V$ $(x_1)_{Ag}$ $(x_2$: part of body $(x_2))_{Go}$ $(x_3)_{Exp}$

    Output: [casser$_V$ REFL (x_3)]$_V$ $(x_3)_{Exp}$ $(x_2$: part of body $(x_2))_{Proc}$

I assume that Experiencer occupies a higher position in the Semantic Function
Hierarchy (it is typically human) so that the syntactic function Subject is

assigned to the Experiencer and not to the Processed. Note that this rule brings about the same Semantic Function Shift as (43).

For the reflexives of class IID I propose the following rule:

(45)   REFLEXIVE (type IID)

Input: $nettoyer_V$ $(x_1)_{Ag}$ $(x_2)_{Go}$

Output: $[nettoyer_V$ REFL $(x_2)]_V$ $(x_2)_\emptyset$ $(y_1)_{Manner}$

The meaning of the output predicate is that x_2 has the property that it can be cleaned in the way indicated by Manner. Note that without Manner the sentence would be ungrammatical. The only exception to this rule is when the argument contains the generic operator (g) (cf. Ruwet 1972: 95f). The property expressed by the predicate then applies to all the members of the set referred to by the nominal predicate. For example:

(46)   Les erreurs ça   se   paie
         the errors   that REFL pays
         'One has to pay for the errors (one makes)'

A tentative formulation covering both cases is given in (47):

(47)   Input: $nettoyer_V$ $(x_1)_{Ag}$ $(x_2)_{Go}$

         Output: $[nettoyer_V$ REFL $(x_2)]_V$ $\begin{Bmatrix} (x_2)_\emptyset \\ (gx_2)_\emptyset \end{Bmatrix}$

The rules put forward in this section account for the seemingly paradoxical behaviour of the reflexives in French. This paradox only obtains if one assumes the existence of a clearcut dichotomy between transitive and intransitive predicates. The notion of argument incorporation makes it possible to describe some intermediate stages in the detransitivizing process which in French takes the form of reflexivization. In the next section I will propose rules for the formation of causative predicates. It will be shown that the rules formulated in this section for the reflexive predicates are capable of predicting their behaviour when they are used as the input for the rules for the formation of causative predicates.

3. *Two strategies for causative predicate formation*

In this section I will propose an analysis of the causative constructions in French which also offers an explanation for the behaviour of reflexives in sentences such as (26a). I will adopt for French the general idea developed in Dik (1980a: ch. 3) for Dutch causative constructions, namely that causatives are complex verbal predicates formed by a transitivizing rule which adds an Agent to the predicate-frame of the input predicate. Theoretically this may result in derived causative predicates with two Agents. Consider for example (48):

$$(48) \quad \text{Input:} \quad \text{partir}_V \ (x_1)_{Ag}$$
$$\quad \text{Output:} \quad [\text{faire}_V \ \text{partir}_V]_V \ (x_0)_{Ag} \ (x_1)_{Ag}$$

According to the Semantic Function Hierarchy the syntactic function Subject can be assigned to either (x_0) or (x_1). The Agent which is not Subject will be realised as *par* ('by') + term, as also in passive predications. In both cases the resultant sentence is ungrammatical:

(49) a.*Jean fait partir par Marie
        Jean makes leaves by Marie

   b.*Marie fait partir par Jean
        Marie makes leave by Jean

Dik (1980a: 68f) resolves the problem by allowing Object assignment to the original Agent if the new Agent (x_0) is assigned the function of Subject. I will not follow him on this point, since French syntax does not seem to have any Object assignment at all. In order to solve the conflicting situation which would arise from rules like (48) French seems to have developed two different strategies: In the first the hierarchy problem of the two Agents is solved by a Semantic Function Shift which remodels the causative predicate-frame according to general patterns for two- and three-place predicates containing an Agent;[3] the other strategy maintains two Agents but ensures that these do not pertain to the same predicate, and treats one of them as an argument and the other as a satellite (see our definition in the Introduction). These two different strategies account for the fact that French has two different causative constructions:

(50)   Jean fera   boire un peu   de vin   à son enfant
        Jean make-FUT drink a little of wine to his child
        'Jean will make his child drink a little wine'

(51)   Jean fera   traduire ce   poème par Eugénie
        Jean make-FUT translate this poem by Eugénie
        'Jean will have this poem translated by Eugénie'

I will first discuss the Semantic Function Shift. This seems to be relevant to
both (50) and (52):

(52)   Jean fait partir Marie
        Jean makes leave Marie
        'Jean makes Marie leave'

In (52) the hypothetical output of (48) seems to have been remodeled according to
the general schema in which there are two human arguments. This schema is illustrated by the example of (53):

(53)   Jean$_{Ag}$ regarde Marie$_{Go}$
        Jean   looks-at Marie
        'Jean is looking at Marie'

The rule accounting for this has to be formulated as follows:

(54)   CAUSATIVE (for one-place predicates)

        Input: partir$_V$ $(x_1)_{Ag}$

        Output: $[faire_V \ partir_V]_V$ $(x_0)_{Ag}$ $(x_1)_{Go}$

The output is the same for one-place predicates in which the argument has another
semantic function (cf. (29) above).

   Let us now consider the case in which the predicate-frame of the input contains two arguments (an Agent and a Goal). This raises the same problem as in
(48):

(55)   Input: boire$_V$ $(x_1)_{Ag}$ $(x_2)_{Go}$ 'drink'

        (Theoretical) output: $[faire_V \ boire_V]_V$ $(x_0)_{Ag}$ $(x_2)_{Go}$ $(x_1)_{Ag}$ 'make drink'

Here the output is a three-place predicate-frame which contains two human argu-

ments (x_0) and (x_1) and one non-animate argument (x_2). The general schema for
this kind of predicate is that can be found in the predicate-frame of *donner*
'give':

(56)   donner $(x_1)_{Ag}$ $(x_2)_{Go}$ $(x_3)_{Rec}$

French seems indeed to have chosen this solution for the problem of (55) so that
the rule we need for them can be formulated as follows:

(57)   CAUSATIVE (for two-place predicates)

          Input: $boire_V$ $(x_1)_{Ag}$ $(x_2)_{Go}$

          Output: $[faire_V \ boire_V]_V$ $(x_0)_{Ag}$ $(x_2)_{Go}$ $(x_1)_{Rec}$

Note that both rules, (54) and (57), account for the fact that the original
Agent is no longer a real Agent in the causative sentences (see (50) and (52))
since it is the 'new' Agent (x_0) that takes the initiative for the realization
of the action (*partir* 'leave' and *boire* 'drink' respectively).

    I will now examine more closely the difference between (50), which is formed
according to rule (55), and (58):

(50)   Jean fera   boire un peu   de vin   à son enfant
          Jean make-FUT drink a little of wine to his child
          'Jean will make his child drink a little wine'
(58)   Jean fera   traduire ce   poème par Eugénie
          Jean make-FUT translate this poem by Eugénie
          'Jean will have this poem translated by Eugénie'

The first thing to be noted is that there is a semantic difference: in (58)
Eugénie is a real Agent since she has to take the initiative for the translation
of the poem. Another point is that the second Agent in (58) (*Eugénie*) has the
status of a satellite according to my criterion (it is not necessarily present
in the sentence). In (50) *son enfant* 'his child' has the status of an argument
since it cannot be omitted. Compare:

(59)   Jean fera   traduire ce   poème (mais il ne   sait pas encore par qui)
          Jean make-FUT translate this poem   but he NEG knows NEG yet   by who
          'Jean will have this poem translated (but he does not yet know by whom)'
(60)   ??Jean fera   boire un peu   de vin (mais il ne   sait pas encore à qui)
          Jean make-FUT drink a little of wine but he NEG knows NEG yet   to who
          'Jean will have a little wine drunk (but he does not yet know by whom)'

The following examples show that the satellite Agent has a special status since it does not have to be omitted in an infinitival term, whereas 'normal' Agents cannot be specified:

(61)   Traduire ce   poème (*par Eugénie) est la meilleure solution
        translate this poem   by Eugénie is the best   solution
        'To translate this poem (*by Eugénie) is the best solution'

(62)   Faire traduire ce   poème (par Eugénie) est la meilleure solution
        make translate this poem   by Eugénie is the best   solution
        'To have this poem translated (by Eugénie) is the best solution'

From (62) I conclude that *Eugénie* is not a constituent pertaining to the complex verb *faire traduire* 'make translate' but only to *traduire* 'translate'. However, it may be concluded from the fact that, if it is a pronoun, the Goal is placed before the complex verb that in (58) *ce poème* is indeed the Goal of the complex predicate *faire traduire*:

(63)   Je le ferai   traduire par Eugénie
        I it make-FUT translate by Eugénie
        'I will have it translated by Eugénie'

For the causative constructions of this type I propose the following rule:

(64)   CAUSATIVE (with Agent-satellite)

        Input: traduire_V $(x_1)_{Ag}$ $(x_2)_{Go}$ 'translate'

        Output: $[\text{faire}_V [\text{traduire}_V (y_1)_{Ag}]]_V (x_0)_{Ag} (x_2)_{Go}$ 'have translated'

The output of this rule show that *traduire* 'translate' has preserved its Agent, but in the form of a satellite (see (62)), whereas the complex predicate *faire traduire* has two arguments: an Agent and a Goal.

   I will now return to the problem of (26a), repeated here as (65):

(65)   La crainte du scandale a fait se tuer le frère du juge
        'Fear of scandal made the judge's brother kill himself'

From the position of the pronouns in (66) and (67):

(66)   *La   crainte du   scandale s'est   fait tuer le   frère   du   juge
        the fear   of-the scandal REFL-is made kill the brother of-the judge

(67)   La   crainte du   scandale l'   a   fait se   tuer
        the fear   of-the scandal him has made REFL kill
        'Fear of scandal made him kill himself'

it may be concluded that, unlike the non-reflexive pronoun *l'* (*le*, 'him') in
(67), the reflexive *se* is not an argument of the complex verb. This can easily
be explained if we look at the predicate formation rule Reflexive of (39). There
it was argued that the reflexive pronoun can best be regarded as an incorporated
argument. Together with its incorporated argument the derived reflexive predicate
se tuer 'REFL kill' serves as the input for rule (54). The result is that the
complex causative predicate contains a verb, here *tuer* 'kill' with an incorporated argument (*se*): *faire (se tuer)* 'make (REFL kill)'. The formation of this
predicate is as follows:

(68)   Input: $tuer_V$ $(x_1)_{Ag}$ $(x_2)_{Go}$

        Output (by rule (39)): $[tuer_V$ REFL $(x_1)]_V$ $(x_1)_{Ag}$ = Input for rule (54)

        Output: $[faire_V$ $[tuer_V$ REFL $(x_1)]_V]_V$ $(x_0)_{Ag}$ $(x_1)_{Go}$

The predication underlying (65) is as in (69):

(69) $[faire_V$ $[tuer_V$ REFL $(x_i)]_V]_V$ $(d1x_j:$ crainte-du-scandale$_N$ $(x_j))_{FoSubj}$

        $(d1x_i:$ frère-du-juge$_N$ $(x_i))_{Go}$

     As a last point I will examine here why there is a strong tendency for the
reflexive pronoun of inherently reflexive verbs (class I) to be dropped out of
the causative constructions, as we saw in (30) and (31). This may be explained
as follows. In sentences such as (70):

(70)   Jean se   tait
        Jean REFL be-silent
        'John is silent'

the reflexive pronoun is not an incorporated argument, but has become a preverbal
particle which agrees with the subject of the sentence just like the verb endings
of French. But in examples such as (71):

(71)   ?*Je le ferai   se   taire
       I him make-FUT REFL be-silent

the unacceptability may be explained as follows. The causative predicate has become a real unit (the place of the personal pronouns can be regarded as an indication that this is indeed the case). The result seems to be that the 'embedded'
verb *((se) taire)* cannot carry any inflection markers: this would explain why
(72) is felt as the correct form:

(72)   Je le ferai taire

In the reflexives of the classes IIA, B, C, D the reflexive pronoun has not become an inflection marker, but has the status of an incorporated argument which
cannot be omitted without changing the meaning of the sentence. Compare:

(73)   Cela le fera   tuer
        that him make-FUT kill
        'That will make him kill'

In (73) *tuer* has completely lost its reflexive meaning: the sentence has to be
interpreted as 'That will make him a killer' (and not: a suicide).

4. Conclusion

In this paper I have proposed formulations for what seem to be the most important
rules for the formation of verbal predicates in French. I have argued that passive and some classes of reflexive predicates are the result of detransitivizing
rules: in Passive, the status of the Agent is affected (it becomes a satellite);
in Reflexive, one of the arguments (Ag, Go, Exp) is incorporated. In Causative,
however, an Agent is added to the predicate-frame of the input, which could result in predicate-frames with two Agent-positions. Such frames are, however, in
conflict with some general convention since they give problems with respect to
Subject assignment, given that both Agents occupy the same rank in the Semantic
Function Hierarchy. This problem is avoided in French with the help of either of
two strategies: a) the Agent of the input predicate undergoes Semantic Function
Shift according to the most general patterns for two- and three-place predicates;
or b) the Agent of the input predicate becomes a satellite. This analysis provides at the same time an explanation for the at first sight paradoxical behaviour of the reflexive pronouns in these constructions.

From a theoretical point of view it seems interesting that satellites turn out to play an important role in the characterization of the conceptual and syntactic properties of the predicate (cf. for example the difference between the passives and the 'Goal-oriented' reflexives of class IIB). Another interesting point is that the notion of argument incorporation can be used to define intermediate stages in detransitivizing processes. The Semantic Function Shift and the argument/satellite shift seem to suffice for the description of the causative formation rules in French.

Some important points remain to be considered. These concern for example possible constraints on the input for the causative rules (some interesting suggestions are given by Dik 1980a: ch. 3), the relationship between reflexive and reciprocal constructions, and the relation between reflexives and pseudo-transitive predicates.

NOTES

*   I would like to thank Brigitte Kampers-Manhe, Anne-Marie de Both-Diez, Arie Molendijk and the editors of this volume for their valuable suggestions.

1   With predicates such as *se laver* 'REFL wash' *lui-même* is interpreted as referring to the Agent rather than to the Goal. This may be due to pragmatic factors. For me it is important that the reading with *lui-même* referring to the Goal is possible with at least some predicates of class IIA.

2   The situation is more complicated, however, and needs more detailed treatment than is possible here. Probably some variants have to be distinguished. There are for example constructions where the Experiencer is incorporated and where the part of the body appears in the form of a Locative, e.g.:

       Pierre s'est   coupé à la main
       Pierre REFL-is cut   on the hand
       'Pierre has cut himself on the hand'

3   Compare also the 'Prototypical Expression Model' proposed by Dik (this volume).

Predicates and features

Casper de Groot
Department of Language and Literature, Tilburg University

0. Introduction

In Functional Grammar (FG), as in many other linguistic models, a distinction is made between basic and derived predicates. Basic predicates are given in the lexicon, derived predicates are formed by productive predicate formation rules. Although 'lexicon' and 'predicate formation' are central notions within the theory of FG, relatively little attention has been paid to questions such as:

(1)   which predicates are basic predicates, and how are they represented
         in the lexicon?

(2)   what constraints exist on predicate formation?

Dik (1980a) lists five types of effect that a predicate formation rule can have on its input, but makes no claim as to the number of such rules, nor does he adduce any criterion for recognizing a predicate formation rule other than productivity. It seems to me that predicate formation is too strong a mechanism and, although it is confined to one well-defined component of the grammar, it resembles the excessively powerful mechanism of transformation in the generative grammar of the sixties and seventies.

In this paper I will give an initial characterization of predicate and predicate formation within FG based on the notions Control, Dynamism, Telicity and Momentaneousness after Dik (1978) and Vester (1983). It will not be possible to give a detailed discussion of all types of predicates and predicate formation here. The paper will be limited to Verbal predicates, and thus will not discuss Adjectival and Nominal predicates (including nominalizations). Although all claims to be made in this paper can be illustrated by examples from many, many languages of the world, I will only use examples from English and Hungarian. The choice between English and Hungarian will sometimes be an arbitrary one, sometimes a matter of exposition. In some cases, however, only one of the two languages provides good illustrative examples.

1. Predicate and predicate formation

When we compare two verbal predicates, A and B, from the same language, their relation may be classified under one of the following three types:

(R1)   *No relation*

The predicates A and B are distinct predicates. They are both given in the lexicon and they do not have any further relation. For instance:

A *tanít* 'teach'
B *oktat* 'teach'

(R2)   *Derivational relation*

Predicate A is derived, directly or indirectly, from predicate B, or vice versa. For instance:

A *sétál* 'walk' → B *sétáltat* 'make walk'

(R3)   *Two representations of the same predicate*

There is only one predicate, which can have two different representations. For instance:

$eszik_V$ 'eat' $(x_1)_{Ag} \{(x_2)_{Go}\}$

where $\{$ indicates optionality.

If we want to reach a better understanding of the organization of the lexicon and predicate formation in FG, we must find criteria which make clear whether the relation between two predicates, or apparently different predicates, is of type (R1), (R2), or (R3).

I suggest the following procedure. First we ascertain whether A and B are two representations of the same predicate (R3) or not. If not, A and B must be two separate predicates and we have to decide what their relation is: either there is a relation of predicate formation (R2), or they are two unrelated predicates (R1).

It seems to me that the criteria which determine the difference between (R3) on the one hand and (R1, R2) on the other are partly of another nature than those which justify a division between (R1) and (R2). As for the latter opposition, it will be largely concerned with productivity and knowledge of the language. Of course, morphology plays an important role here, because differences between classes of verbs can very often be associated with morphological differences. However, a systematic morphological difference between predicates alone is not a sufficient criterion to determine a relation of predicate formation. In

section 5 below, I will give an example which shows that the application of a
particular morpheme in Hungarian sometimes reflects predicate formation and in
other cases it fails to do so.

In the remainder of this paper I will concentrate on the criteria which distinguish between (R3), where A and B are two representations of one predicate
and (R1, R2), where A and B are two different predicates.

2. *The approach*

In FG, predicates are held to designate sets of states of affairs (SoAs). However, SoAs do not seem to be determined by predicates only. Sometimes, properties
of arguments or even satellites contribute to the determination of SoAs
(Verkuyl 1972). Consider:

(3) a.   Elmer reached the summit of the mountain *in an hour/*for hours*
     b.   *Elmer reached summits of mountains *for hours/*in an hour*
(4) a.   Peter wrote letters *for hours/*in an hour*
     b.   Peter wrote the letters *in an hour/*for hours*
(5) a.   Charles walked *for hours/*in an hour*
     b.   Charles walked to the station *in an hour/*for hours*

The extension with the adverbial phrase *for hours/in an hour* is determined by the
predicate in (3), the Goal argument in (4), and by the presence of the satellite
in (5). Examples like (3) through (5), and many others, motivate a view in which
predications are taken as a point of departure for establishing a typology of
SoAs, and not *predicates*. Predicates, then, can be characterized in terms of the
parameters/features determining the typology of SoAs.

If a feature, let us say feature (α), controls the extension with adverbial
phrases, such that (+α) allows *in an hour* and (-α) allows *for hours*, the predicate *reach* can be characterized as a (+α) predicate, because it only allows the
in an hour adjunct. The predicates *write* and *walk*, then, can be characterized as
($\pm\alpha$) predicates, because they allow both phrases.

Assume that four features are necessary and sufficient for establishing the
typology of SoAs. Depending on which part of the SoA the predicate controls, we
can get for instance the following picture of predicates:

(6)   features of SoA   α   β   γ   δ

        predicate 1   +   +   −   −
        predicate 2   +   +   −   ±
        predicate 3   −   +   ±   −
        etc.

It may then be possible to formulate criteria which distinguish between (R3) and (R1, R2) in terms of different features of predicates. For instance: predicate 1 and predicate 3 are different predicates, because they have oppositie α-values; predicate 2 can have two representations, one figures in a SoA with the value $(+\delta)$, and one in a SoA with the value $(-\delta)$.

3. The features

Vester (1983) reconsiders the typology of SoAs given in Dik (1978), which makes crucial use of the parameters Control and Dynamism. Vester convincingly argues that the typology of SoAs can be made more precise by adding Change and Momentaneousness, based on the works of Vendler and Dowty, to the parameters mentioned.[1] I will therefore use these four features, which I will briefly summarize here together with one test-frame for each of these features:

(7)   *Control*

        A test which distinguishes between (+Co) and (−Co) is based upon the consideration that (+Co) occurs in the true imperative. For instance:

        a.   go!   (+Co)

        b.   *know!   (−Co)

(8)   *Telicity*[2]

        Telic SoAs can be extended with the *in an hour* phrase, atelic SoAs cannot.[3] For instance:

        a.   reach x in an hour   (+Tel)

        b.   *work in an hour   (−Tel)

(9)   *Dynamism*

        A manner adverb such as *slowly* can help us to decide whether a SoA is dynamic or non-dynamic. Consider:

        a.   walk slowly   (+Dyn)

        b.   *stand slowly   (−Dyn)

(10)   *Momentaneousness*

A test which distinguishes between (+Mom) and (-Mom) is the so-called
almost-test.[4] Consider the following two sentences:

a.   John almost reached the summit   (+Mom)

b.   John almost read a book   (-Mom)

The first sentence tells us that John did not reach the summit. The
second example is ambiguous in the following fashion:

- John intended to read a book but changed his mind and did nothing
  at all;

- John began to read a book and he almost but not quite finished
  reading it.

It seems, however, that not all combinations of features within one SoA are
possible. Some features entail others (cf. Vester 1983; ch. 2; De Groot 1983a).
Consider:

(11) a. (-Dyn) > (-Tel)

     b. (+Mom) > (+Tel)

4. Predicates and features

Let us now consider the relation between predicates and features.

4.1. Inherent features

The features Dynamism and Momentaneousness seem to be directly related to predicates. Predicates only occur either in dynamic SoAs or in non-dynamic SoAs, or
either in momentary SoAs or in non-momentary SoAs. Consider:

(12) a. Péter fut   (+Dyn)
        Peter runs

     b. Mari áll   (-Dyn)
        Mary stands

(13) a. Lajos üti Károlyt   (+Mom)
        Louis hits Charles

     b. Anikó olvasta az újságot   (-Mom)
        Anikó read   the newspaper

Note that there are no (-Dyn) SoAs in which *fut* occurs, or (+Dyn) SoAs with *áll*.
The same holds for the incompatibility of (-Mom) SoAs, with *üt* and (+Mom) SoAs
with *olvas*. Thus, predicates do not have the options ±Dyn, or ±Mom. Therefore,
we shall call those features inherent features of predicates. We can now formulate a first claim concerning predicate and predicate formation:

(14)   If A and B differ in the values Dynamism or Momentaneousness, A and B
          are two predicates.

Examples that illustrate (14) are:

(15) a. pattan   'to crack once'   (semelfactive)   (+Mom)

     b. pattog   'to crack'   (iterative)   (-Mom)

(16) a. ül   'to sit'   (-Dyn)

     b. leül   'to sit down'   (+Dyn)

The criterion given in (14) may also discriminate between different 'passive'
constructions in English, but also in many other languages, as given in (17):

(17) a. The door is painted   (+Dyn)

        $paint_V (x_1)_{Ag}$ (the door)$_{GoSubj}$

     b. The door is painted   (-Dyn)

        be_V $painted_A$ (the door)$_\emptyset$

4.2. Contingent features

Contrary to what we saw in section 4.1., there are predicates which can occur in
both controlled and non-controlled SoAs. For instance:

(18) a. Mari áll   a sarokban   (+Co)
        Mary stands in the corner

     b. A szekrény áll   a sarokban   (-Co)
        the cupboard stands in the corner

The predicate *áll* might be represented in the lexicon as either (19a) or (19b):

(19) a. $áll_V (x_1)_{Pos}$
                $\emptyset$

     b. $\pm Co$ $áll_V (x_1)$

There are also predicates which can occur in both telic and atelic SoAs. Consider:

(20) a. János olvas   (-Tel)
        John reads

     b. János könyvet olvas   (-Tel)
        John book   reads

     c. János olvassa a   könyvet   (+Tel)
        John reads   the book

The question of how the predicate *olvas* must be represented in the lexicon cannot easily be answered. I will return to this matter later.

Since there are predicates which can occur both in controlled and non-controlled and in telic and atelic SoAs, I conclude that Control and Telicity cannot be considered to be inherent features of predicates. We shall call them contingent features. The fact that they are contingent does not mean they cannot be used for our purposes. It is correct to say that predicates can be free to choose the value of Control and Telicity, but there are also limitations: some predicates only allow controlled SoAs and others allow only non-controlled SoAs. The same holds for Telicity. We will also see that Control and Telicity can be associated with particular arguments and satellites.

4.2.1. Control

In this paper, I will not go into matters such as 'the degree of control' and 'selection restrictions on argument positions'. I will only point here to one relevant property of Control: Control always affects the first argument of a predicate and not any other. Let us say that in any SoA, Control binds the entity referred to by the first argument. Consider:

(21) a. give_V $(\text{John})_{Ag}$ $(\text{the book})_{Go}$ $(\text{Mary})_{Rec}$ $\qquad$ (+Co)

$\quad$ b. receive_V $(\text{Mary})_{Proc}$ $(\text{the book})_{Go}$ $(\text{John})_{So}$ $\qquad$ (-Co)

Example (21) may also illustrate the point I want to make here. The entities bound by Control in (21a) and (21b) (*John* and *Mary* respectively) are not the same participants in the same SoA. This tells us that two different predicates are involved. When we apply this criterion to the less transparent example (22), it emerges that there are two predicates *march* and not one, because the controller in (22a) is not the controller in (22b). Consider:

(22) a. The soldier marched
$\quad$ b. The sergeant marched the soldiers

The predicate-frames underlying these two expressions may be represented as follows:

(23) a. march_V $(x_1)_{Ag}$

$\quad$ b. march_V $(x_0)_{Ag}$ $(x_1)_{Go}$

Compare now (24), which at first sight displays similar structure differences to those in (22). However, the controller in (24a) is the same as in (24b):

(24) a. John is reading
     b. John is reading the newspaper

From an application of the criterion proposed here it does not follow that there are two predicates *read*.

4.2.2. Telicity

The last feature I will discuss here is Telicity, probably the most difficult and interesting feature. I will interpret the notions Telic and Atelic in the sense of Comrie (1976c) in the following way: if a SoA has built into it a terminal point, the SoA has the feature +Telic; if not, the SoA has the feature -Telic.

   Telicity, which is sometimes also described as 'goal-orientedness', can be associated with those arguments or satellites of predicates which set the terminal point in the SoA. To use the word 'bind' again, we can say that in general, Telicity binds the Goal argument of a predicate (or better, the argument affected by the predicate) or the Directional argument/satellite in a predication.[5] Consider the following examples where the italicized phrases define the terminal point:

(25) a. John read the *newspaper*$_{Go}$
     b. Mary receives *the letter*$_{Go}$
     c. Peter walks *to the station*$_{Dir}$

The relation between Telicity and arguments/satellites in (25) can be represented in the following way:[6]

(26) a. +Tel read$_V$ $(x_1)_{Ag}$ $(x_2)_{Go}$

     b. +Tel receive$_V$ $(x_1)_{Proc}$ $(x_2)_{Go}$

     c. +Tel walk$_V$ $(x_1)_{Ag}$ $(y_1)_{Dir}$

Before we discuss the relation between Telicity and other arguments, let us return to the predicate *read*:

(27) a. Peter is reading

    b. Peter is reading the book

Brigden (1984) suggests relating predications such as (27a-b) by means of a predicate formation rule. The idea is that a (-Tel) predicate can be made (+Tel) by adding a definite Goal argument or Directional argument/satellite. In other words, *read* in (27a) is considered to be a one-place verb and *read* in (27b) a two-place verb. It seems to me that this approach is not correct, for at least two reasons. Firstly, the occurrence of a Goal argument in atelic SoAs is not accounted for, or must be accounted for by a different rule. For instance:

(28)   Mari könyv-et olvas két órán át   /*két óra alatt
         Mary book -acc reads for two hours/ in two hours

Note that (28) does not exhibit a case of 'Object-incorporation'. This is illustrated, *inter alia*, by the application of the accusative case. Secondly, there are even predicates which cannot leave the Goal argument empty, neither in telic nor in atelic SoAs (cf. Hetzron 1969). For instance:

(29) a.*a   fiú vesz
      the boy takes/buys

    b. a   fiú (a)   kenyeret vesz(i)
       the boy (the) bread   takes/buys (it)

I suggest the following approach. The predicate *read* is in all cases one and the same two-place predicate and is given as such in the lexicon. When the feature (+Tel) is applied, it binds the Goal argument, which then must fulfil certain requirements, such as specificity.[7] There remains, however, the problem of how to account for the fact that some predicates can leave their Goal argument empty and others cannot. Does this have to be accounted for in the lexicon?

We have seen that the occurrence of a predicate in both telic and atelic SoAs does not entail that two predicates are involved. We will now have a look at three examples in which Telicity can be used as a criterion to distinguish between (R3) and (R1, R2). Compare (30a) and (30b):

(30) a. János esik (a   föld- re)   a'. $\text{esik}_V \ (x_1)_{Proc} \ \{(y_1)_{Dir}\}$
       John   falls (the floor-on)

    b. Mari szépül   b'. $\text{szépül}_V \ (x_1)_{Proc}$
       Mary grows pretty

Esik and *szépül* are both one-place predicates. When we put them in a telic SoA, however, they behave differently: *esik* needs a satellite to set the terminal point, whereas *szépül* does not need a satellite, because the first arguments gives the terminal point. Thus, Telicity can distinguish between types of one-place Process predicate:

(31) a. +Tel esik$_V$ (x$_1$)$_{Proc}$ (y$_1$)$_{Dir}$

b. +Tel szépül$_V$ (x$_1$)$_{Proc}$

Let us consider as a second case the following sentences:

(32) a. Vilmos ruhá- t   mos   (-Tel)
        Bill   cloth-acc washes

b. Vilmos mossa a   ruhá- t   (+Tel)
   Bill   washes the cloth-acc

c. Vilmos mossa magá-   t   (+Tel)
   Bill   washes himself-acc

d. Vilmos mos-   akodik   (+Tel)
   Bill   washes-refl

The predicate *mos* in Hungarian is a two-place predicate which can occur in telic and atelic SoAs. Telicity again affects the Goal argument:

(33)   +Tel mos$_V$ (x$_1$)$_{Ag}$ (x$_2$)$_{Go}$

Example (32d), however, shows a verbal reflexive, which together with verbal reciprocals belongs to a distinct category of predicates: the first argument is not only the controller of the Action, it is also the Goal and therefore the argument affected by the feature Telicity:

(34)   +Tel mosakodik$_V$ (x$_1$)$_{Ag}$

This time, Telicity distinguishes between two reflexive constructions.[8] A last example concerns three-place predicates. Consider:

(35) a. János kenyér-re   keni   a   zsír-t   (+Tel)
        John bread- onto smears the fat- acc

b. János zsír-ral keni   a   kenyer-et   (+Tel)
   John fat- with smears the bread- acc

In De Groot (1984), I argued that the predicates in (35a-b) are different predicates with a different predicate-frame. In both cases, it is the Goal argument
which is bound by the feature Telicity. Note the semantic function shift between
the second and third arguments:

(36) a. +Tel ken$_V$ $(x_1)_{Ag}$ $(x_2)_{Go}$ $(x_3)_{Dir}$

   b. +Tel ken$_V$ $(x_1)_{Ag}$ $(x_3)_{Go}$ $(x_2)_{Instr}$

The examples given in this section, now, justify the following claim:

(37)   If Control binds different entities, or Telicity binds different
         arguments in A and B, A and B are different predicates.

As was mentioned earlier, there are also predicates which only occur in either
controlled or non-controlled, or either in telic or atelic SoAs. Rule (37), then,
does not account for the recognition of different predicates in (38a) and (38b):

(38) a. játszik   (-Tel)
        play

   b. megjátszik   (+Tel)
      pretend

In order to make claim (37) more precise, we can formulate the following rule
which resembles rule (14):

(39)   If A and B do not have the option ±Co or ±Tel and A and B differ
         in the values Control or Telicity, A and B are two predicates.

5. *An application*

In the previous sections, I have developed a general theory of predicates and
predicate formation in terms of the features of SoAs. I have formulated three
criteria which can, regardless of morphological information, predict whether A
and B are two representations of one predicate or two different predicates. I
will now test the criteria on a small sample of pairs of verbs in Hungarian. The
verbs in column I in (40) differ morphologically from the verbs in column II
only in that the latter verbs have a prefix *meg-*. The prefix *meg-* has no meaning
of its own and is usually referred to as the perfectivizing preverb. Note that
in Hungarian perfectivity is an aspectual category according to Comrie's

definition: 'Perfective situations are characterized as those dynamic situations whose internal time structure is indivisible, i.e. no reference can be made to a time point within the temporal structure of those situations.' (Comrie 1976c: 3). Note also that in Hungarian a SoA must by definition be telic for perfective aspect to apply. Here are the verbs:

(40)   I   II

a. $ismer_V$ $(x_1)_\emptyset$ $(x_2)_{Go}$ $meg\text{-}ismer_V$ $(x_1)_{Ag}$ $(x_2)_{Go}$

        −Co   +Co
        −Dyn   +Dyn
        −Mom   +Mom
        −Tel   +Tel

b. $ír_V$ $(x_1)_{Ag}$ $(x_2)_{Go}$ $meg\text{-}ír_V$ $(x_1)_{Ag}$ $(x_2)_{Go}$

        +Co   +Co
        +Dyn   +Dyn
        −Mom   −Mom
        ±Tel   +Tel

c. hal_V $(x_1)_{Proc}$ $meg\text{-}hal_V$ $(x_1)_{Proc}$

        −Co   −Co
        +Dyn   +Dyn
        +Mom   +Mom
        +Tel   +Tel

d. $szépül_V$ $(x_1)_{Proc}$ $meg\text{-}szépül_V$ $(x_1)_{Proc}$

        −Co   −Co
        +Dyn   +Dyn
        −Mom   −Mom
        ±Tel   +Tel

e. $beszél_V$ $(x_1)_{Ag}$ $meg\text{-}beszél_V$ $(x_1)_{Ag}$ $(x_2)_{Go}$

        +Co   +Co
        +Dyn   +Dyn
        −Mom   −Mom
        −Tel   +Tel

f. $csókol_V$ $(x_1)_{Ag}$ $(x_2)_{Go}$ $meg\text{-}csókol_V$ $(x_1)_{Ag}$ $(x_2)_{Go}$

        +Co   +Co
        +Dyn   +Dyn
        −Mom   +Mom
        −Tel   +Tel

Rules (14), (37) and (39) predict that the predicates given in (40a) (−Dyn versus +Dyn), (40c) (−Tel versus +Tel), and (40f) (−Mom versus +Mom) are different predicates. We may then expect in (40b-d) the predicates in column II to be the perfective counterparts of the predicates in column I. The prediction and expectation are correct.

(40a) *ismer* 'know', 'be acquainted with' clearly differs from *megismer* 'to get to know': they have four opposite features. There seems to be a productive relation between verbs of perception and cognition such as *ismer* and momentary verbs such as *megismer* in Hungarian.

(40b) shows an example of imperfective *ír* 'write' and perfective *megír* 'write'.

(40c) *hal* and *meghal* both mean 'die' and are both perfective. From the features one cannot deduce whether there is only one predicate or not; the lexicon must account for that.

(40d) also exhibits a clear case of an imperfective/perfective pair *szépül* and *megszépül* 'become pretty'.

(40e) *beszél* 'talk' cannot figure in a +Tel SoA, whereas *megbeszél* 'discuss' always will.

(40f) *csókol* 'kiss' has a habitual/iterative reading; *megcsókol* 'kiss once' on the other hand has a semelfactive Aktionsart.

6. *Conclusions*

The relation between predicates and features, of course, is only a part of a general theory of predicates and predicate formation. It will interact with morphology and a theory of predicate-frames. Nevertheless, the theory developed so far already accounts for several facts concerning differences between predicates; it gives a first answer to questions such as: how are predicates represented in the lexicon, and what constraints exist on predicate formation? It also offers wider perspectives with regard to the formulation of predicate formation rules.

NOTES

[1] See for a discussion of the relation between the features (hierarchy or matrix) Pinkster (1983), Vester (1983) and De Groot (1983a).

[2] I will use Telicity instead of Vester's Change (Vester 1983).

[3] See Declerck (1979) for a discussion of this test.

[4] The *almost*-test is not adequate in all cases. See De Groot (1983a).

[5]   Of course, the notion Telicity and the relation between that feature and predicates, arguments, and satellites are very complicated. I deliberately do not go into a detailed discussion here, because it would confuse the discussion at issue. See Verkuyl (1972), Dowty (1979), Dahl (1981) and also Lindstedt (1984). It seems to me that the treatment of Telicity within the theory of Functional Grammar is compatible with Lindstedt's concept of 'nested aspects'.

[6]   I consider *to the station* in (25c) a satellite and not an argument of the predicate *walk*.

[7]   I agree with Brigden that predicate formation is involved in the case of the opposition in the features (±Inch) (= ±Mom).

[8]   Genuine verbal reflexives, as occur for instance in Hungarian, can be characterized as +Co/+Tel one-place predicates; pseudo-reflexives as -Co/+Tel one-place predicates (cf. Dik 1983a).

[9]   See Kiefer (1982), also for the discussion of *meg-* and aspect in Hungarian.

Chapter 5

The place of morphology in functional grammar: the case of the Ejagham verb system

John R. Watters
Summer Institute of Linguistics, Cameroon

0. Introduction

The primary concern in this paper is with the place of morphology in Functional Grammar (FG). Up to the present little attention has been given within FG to the overall shape and internal structure of words. Most attention has been given instead to questions concerning the overall shape and internal structure of sentences, with special attention given to how pragmatic, syntactic and semantic functions account for their derivation. However, there are a few studies where morphology has been discussed or alluded to, e.g. Dik (1979b, 1980a: 26ff, 1980b).

In the introductions to the overall structure of FG found in Dik (1978, 1980a, 1983b) there is no mention of a 'morphological component' as such. Not that there must be in terms of the theory itself. In a certain sense one might claim that it is irrelevant to discuss 'morphology' as such in terms of the structure of the theory since the significant components have a much broader scope than the internal structure of the word.

However, morphological phenomena seem to be inherently distinct from other phenomena and so deserve to be studied in their own right. In addition, concern about the place of morphology in FG arises in a theory-independent sense when one attempts to treat the morphology of a given language following the standard descriptive division of a language into its phonology, morphology and syntax. In such a case, what would it mean to do morphology within the FG framework?

The presentation will develop as follows. In section 1 the age-old distinction between derivational and inflectional morphology will be discussed. The question is whether or not there is a principled way to distinguish between these two types of morphology in relation to FG, assuming that there is a difference to be made. In section 2 the question of what constitutes a morphological representation and what its form might be is discussed. Is it possible to have a single notion of such a representation in order to unify the derivational and inflectional fields, or must each type of morphology have its own? In addition, what are the relevant morphological features, if any, within FG morphology? In section 3 the question as to how inflectional systems should be internally organized is addressed. How should they be structured and how should forms within the paradigm be derived? In

each of these sections, the (Western) Ejagham verb system (Watters 1981) will
serve as a primary data base for exemplifying certain possible proposals.

1. Derivational and inflectional morphology

Lyons (1968: 195) and Robins (1967: 50) point out that the basic distinction between derivational and inflectional systems dates back to classical grammars.
However, despite its antiquity, it has proved problematic to provide an independent, universal definition of the difference. Matthews (1974: 37ff) carefully
demonstrates this fact, and a cursory look at the distinguishing features which
Nida (1949: 99) suggests to differentiate the two only confirms the feeling that
we are dealing with 'tendencies' and not an absolute distinction.

1.1. A proposal for morphological types within GB

The basic question is how to distinguish between inflectional and derivational
morphology in a principled way without reference to relative criteria such as
'tendencies'. One suggestion is that of Anderson's (1982), who approaches this
question from within the framework of Government-Binding Theory (GB), and more
specifically using the Extended Word-and-Paradigm model (EWP). He points out
that the search for an independent definition which would distinguish these two
types of morphology has so far been unsuccessful. Some have distinguished between
the two on the basis of their relative productivity: inflection being completely
productive and derivation being idiosyncratic. Others have distinguished them in
terms of word-class membership: inflection specifying an item within the same
word-class and derivation specifying an item of a different word-class. Others
have distinguished them in terms of the paradigm: inflection being what happens
within a paradigm of a single lexical item and derivation being what happens
when entirely new lexical items are made from old ones. However, in the first two
cases these are only tendencies and not absolute distinctions since in each case
there are clear exceptions to the given distinction. In the third case, there is
no independent basis to determine whether two different forms of a given word
belong to the same or different paradigm. As a definition it is subject to
vicious circularity.

Because of the failure of these past attempts to arrive at an acceptable
definition, Anderson abandons the idea that a universal, theory-independent
definition for the distinction is possible, and proposes instead that the solution is to be found in making the distinction strictly a theory-internal one. In
the case of GB and EWP he suggests the following general definition:

(1)   Inflectional morphology is what is relevant to the syntax

This definition of inflectional morphology complements Aronoff's (1976: 2) definition of derivational morphology as paraphrased in (2):

(2)   Derivational morphology is what is relevant to the lexical category

As Anderson notes, the definition in (1) is potentially subject to a fatal
problem: namely, a hopeless circularity. The potential circularity might be
stated as follows: 'form *x* is inflectional because it is relevant to the syntax;
form *x* is relevant to the syntax because it is inflectional.' In order to avoid
this crippling circularity, an independent criterion for 'syntactic accessibility'
has to be found.

   The independent criterion lies in a literal rendering of the notion 'syntax':
namely, that syntax is concerned with inter-relations between words and not with
the internal structure of words. Thus, any morphological phenomenon which is determined by reference to the larger syntactic structure in which it occurs is
inflectional. Such phenomena would include case marking, verbal forms restricted
to certain syntactic structures, agreement properties, etc. This type of definition is not far from what Hockett (1958: 209) implies by equating inflectional
affixes with syntactic markers and from what Lyons (1968: 195) claims to have
been the working definition of classical grammar.

   Given this criterion for distinguishing derivational and inflectional morphology in GB, at least two implications follow:

a.   The same morphological category may be derivational in one language and
        inflectional in another
b.   The traditional inflectional categories of tense and aspect are no longer
        clearly inflectional

An example of the first implication is that of the category 'diminutive'. In
many languages, such as English and Dutch, the diminutive is a derivational
category, its word-internal realization having nothing to do with the larger
syntactic structure in which it occurs. However, in languages such as Fula and a
variety of Benue-Congo languages the diminutive (along with the augmentative) is
an inflectional category in that various agreement rules within the noun phrase
and the sentence are sensitive to its presence.

The second implication follows from the fact that on the surface it is not apparent how tense and aspect in many languages can be considered syntactically relevant. Instead, they appear to be derived independently of the given syntactic structure. This being the case, they may have to be considered derivational, a conclusion which is certainly non-traditional.

However, in the case of GB, Anderson points out that a series of proposals from the 'Tensed-S Condition' (Chomsky 1973) through to the 'Nominative Island Condition' (cf. Chomsky 1980: 13) argue that the category *Tense* is relevant to the type of syntactic domain. This is because *Tense* is viewed as a constituent of the category *Infl* which is itself the head of *S*, an unambiguously syntactic domain. Thus, the traditional inflectional categories are relevant to a larger syntactic structure and are therefore inflectional within GB by definition (1).

1.2. A proposal for morphological types within FG

Given this theory-internal distinction between derivational and inflectional morphology in GB, what are the possibilities of having a theory-internal distinction in FG? Is it possible to carry over the idea of 'syntactic accessibility' into FG? This would assume that a comparable notion of syntax is held by the two theories.

In terms of FG as outlined by Dik (1978; 1980a), the first place to look for 'syntax' would be in the expression rules, specifically the rules ordering the constituents. If these are comparable to the 'syntax' mentioned in (1), then (1) could be said to hold in FG as well. However, it is probably misleading to compare the two theories in terms of syntax since they each assume substantially different structures in the derivation of a given sentence. GB assumes a formal syntactic structure which follows closely the surface word order throughout the derivation, while FG assumes a functional non-syntactic structure which does not necessarily bear a close relationship to the surface word order throughout much of the derivation. Given this fundamental difference, it might be more appropriate to follow Anderson's more general proposal of basing the distinction on a theory-internal criterion rather than to follow his more specific proposal for GB as stated in (1). Thus, in the case of FG, a criterion such as the following might be more appropriate:

(3)   Inflectional morphology is what is relevant to the *expression rules*

Again, one has to be sure that there is not a vicious circularity involved in
this criterion. In this case an independent criterion for 'expression rule
accessibility' is possible: that is, any rule which is necessary to provide the
formal realization of the fully specified predication. Some of these rules will
involve morphological (i.e. word internal) structures and others will involve
non-morphological structures.

   Given that this is the case for inflectional morphology, where would one find
derivational morphology in FG? One could say that all other morphology which is
irrelevant to the expression rules is derivational, but FG actually offers the
possibility of a more positive statement. Derivational morphology within FG
could be characterized as follows:

(4)   Derivational morphology is what is relevant to the *fund*

The fund consists of the terms and predicates found in the lexicon plus those
terms and predicates derived by formation rules. Given the criterion in (4),
derivational morphology becomes a sub-domain of the predicate (but not term)
formation processes found within the fund, since such processes involve not only
the internal structure of words but also structures larger than a single word.

   Assuming such a distinction can hold, it is again implied that the same morphological category may be derivational in one language and inflectional in
another. However, in the case of the traditional inflectional categories of tense
and aspect, it appears that they can only be formally realized in the ·expression
rules and therefore by (3) can only be considered inflectional within FG.

   Thus, FG provides a natural, theory-internal distinction between derivational
and inflectional morphology. Derivational morphology is that morphology found in
the Fund and inflectional morphology is that morphology found in the Expression
Rules. As such, morphology within FG is diffuse, not being localized in any one
part of the theory. This reflects the fact that the internal structuring of
words is not functionally homogeneous. At one point new predicates are formed,
at another point operators and functions are expressed. It should also be noted
that these two types of morphology are distinct in terms of their ordering
within complex words. This ordering can be specified by the following schema
(Dik, p.c.) which by and large holds across languages:

(5)   [inflection [derivation [stem/root] derivation] inflection]

2. Morphological representation within FG

Anderson (1982: 592) points out that in the GB/EWP theory derivational and in-flectional morphology proceed independently of one another but that they do have in common the *morphosyntactic representation*. This representation occurs as the terminal node of a phrase marker in the form of a complex symbol of morphological features. It is this symbol which links the phrase marker with the lexical in-sertion process by means of common features assigned to both lexical items and terminal nodes, and so serves as the unifying factor between derivational and inflectional morphology.

By contrast, there is no such complex symbol in FG which unites derivational and inflectional morphology, since there are no terminal syntactic nodes needing feature specifications in order to control lexical insertion. Instead, what unites the two types of morphology in FG is the *predication*. But this union is only derivative in that the predication basically unites the Fund and the Expression Rules, the two types of morphology being sub-domains of these larger components. The derivational morphology deals with predicates which serve as the initial content of the predication. Then syntactic and pragmatic functions are assigned as well as term and predicate operators, giving a fully specified pred-ication. It is at this point that inflectional morphology comes into play.

In order to make explicit the nature of these types of morphology and the link between them, it is necessary to specify how the following aspects of the theory relate to morphology: the lexicon (2.1.), the formation processes (2.2.), the function and operator assignment processes (2.3.), and finally the expression rules (2.4.).

2.1. The lexicon: basic features relevant to morphology

Dik (1978, 1980a) suggests that five types of information are included in the lexical form of a verbal, nominal or adjectival predicate:

(i)   the lexical form of the predicate
(ii)   its syntactic category (V, N, A)
(iii)   the number of obligatory arguments
(iv)   the selection restrictions relevant to the arguments
(v)   the semantic functions filled by the arguments

According to the above specifications, the lexical form of the predicate has associated with it the syntactic category (number ii above) and certain speci-fications concerning associated arguments (numbers iii-v above), any of which

could be potentially relevant to the morphology of a given language. The 'lexical'
form is not an abstract entity, but bears a fairly direct correspondence to the
systematic phonological form of the given stem. This stem will include all of the
pre-phonological material apart from the inflectional material. The given stem
may be either basic or derived. The lexical form also specifies the set of non-
predictable forms of the predicate, as in (6b) as opposed to (6a) (Dik 1979b):

(6) a.   {love$_V$} (x$_1$) (x$_2$)

    b.   {buy$_V$, Past bought$_V$, Past Part bought$_V$} (x$_1$) (x$_2$)

    Thus in (7) below the lexical form of the Ejagham verb stem *kàdέ*[1] 'to give'
could be assumed to correspond in a fairly direct way to the phonological form
[kàdέ]. Associated with this phonological form are certain non-phonological but
potentially morphologically-relevant features such as *V*, cf. (7):

(7)   kàdέ$_V$ (x$_1$: human (x$_1$))$_{Ag}$ (x$_2$)$_{Go}$ (x$_3$: animate (x$_3$))$_{Rec}$

The feature *V* may be further specified for relevant sub-categorizations in the
given language. For example, in (Western) Ejagham there is a set of defective
stative verb stems which have only one paradigmatic form rather than the multiple
modal and aspectual paradigmatic forms found with other stative (and non-stative)
verb stems. This set includes:

(8) a.   rǐ   'to be'
    b.   dɜ̌   'to be from'
    c.   nɜ̌ŋ   'to be lying down'
    d.   kɜ̌n   'to be seated'
    e.   gím   'to be standing'

This set of verbs would have to be sub-categorized by means of a diacritic such
as α, giving a category label *V$_α$*.
    To take another case, in (9) below the lexical form of the Ejagham noun stem
-nὲ 'person' could be assumed to correspond in some fairly direct way to the
phonological form [nὲ] while having associated with it the non-phonological but
but potentially morphologically-relevant features such as the syntactic category
N and certain semantic selection features like 'animate' and 'human' which are
needed for term insertion, cf. (9):

(9) $-n\grave{\varepsilon}_N$ (x_i) [...count, animate, human...]

Again, the feature N may have to be further subcategorized for relevant features. For example, Ejagham is a noun-class language and each noun stem has to be further subcategorized for its given gender. Thus, $-n\grave{\varepsilon}$ in (9) has to be subcategorized for the gender 1/2 as in (10), where class 1 is used for the singular and class 2 for the plural:

(10) $-n\grave{\varepsilon}_{N1/2}$ (x_i) 'person' [...count, animate, human...]

It is on the basis of such entries in the lexicon that all discussion of derivational and inflectional morphology in FG must begin.

Besides noting the form of the lexical representation, it is also important to note what types of stems are included in the lexicon. From the relevant reading, it would appear that the lexicon includes all and only the basic nominal, verbal and adjectival predicates of the language. Categories such as prepositions, conjunctions, demonstratives, etc. would be specified by expression rules or inserted as operators. Thus, the lexicon of a given language would consist of a comprehensive list of basic nominal, verbal and adjectival stems specific to that language.

2.2. Formation processes: the domain of derivational morphology

The fund in FG consists not only of the lexicon with its basic predicates and basic terms, but also of formation processes. These processes create new predicates, some of which involve the internal alteration of a given stem or the formation of an entirely new stem, while others involve configurations larger than a single stem. Those formation processes which specifically create new or altered stems fall within the domain of derivational morphology.

An important notion with regard to the fund and the distinction between a formation process and a lexical item is that of the 'synchronically productive rule' (Dik 1980a: 25f). This notion claims that for a process to be included as a formation process, it cannot enumerate the specific items to which it applies. If such enumeration is necessary, then the process cannot be included as a synchronically *productive* one. In such cases the forms which would have been produced by the process are instead listed separately in the lexicon. Note also that the productivity must be both formal and semantic. Thus, the scope of

derivational morphology is narrowed to those processes which are significantly
productive, for which, if specific forms need to be listed, they would be the
exceptions rather than the rule. This represents a position between the extreme
transformationalist and extreme lexicalist positions (Dik 1980a: 27).

(Western) Ejagham has two sets of verbs which bear such a limited productive
relationship to one another. It was no doubt historically a productive process.
However, in a synchronic description within FG it could no longer be considered
a productive formation process, given the notion of 'synchronically productive
rule'.

The process is that of causativization, the verbs being related by the
causative suffix -*i*, a Proto-Bantu suffix (Meeussen 1967: 92) which is still
widely productive throughout much of the Bantu zone. Consider the following,
where in some cases the suffix has assimilated to the preceding vowel by
becoming -ɛ:

(11) a. -bɛ́d   -bɛ́dɛ́
          'to be hidden',   'to cause *x* to be hidden',
          'to hide'   'to cause *x* to hide'

     b. -bíb   -bíbí
          'to be spoiled'   'to cause *x* to be spoiled'

     c. -chág   -chágɛ́
          'to be torn'   'to cause *x* to be torn'

     d. -ríg   -rígí
          'to be burnt'   'to cause *x* to be burnt'

     e. -tán   -tánɛ́
          'to be lost'   'to cause *x* to be lost'

Today this derivational process applies to no more than about a dozen verbs.

By contrast, the synchronically productive causative does not involve a morphological process but instead involves the formation of a syntactic construction
using the verb -*yĭm* 'to do, make' as in (12):

(12)   à-yĭm   yê à-năm   à-kɔ́
        p3: make$_{pf}$ p3 p3: buy$_{hort}$ 6-oil
        'She made him buy oil'

This form of the causative can be derived along the lines of Dik's (1980a: 66ff)
Causative Predicate Formation rule. It is important to note that the historical
derivation of causatives, using the morphological process of suffixing -*i* to a
verb root, and the synchronic derivation of causatives, using the syntactic

process of *-yĭm* in serial construction with another verb, both involve formation
processes. These rules are necessary to form new predicates independently of
whether they involve morphological or syntactic structures. Thus, the definition
of derivational morphology in FG as involving formation processes is not circular
but built on the independently motivated notion of the 'formation process'.

It happens to be the case that in the synchronic grammar of Ejagham there are
no morphological derivational processes which make new verbal predicates out of
old ones. However, there are certain morphological processes which derive nominal
predicates from partially specified predications. Take for example the following
agentive nominals:

(13) a. nkpaŋa-ɛbĭn   'farmer'   (lit: 'hoer of farm')

   b. nkaga-ɔbɔ   'helper'   (lit: 'putter of hand')

   c. nkíga-ntí   'treasurer' (lit: 'keeper of money')

These nominals have the following lexical form and derive from the corresponding
predicate-frame:

(14) a. input: kpaŋ_V $(x_1:$ human $(x_1))_{Ag}$ $(x_2: -\text{bĭn}_{N5/8}$ $(x_2))_{Go}$

   output: $\{-\text{kpaŋ}_V\text{-a+ } -\text{bĭn}_{N5/8}\}_{N1/2}$ (x_i) 'farmer'

         hoe-SFX+ -farm

   b. input: kag_V $(x_1:$ human $(x_1))_{Ag}$ $(x_2: -\text{bɔ}_{N14/6}$ $(x_2))_{Go}$

   output: $\{-\text{kag}_V\text{-a+ } -\text{bɔ}_{N14/6}\}_{N1/2}$ (x_i) 'helper'

         put-SFX+-hand

   c. input: kí_V $(x_1:$ human $(x_1))_{Ag}$ $(1x_2: -\text{tí}_{N3}$ $(x_2))_{Go}$

   output: $\{-\text{kí}_V\text{-ga+ } -\text{tí}_{N3}\}_{N1/2}$ (x_i) 'treasurer'

         place-SFX+-money

In each case there is a process of Goal-incorporation and a process of agent-
nominal formation. Ignoring the possibility of a two-stage process to account
for alternate forms like *nkpaŋá-kpáŋá* 'farmer', the rule might be specified as
follows:

(15)   AGENTIVE NOMINAL DERIVATION

    a. input: $\varphi(=CV)_V$ $(x_1:$ human $(x_1))_{Ag}$ $(x_2: \varphi_{Na/b}$ $(x_2))_{Go}$

       output: $\{\varphi(=CV)_V\text{-}ga\text{+}\varphi_{Na/b}\}_{N1/2}$ $(x_1)_\emptyset$

    b. input: φ_V $(x_1:$ human $(x_1))_{Ag}$ $(x_2:\varphi_{Na/b}$ $(x_2))_{Go}$

       output: $\{\varphi_V\text{-}a\text{+}\varphi_{Na/b}\}_{N1/2}$ $(x_1)_\emptyset$

Formation process (15) consists of two disjunctive rules. These rules take any
verbal predicate φ with two terms, one being a human Agent and the other being a
Goal selected for that predicate, adds a suffix to the verbal predicate, incor-
porates the Goal as part of the nominal predicate, and assigns the new form to
the category of 'noun' and the subcategory of gender 1/2. This gender is specific for humans, including human agents. It should be noted that no additional
information is needed other than that which is already available in the partially
specified predication. In addition, note that rule (15a) is specific to CV verb
stems, assigning the suffix -*ga*, while rule (15b) is general for all other verb
stems, assigning the suffix -*a*.[2] As such, (15a) must apply before (15b), and if
(15a) does apply it blocks the further application of (15b).

*2.3. Function and operator specifications: potentially relevant features to
    morphology*

Once a predicate-frame is chosen and terms are inserted, various syntactic and
pragmatic functions can be assigned, as well as predicate and term operators.
Each of these are necessary for reasons independent of morphology, but each can
have implications for the morphology of a given language. For example, in terms
of syntactic functions, the Subject function controls subject agreement on verbs
in Ejagham. In terms of pragmatic functions, the Focus function controls the
occurrence of certain verbal forms in the Ejagham perfective and imperfective
aspects.

    In terms of term operators which specify values for items such as quantity,
number, definiteness, deixis, etc., an example in Ejagham of their relevancy to
morphology would be the number operator. This operator determines which prefix
the given nominal stem will be assigned. Take the nominal stem -*tɛm* 'friend' in
(16):

(16)   -$\text{t}\varepsilon\text{m}_{N1/2}$ (x_i) [...count, animate, human...]

If it co-occurs with a number operator specifying singular as in (17a), then the
stem takes the homorganic nasal prefix *N-* of class 1. If the number operator
specifies plural, then the stem takes the prefix *a-* of class 2 as shown in (17b):

(17) a. $(1x_i: -t\varepsilon m_{N1/2} (x_i))$ Ñ-tεm 'friend'

     b. $(mx_i: -t\varepsilon m_{N1/2} (x_i))$ à-tεm 'friends'

    Predicate operators, on the other hand, would specify such notions as mood,
aspect and tense. A number of these would have morphological realizations
in Ejagham. A crucial question with regard to the assignment of these predicate
operators concerns the exact place of their assignment within the derivation of
a given predication. Dik (1980b) suggests that they are assigned after the syntactic functions but before the pragmatic functions. However, this choice was
not based on any principled reason.

    Of the various possibilities for assigning predicate operators, the most
promising is that of assigning them immediately after predicate-frame selection
and term insertion have taken place, rather than after syntactic function assignment. There are various reasons for this.

    First, from the pragmatic viewpoint, the assignment of these operators reflects
a choice made by the speaker (see Matthiessen 1983 for the use of a 'chooser' in
a text generation system). For tense, the choice involves assigning a temporal
deixis to the given situation. For aspect, the choice involves treating the situation as a unit or breaking it up into its internal temporal constituency in
various ways (cf. Comrie 1976c), the choice based on how the given situation
relates to other situations. For mood, the choice might involve treating the
situation as real or unreal, and so on. For example, in Ejagham the choices that
are possible for predicate operators are made along the lines of the systematic
chart in Figure 1. The categories basically follow Comrie's (1976c) theory of
aspect.

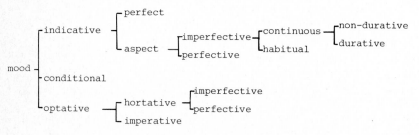

Figure 1: Ejagham predicate-operator selections

Choices are made in Figure 1 from left to right, along the branching nodes,
until no further choices are possible.

However, for the speaker to make such choices the predication must be minimally specified in terms of its predicate and terms (see Matthiessen 1983: 377
for his comparable notion of a 'conceptual locus' for verbal categorial choices).
To claim that the choices are made before the predicate and term are minimally
specified would mean that the linguistic context of the utterance is irrelevant
to predicate-operator selection, which is clearly not the case.

Secondly, from the semantic viewpoint, tense, aspect and mood systems vary
from language to language. Although they share many common features across languages, each system also often has its own idiosyncracies which are specific to
the given language. In this way, a verbal system is like the lexicon, which shares
certain features across languages but has many features which are also specific
to the given language, rather than being like the syntactic and pragmatic functions, which are assumed to be universal. It would seem that just as FG blocks
the infinite regression of lexical decomposition by accepting the lexical items
of a given language as they are, it would be appropriate to accept a given language's verbal system as it is rather than try to decompose it into a universal,
semantic system. Given this inherent nature of verbal systems, it would be best
to treat it as close as possible to the idiosyncratic end of the derivation,
which is the fund in this case, rather than in the middle of the area of universal functions.[3]

Of course, evidence from a given language could show otherwise. Such evidence
would involve cases where the choice of predicate operators could not take place
until the syntactic functions had been assigned. However, I am presently unaware
of any such evidence.

2.4. Expression Rules: the domain of inflectional morphology

As Dik (1978, 1980a) specifies, the expression rules are needed to determine the
form of terms and predicates, the order of constituents, and the placement of
stress and intonation. It is in the area of specifying the form of terms and
predicates that inflectional morphology would be found.

In the case of the expression rules the fully specified predication serves as
the input, unlike the case of the formation processes where at most a partially
specified predication served as input. It is assumed that the expression rules
have unlimited access to the information included within the fully specified
predication, just as the formation rules had unlimited access to the information

in the partially specified predication as in (14) above.

One implication of this unlimited access to the fully specified predication
is that the question which arises in the EWP theory (Thomas-Flinders 1981;
Anderson 1982) concerning the internal structure of the complex symbol used for
morphological representation is not relevant. An example of the problem posed
for Anderson is the Georgian verb form *m-xedav-s* 'he sees me', in which both
object and subject agreement occur (Anderson 1982: 598). The problem is to make
sure that the features specifying the Subject are not merged in an unordered
way with the features specifying the Object, but instead are ordered and therefore differentiated. Thus, he proposes the following complex symbol for this
verb form (his example (20)):

(18)

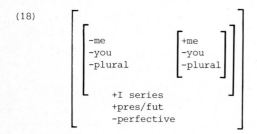

The innermost [+me...] specifies the *m-* 'me' prefix, while the outer [-me...]
specifies the *-s* 'he' suffix. The other features indicate the verbal paradigm
to which this form belongs, namely, the first series (+I) of the present/future
tenses. In FG, however, there is no need to make further distinctions within the
fully specified predication since the object and subject are already uniquely
identified in the predication, allowing the agreement affixation on the verb to
be unambiguously specifiable.

Thus, the occurrence of the stem, whether verbal, nominal or adjectival,
within a fully specified predication is sufficient for the application of inflectional processes. At this level one may distinguish between non-morphological
processes and morphological (inflectional) processes by defining inflectional
systems as treating ordered pairs of the form {P,S}. S is a specific lexical stem
(whether a verbal, nominal or adjectival predicate) which consists of its lexically specified phonological shape plus the non-morphological features discussed
in 2.1. P is the fully specified predication in which the given stem occurs.
According to the inherent, lexical features of S (phonological and otherwise)
and the assigned features in P, S is systematically altered by the inflectional
rules to become a well-formed word (if it is not such already).

In Ejagham inflectional rules specify such word-internal features as noun
prefixes, agreement affixes on dependent word classes, and aspectual and modal
affixes. For example, the processes in (17a) and (17b) could be realized by
rules such as those in (19a) and (19b), respectively:

(19) a. input: $(1x_i: \varphi_{N1/2} (x_i))$

     output: $(1x_i: N\text{-}\varphi_{N1/2} (x_i))$

  b. input: $(mx_i: \varphi_{N1/2} (x_i))$

     output: $(mx_1: a\text{-}\varphi_{N1/2} (x_i))$

In the case of the verbal predicates in Ejagham two different types of morphology
are involved. First, there is the assignment of the prefix which agrees in
person/class and number with the term specified as the Subject in the given predication. Secondly, there is the assignment of the correct aspectual and modal
forms which involves both segmental and tonal affixes.

    Consider the following first person, singular forms for various verbal para-
digms in Western Ejagham. Segmentally this person is marked by a homorganic
nasal $N\text{-}$:

(20) a.   Ń-yɛn   'I have seen'

    b.   Ǹ-kɪ́'-yɛn   'I am seeing'

    c.   Ǹ-kɪ́'-yɛn-â   'I am seeing continuously'

    d.   Ǹ-yɛn-á   'I see habitually'

    e.   nji   Ń'-yɛn-á   'when I see'

    f.   Ǹ-yɛ̂n   'I saw'

    g.   nji   Ǹ-yɛn'-ɛ   'when I saw'

    h.   Ń'-yɛn   'if I see'

    i.   Ń-yɛn   'I should see'

    j.   Ń-kà-yɛn   'I did not see'

    k.   Ń-bɔ́'-yɛn   'I am not seeing'

In this case, there are three different forms for the first person, singular
subject, namely (a) $Ǹ\text{-}$; (b) $Ń\text{-}$; and (c) $Ń'\text{-}$. The tone in the case of form (c)
occurs throughout the given paradigm and is best treated as a marker of the mood
or aspect and not the person. This leaves tone in forms (a) and (b) of which (a)
appears to be the most general form. On the basis of these facts, an expression

rule for realizing the first person, singular could be formulated as follows:

(21)   SUBJECT PREFIX EXPRESSION RULE: FIRST PERSON, SINGULAR

a. $´'-\varphi_V$ $(1x_1: {}^1P_{N1}$ $(x_1))_{Subj}$ $\rightarrow \acute{N}'-\varphi_V \ldots$

b. $\left\{\begin{array}{l} \text{perfect} \\ \text{hortative} \\ \text{negative} \end{array}\right\}$ φ_V $(1x_1: {}^1P_{N1}$ $(x_1))_{Subj}$ $\rightarrow \acute{N}-\varphi_V \ldots$

c. φ_V $(1x_1: {}^1P_{N1}$ $(x_1))_{Subj}$ $\rightarrow \grave{N}-\varphi_V \ldots$

In (21a) the toneless form of the prefix, N, is assigned. In this case the predicate has already had the mood-aspect rule in (22) below apply, assigning a high
followed by downstep to the subject prefix. In (21b) the prefix $\acute{N}$- is assigned
when the predicate operator includes one of the following: perfect (20a),
hortative (20i) or negative (e.g. 20j, 20k). Otherwise, the general rule (21c)
applies, assigning prefix $\grave{N}$-. What (21) presents is a set of disjunctively ordered rules which can be treated along the lines specified by Kiparsky (1973)
and Anderson (1974).

Note that since the disjunctive set in (21) applies only after the mood-aspect
rule in (22), there is also an implied order of rule application which parallels
the linear order of formatives, from stem on out. The specific rule involved for
the conditional (20h) is specified in (22).

(22)   MOOD-ASPECT EXPRESSION RULE: CONDITIONAL MOOD

conditional φ_V $\ldots \rightarrow$ conditional $´'-\varphi_V$ $\ldots$

In (22) the presence of the operator 'conditional' results in the assignment of
a high tone followed by a downstep feature to the subject prefix. This rule
applies to all persons and classes, both singular and plural.

3. The structure of inflectional systems within FG

If inflectional systems are defined as treating ordered pairs of the form $\{P,S\}$,
then the question arises as to the organization of inflectional systems which
treat concurrently both P and S. What kind of rule ordering is entailed, if any?
Are the results of these rules cumulative, adding further to the fully specified
predication, or do they replace the features controlling their application? What
is the place of irregular or suppletive stem forms? What is the final pre-

phonological shape of a given word? It is not possible to answer all of these
questions in depth as each of them would require a separate study, but I would
like to suggest the following.

First, in order to economize on the structural description of inflectional
rules, they could be ordered to mirror the order of the formatives used to make
up the given word, as pointed out in 2.4. for the relation of the conditional
mood to subject prefix assignment. For another example, take the third person
plural of the continuous, repetitive verb form in Western Ejagham, *á-kí*
'*kpɔ́-jí* 'they are going again'. This form would be constructed by first applying
the rule which is sensitive to the operator 'repetitive', giving *kpɔ́*-, then the
operator 'continuous', giving *kí*'-, and finally the rule giving the subject
prefix *á*-. Of course, in languages which are less agglutinating than Ejagham
more than one operator may be needed to specify the occurrence of a given
formative.

Furthermore, there will be times when a general rule can apply to all stems
of a given specification except for a few which need to have their own more
specific rule. In these cases the process of disjunctive rule application
(Kiparsky 1973, Anderson 1974) can be followed. One example has been given in
the set of rules in (21) above. For another example, the rule for the imperfective suffix in Western Ejagham could be specified as follows:

(23)   input: imperfective $(...\varphi_V...)$

        output: imperfective $(...\varphi_V\text{-}á...)$

This rule results in forms like *a-kpaŋ-á* 'he hoes' and *a-káŋ-á* 'she fries'.
However, if this rule were applied to CV verb stems in Western Ejagham it would
give wrong results since the CV class of stems does not take the suffix -*á* but
-*g*. Therefore, a rule like (24) is needed for these:

(24)   input: imperfective $(...\varphi(=CV)_V...)$

        output: imperfective $(...\varphi(=CV)_V\text{-}g...)$

Rule (24) gives forms like *a-gbɔ́-g* 'he falls' and *a-kpí-g* 'she learns'. In this
case, rule (24) would be disjunctively ordered in relation to (23), with the
more specific (24) applying first and blocking the application of (23) to CV
stems. The notion of 'more specific' means that the structural description of

the rule is more fully specified than that of another rule. Thus, there appears
to be ordering both in terms of the formal ordering of the formatives within the
word and in terms of the disjunctive ordering of rules to a common set of stems.

Secondly, whether the results of inflectional rules are cumulative or replacive depends on the notion of rule application. If it is true that at least
some rules must apply in an ordered way, then all rules cannot apply simultaneously. In addition, of two (or more) successively ordered rules, two rules
might need the same or overlapping feature specifications in their structural
descriptions, so it would be impossible to treat the rules as replacive. For
example, in the third person plural of the repetitive conditional $á'$-$kpɔ'$-$jǐ$
'if they go again', the form of the 3p plural subject prefix $á'$- needs to refer
to the feature 'conditional' as does the form of the repetitive prefix $kpɔ'$-.
If the expression rule for the repetitive prefix replaced the operator 'conditional', it would be impossible to derive the correct expression for the 3p
plural subject prefix. Thus, it appears that inflectional rules must be cumulative in their application and that in order to block their unwanted iterative
application they can apply only once, unless otherwise specified.[4]

Thirdly, it is clear from Dik (1979b) that irregular or suppletive stem forms
are specified in the lexical entries as disjunctive forms. However, the actual
selection of the correct stem form will only occur in the expression rule, after
the specification of predicate operators. In this way, inflectional rules divide
into two classes: those that specify affixation processes and those that select
predicate stem forms from disjunctive sets. Thus, in Ejagham the disjunctive set
in (25) would have to undergo a selection rule like that in (26):

(25)
$$\left\{ \begin{matrix} \text{dur} \\ \text{hab} \\ \text{pf} \\ \text{hort impf} \end{matrix} \right\} \quad \text{jǎg}_V, \; \text{jǐ}_V \} \; (x_1)_{Ag} \qquad \text{'to go'}$$

(26)
input: $\text{pf} \left\{ \begin{matrix} \text{dur} \\ \text{hab} \\ \text{pf} \\ \text{hort impf} \end{matrix} \right\} \quad \text{jǎg}_V, \; \text{jǐ}_V \} \; (x_i)_{Ag}$

output: $\text{pf} \{\text{jǎg}_V\} \; (x_1)_{Ag}$

Finally, how far does the inflectional process continue? One way to specify
unambiguously such a limit would be to assume within the theory that the phonological component concerns only phonological processes. Thus, phonological rules
would not make any reference to functions, categories or operators. If a rule

made such a reference, then it would be by definition an Expression rule. Thus, by extension, the pre-phonological form which is passed on to the phonological component after the Expression rule is a form fully specified except for certain purely phonological and phonetic processes. However, claims (Anderson 1975) that some phonological and morphological rules within a GB framework have to be interspersed with one another remain to be studied within a FG framework to see if these claims also hold in FG.

4. Conclusion

In determining the place of morphology within FG, it has become clear that it is not located in any one component of the grammar. Instead it is divided into two areas. One area is the fund and the other is the expression rules. It was noted that this division of morphology into two different components corresponded to the traditional distinction between derivational and inflectional morphology, the fund being the location for derivational morphology and the expression rules being the location for inflectional morphology. In fact it was argued that this correlation between derivation and inflection and two theory-internal components provided a principled way of distinguishing between the two types of morphology, providing a solution to the age-old problem of distinguishing between them. The general argument was based on a similar argument of Anderson's (1982) for GB.

It has also become clear that all stages involved in the derivation of an utterance are potentially relevant to the morphology of a given language. These stages include the form of the lexicon, the formation processes, the operator and function assignment processes, and finally the expression rules. It is the predication, whether partially or fully specified, that unites the various morphological processes. It is the whole set of features specified in the predication that are available for specifying morphological phenomena. And it was noted that some of these phenomena involve disjunctively ordered rules.

Finally, certain features about the structure of inflectional systems within FG were suggested. These features included the fact that certain types of rule ordering processes were necessary, that inflectional rules are cumulative and not replacive with regard to the operators or other features which motivate them, that irregular predicate stems have to be accounted for in the inflectional rules, and that all processes which are not purely phonological probably should be considered inflectional, that is, as part of the expression rules.

NOTES

[1]   Tones in Ejagham are indicated as follows: high ´, low `, downstep ',
falling ^ and rising ˇ. Ejagham is spoken by about 80,000 people in the
forest area of southwest Cameroon and southeast Nigeria. The Ministry for
Higher Education and Scientific Research, the Institute of Human Sciences
and the Center for Anthropological Research and Studies in Cameroon are
thanked for permission to pursue the study of this language.

[2]   An alternative would be to form one rule with suffix {GA} and specify the
exact form of the suffix by a morphophonemic rule which takes into account
the syllabic structure of the stem. The choice between these alternatives
depends in part on the position taken regarding the concreteness of morphological forms.

[3]   The ordering relationship between term operator assignment and predicate
operator assignment is not clear to me at this point. However, note that
Dik (1980a: 10) implies that term operators are assigned in the fund.

[4]   An alternative (Dik, p.c.) is to replace all information except that which
is specifically needed for a later rule application.

Chapter 6
Anaphoric agreement in Aleut

Michael Fortescue
Institute for Eskimology, University of Copenhagen

0. Introduction

An unusual but pervasive aspect of Aleut grammar whereby verbal inflection may
indicate the anaphoric status of clausal terms or their possessors irrespective
of logical transitivity relations - even across clause boundaries - represents
something of an embarrassment for current syntactic theory. Krauss (1976: 185)
cites the work of Knut Bergsland, the leading authority on Aleut today, when
suggesting that fundamental aspects of Aleut grammar may be incompatible with
phrase structure *and* generative theory.[1] Functional Grammar, based as it is on
underlying semantic representations that can easily accommodate referential
features such as anaphoricity to trigger the appropriate expression rules
promises a more satisfactory treatment of the data than appeals to a syntactic
'anaphoric/referential transformation'.

I should first present some facts about the grammar of Aleut relevant to the
analysis which follows. As a first approximation one can state that Aleut is a
strict SOV language. Nominal terms consist of stems plus (optional) derivational
suffixes plus inflectional endings to mark number, case and/or pronominal possessor, and verbal forms consist of stems plus (optional) derivational suffixes
plus inflections divisible into mood/tense markers such as 'present-indic.' and
person/number markers for the subject. In the case of the anaphoric construction
central to this paper, the number of an object (or locational) term or its possessor is also indicated in the inflection of the verb. The nominal cases are:
absolutive (simple number markers), relative (for possessor or 'ergative' subject), and on pronominals also locative/allative and ablative/prosecutive. Other
case relations are expressed by postpositional constructions (Bergsland's 'local
complement') consisting of a special set of possessed nominal stems. Demonstrative stems may appear either uninflected (adverbially or as 'Tail') or inflected
(within the predication, e.g. before a head noun). 3rd and '4th' (reflexive)
person are distinguished in both nominal (possessive) and verbal (subordinate)
forms. Besides the simple mood/tense forms of verbs there are a number of compound forms involving auxiliary verbs such as *aĝi-* 'go/put/give' following particular forms of the main verb. Grammatically subordinate clauses always precede

the main verb, which takes full inflectional endings regardless of whether it is semantically superordinate or not. Subordination is generally marked by participial forms of the verb (apart from specific mood paradigms for the conditional, conjunctive, etc.); some of these forms overlap with superordinate clause mood/tense markers.

In section 3, I shall demonstrate that it is probably preferable to distinguish Topic and various semantic functions of terms standing before the verb (as well as Theme and Tail) rather than Subject and Object. In sections 1 and 2, however, subject and object will be employed as informal indications corresponding to their use in existing accounts of Aleut.

1. *The data*

The basic facts of anaphoric ('referential number') agreement in Aleut are as follows. A verb may take either of two sets of person/number inflections, one marking subject only for semantically intransitive verbs *or* for transitive ones when a 3rd person object term is overt, and the other for transitive verbs when the object (or its possessor) is absent - anaphorically referred to as understood - or stands in a position other than between the subject and the verb. The first set requires absolutive case marking on the subject whereas the second requires morphological ergativity (relative case) of the subject if it is overtly expressed as a term. The following examples are for singular/plural object respectively; in (1a) and (2a) there is normal (non-anaphoric) number-agreement between subject and verb.[2]

(1) a. asxinu-x̂   kidu-ku-x̂
        girl-abs sg help-pres-3sg
        'He is helping the girl'

    b. kidu-ku-u
        help-pres-3sg anaph
        'He is helping her'

(2) a. asxinu-s   kidu-ku-x̂
        girl-abs pl help-pres-3sg
        'He is helping the girls'

    b. kidu-ku-ngis
        help-pres-3pl anaph
        'He is helping them'

The two constructions correspond respectively to Eskimo intransitive and transitive inflection types, though both sentences here would require transitive inflection in Eskimo: Aleut has preserved a state of affairs out of which Eskimo

has developed a straightforward transitivity system. With overt subject the
first two sentences above (1a-b) would appear as (3a) (with *Piitra-* in the
absolutive case), and (3b) (with *Piitra-* in the relative) respectively:

(3) a. Piitra-x̂   asxinu-x̂   kidu-ku-x̂
        Piitra-abs sg girl-abs sg help-pres-3sg
        'Piitrax̂ is helping the girl'

  b. Piitra-m   kidu-ku-u
        Piitra-rel sg help-pres-3sg anaph
        'Piitrax̂ is helping her'

    Observe also the following, where the object is respectively thematized in
initial position, (4a), or placed after the verb, (4b), (where deictic subjects
or objects represented by non-inflected demonstrative stems stand if not em-
phasized contrastively):

(4) a. asxinu-s   Piitra-m   kidu-ku-ngis
        girl-abs pl Piitra-rel sg help-pres-3pl anaph
        'The girls, Piitrax̂ is helping them'

  b. Piitra-m   kidu-ku-ngis   hinga
        Piitra-rel sg help-pres-3pl anaph that
        'Piitrax̂ is helping them'

    Bergsland has suggested (1969: 26-27) that the referee of an anaphoric express-
ion is in *his* terms the 'subject' (in FG terms read: Theme) with which the predication is concerned. In fact he describes the basic structure of the Aleut
sentence as 'Subject + Predicate' (read: Theme + Predication) and this covers
both the covert object construction and the overt one illustrated in (4), where
asxinus and *hinga* can thus be characterised as optionally realized Theme. It
should be pointed out also at this stage that the anaphoric construction in
Aleut is exactly parallel to the ordinary nominal possession construction. Thus
the expression (5) has the same relative case marker on the possessor and 3rd
person 'referential number' marker on the possessum (it appears as *u* rather than
a following *ku*, however, since the morpheme is realized as vowel length):

(5)   Piitra-m   ukina-a
        Piitra-rel sg knife-3sg anaph
        'Piitrax̂'s knife'

    So far so good: the anaphoric inflections illustrated above look like fused
subject-object markers (they exist for all person subjects) and do not reflect

any 'displacement' of underlying relations. Consider, however, the following:

(6) a.   ada-a   kidu-ku-u
          father-3sg anaph   help-pres-3sg anaph
          'He$_i$ is helping his$_j$ father'

    b.   ada-ngis   kidu-ku-ngis
          father-3pl anaph   help-pres-3pl anaph
          'He is helping their father'

Even though the object is overt and in normal position the construction is anaphoric: the 3rd person marker on the verb does not refer to the object term at
all but rather to its possessor, as can be seen from the number agreement. Anaphoric agreement in connection with an 'understood' possessor only occurs when
the possessum is the object of a transitive verb or a 'postpositional' location
term (not a subject) and only concerns 3rd person possessors, not 4th (reflexive
3rd) person. Similar conditions hold in the postpositional construction illustrated below, where an anaphoric inflection is required on the verb even though
it is semantically intransitive:

(7)   qalgada-m   kug-an   a-ku-u
       food-rel sg top-3sg loc   be-pres-3sg anaph
       'The food is on it'

As expected, the anaphoric marking is absent if the 'possessor' of the location
term is overt, thus (8) with absolutive case subject:

(8)   qalgada-x̂   stuulugim kug-an   a-ku-x̂
       food-abs sg   table   top-3sg loc   be-pres-3sg
       'The food is on the table'

   A further degree of complexity is introduced by a rule which ensures that if
a relative case *subject* or possessor of a subject term is omitted as understood,
its number - if plural (or dual) - will show up on the verb, overriding that of
any singular anaphoric object inflection. Note that absolutive and relative case
are not distinguished morphologically in the plural.

(9) a.   asxinu-s   kidu-ku-u
          girl-rel pl   help-pres-3sg anaph
          'The girls are helping him'

    b.   kidu-ku-ngis
          help-pres-3pl anaph
          'They are helping him'

This is parallel to nominal (10a), but note (10b):

(10) a. hla-s   ukina-a
        boy-rel pl   knife-3sg anaph
        'The boys' knife'

     b. ukina-ngis
        knife-3pl anaph
        'Their knife/knives (also 'his knives')'

This 'subject(possessor)-deleting' rule contributes to such 'illogical' sentences as the following, where the verb in (11) is marked as *plural*; that in (12)
on the other hand is marked as *singular* (according to the usual rules of anaphoric agreement):[4]

(11)   ada-ngis   awa-ku-s
        father-3pl anaph work-pres-3pl
        'Their father is working'

(12)   huyu-ngis   kidu-ku-ng
        brother-3pl anaph help-pres-1sg 3sg anaph
        'I am helping her brothers'

   It is in fact possible to have not just two but three terms omitted as understood: subject, object and a location term possessor. However, the 'deleted'
subject is, as usual, not referred to anaphorically by the remaining verb inflection (cf. the optional presence of the subject in (1) and (2)), and only
affects the latter as regards number marking, as explained above. Thus the subject can be omitted without further effect in the following:

(13)   (Ivaana-m)   nag-an   aĝi-ku-ngis
        (Ivaana-rel sg)   inside-3sg loc   put-pres-3pl anaph
        'He (Ivan) is putting them into it'

Since the verbal inflection can only indicate number once there is obviously
going to be conflict if the anaphoric referees are of differing number (if both
are singular so is the inflection). What occurs is that (any) plural overrides
(any) dual, in turn overriding (any) singular marking in the sentence.[5] Thus
the plural marking of the indirect object (the possessor of the postpositional
term) shows up on the verbal inflection in the following sentence (whereas it
was that of the object that did so in (13)):

(14)   hla-s   ngiin   aĝi-ku-ngis
        boy-rel pl   to them   put/give-pres-3pl anaph
        'The boys are giving it to them'

Again the subject may be omitted without otherwise affecting the sentence. If
the subject were singular, omitting it would not cause the verbal inflection to
revert to singular to agree with it.

    Finally, the following sentence illustrates the extension of the facts pre-
sented above to more complex interclausal constructions:

(15)   su-gumiz-aan   txin sihmi-ingan   aĝi-ku-ng
        take-2sg condit-(to) it   thou spank-1sg intent   do/put-pres-1sg 3sg anaph
        'If you take it I'll spank you'

The enclitic morpheme -*aan* (literally 'to it') is added to the subordinate verb
here to indicate an anaphoric object not coreferential with the subject or object
of the main verb. Independent pronouns for 1st, 2nd and '4th' person exist, as
can be seen here, such objects not being marked for agreement in the verbal inflection. Further examples of anaphoric agreement across clause boundaries are
discussed in Bergsland (1969).

2. *Towards an FG characterization of the data*

The immediate question presenting itself when one attempts to apply a Functional
Grammar analysis to the Aleut data presented above is as to where anaphoricity
is to be introduced and how to relate it to such notions as Theme and Topic.
Dik (1981a: 21) has suggested that a term operator 'A' can be introduced by term
formation at an early stage and I see no reason not to adopt this practice in
the present analysis. It must at all events be present prior to the expression
rules in order to trigger anaphoric agreement. More problematical is the involvement of the pragmatic functions of Theme and Topic. As I have suggested in section 1, we are dealing here in fact with the function 'Theme'. In FG terms (see
the end of section 3) this is generally taken to be a constituent outside of the
predication proper right from the outset, in contradistinction to Topic, which
is a constituent within the predication marked at the pragmatic function level as
the 'entity about which the predication predicates something'. In a sense this
latter can be said to characterize what I call Theme in Aleut: such a term,
though appearing outside the predication proper in position P2, is always one of
the entities referred to within the predication. This is not the case in such

languages as Chinese and Japanese, where Theme can be characterized well by
Dik's definition as 'domain or universe of discourse with respect to which it is
relevant to pronounce the predication that follows'. Of course Dik's definition
does also cover Themes coreferent with elements within the predication.

The oddity of Aleut here, if one accepts that we are dealing with Theme in
both the overt and covert (anaphoric) constructions described, is that such a
Theme may be and usually is omitted, referred to solely by verbal inflection,
and moreover, that there may be more than one such entity per sentence/clause.
The latter suggests an FG Topic rather than Theme, since, as De Groot (1981: 45)
has shown, there are languages which do appear to allow more than one Topic per
sentence; furthermore, there is a clear constraint on *which* terms can be marked
as Theme in Aleut (specifically not the subject). If one prefers to use the label
Topic here, one is still left with the basic fact that this entity is, unlike
such terms in FG theory, clearly outside the predication in Aleut and - if it is
overt - is always in the absolutive case, irrespective of the role it plays within the predication (compare sentence (4a) and the two sentences with *itx̂aygix̂* in
footnote 3), i.e. is otherwise a typical FG Theme. One thing is reasonably clear:
there is no room in Aleut for a syntactic function Subject as well as Topic if
one accepts the Theme analysis. I shall return in section 3 to the possibility
of a Topic analysis which does away with the need for Subject-assignment entirely.
I shall also touch on the terminological confusion surrounding this whole area,
which allows one to say that Aleut is more 'topic-prominent' than Eskimo - on the
understanding that Li & Thompson's (1976) term 'topic' corresponds more closely
to the FG term 'Theme'.[6] What is essential to grasp is the close connection between anaphoricity and Theme in Aleut: in a sense it is Theme rather than anaphoric marking as such that triggers the anaphoric rules. It will be seen that
these rules account for all manifestations of the phenomenon without resorting
to the notion of displacement.

2.1. *Analysis of the basic sentences*

Let me at once suggest underlying predications for the basic sentences we are
concerned with:

(16) a. (= 1a)   Pres kidu-$_V$ (A1x_i)$_{Ag}$ (1x_j: asxinu-$_N$(x_j))$_{Go}$

b. (= 1b)   (Ax_j)$_{Th}$ Pres kidu-$_V$ (A1x_i)$_{Ag}$ (A1x_j)$_{Go}$

The predications underlying (2a-b) are the same, but with plural-marked Goal terms. Consider now the representations for (4a-b):

(17) a. (= 4a) $(mx_j: asxinu\text{-}_N(x_j))_{Th}$ Pres $kidu\text{-}_V$ $(1x_i: Piitra\text{-}_N(x_i))_{Ag}$ $(Amx_j)_{Go}$

During term-formation the Goal term would have to be assigned the A operator here - this suggests that the latter operation depends already on the selection of a Theme term (with which the Goal term is coreferential).[7]

(17) b. (= 4b) $(x_j: hinga_{Dem}(x_j))_{Th}$ Pres $kidu\text{-}_V$ $(1x_i: Piitra\text{-}_N(x_i))_{Ag}$ $(Amx_j)_{Go}$

In the last predication it may seem superfluous to assign a Theme term at all in so far as non-focused subject/object demonstratives must anyway be placed after the verb by an expression rule. The advantage of the analysis here is that the anaphoric agreement rules will be triggered by such a term (but not by a demonstrative subject), as by all other Themes - with one exception discussed under 2.2. - and deixis is moreover closely related semantically to anaphoricity. One might wish, however, to talk of (de-emphasized) Tail rather than Theme here, since only such demonstratives may fill the P3 slot, though this is not really a matter of 'afterthought' by right-dislocation, Dik's (1978: 53) sense of the term.

    If syntactic function assignment were relevant, all the terms marked 'Ag' would be selected for subjecthood and those marked 'Go' for objecthood in the above predications;[8] nothing further would occur at the pragmatic function assignment level. The expression rules needed to produce the corresponding surface sentences include an overall placement 'template' - as a first approximation (leaving out the possibility of Focus-marked demonstratives) consider (18) - plus various case and number-assigning rules such as (19a), and of course (19b):

(18) (Th_N) (S_N) (O_N) V (S/O_{Dem})

(19) a. mN → N-s

    b. Ax → ∅

The rules that interest us most however are those for verbal agreement. In the case of sentences (1a) and (2a) the rule may be informally expressed as follows:

(20)   V → V-x̂/s   in the context of $(1/mx)_{subj}$

where x is a noun (or demonstrative), plain or anaphorically possessed (= ordinary subject agreement).[9] In (1b) and (2b), however, the Theme term triggers a rule of the following form:

(21)   V → V-u/ngis in the context of $(1/mx_j)_{Th}$

This rule is linked to another which assigns the correct case (relative) to the subject term. These can be combined thus (for singular nominal subject):

(22) $(1x_i)_{subj}$ V → x_i-m V-u/ngis in the context of $(1/mx_j)_{Th}$

Of course this is only part of a more complex rule allowing for all possible persons and number of the subject term. As will become clear in section 3, 'subj' in rules (20) and (22) will have to be replaced by 'Top(ic)' in a more formal analysis.

At this point I would like to indulge in a brief excursion concerning the nature of expression rules in general, in particular their relative ordering - a matter not yet fully explored in FG (see Dik 1981a: 16). It might, for instance, prove problematical to interweave the placement template (or rule) alluded to above with form rules such as (22). I should make clear my own bias in this area at once: I feel that the issue of psychological plausibility is relevant here and that FG seems to me interpretable as a model of real-time sentence-production (this is of course not the only way it can usefully be envisaged). Now there is evidence that human language processing, like other cognitive activities, involes at least some parallel, non-sequential processing (see for example Boomer 1965), and I believe it makes sense to interpret FG expression rules as pathways within a one-pass Augmented Transition Network, or the like, comprising a small set of overall syntactic templates whose 'slots' are filled out by specific subroutines triggered by individual features (e.g. for agreement, case-marking, etc.) by and large simultaneously and/or with heterarchical cross-summoning.[10] From this point of view the question of expression-rule ordering within FG loses much of its point, since any placement rule can be suspended while the case-marking, etc., of its constituents are being filled out, ready in turn to trigger agreement rules, for example, at the level above, once all the necessary triggering conditions are elaborated at lower levels. What this suggests is not so much specific rule orderings held always to apply within the language, but the

assembling of specific rule sequences or bundles that can be regarded as subroutines of the implementation of the overall syntactic template 'program' (compare this with Linell's concept (1979) of 'morphological operations' as semi-
independent productive chains of rules). Form-assigning expression rules need
never precede the inception of placement rules from this perspective, although
the latter may have to be suspended until certain sub-routine rules are worked
out in order to be completed.[11] The question is simply how to formalize these
form-assigning rules and how general to make them, since a rule such as (22) can
be envisaged as 'hooked on' to the overall placement template via the triggering
category which supplies its context of application. However redundant the human
mind may be in its workings, descriptive economy of course demands maximal gen-
erality and the presentation of individual linear rules cut out, as it were,
form the larger network - and this is presumably the situation also with FG.

2.2. Sentence types where displacement appears to be involved

Proceeding now to the example sentences involving a possessor, I would suggest
the following underlying predications, where *ada-* is a two-place nominal predicate. A-assignment again has taken place in term-formation:

(23) a. (= 6a) $(A1x_k)_{Th}$ Pres kidu-$_V$ $(A1x_i)_{Ag}$ $(1x_j: ada-_N(x_j)(A1x_k))_{Go}$

     b. (= 6b) $(Amx_k)_{Th}$ Pres kidu-$_V$ $(A1x_i)_{Ag}$ $(1x_j: ada-_N(x_j)(Amx_k))_{Go}$

(24)   (= 7) $(A1x_j)_{Th}$ Pres a-$_V$ $(1x_i: qalgada-_N(x_i))_{\emptyset}$ $(A1x_j)_{Loc-on}$

The 'subjects' of these sentences are then the Agent terms in (23a) and (23b)
and the Ø-term in (24). The function 'Loc-on' in the latter is shorthand for the
triggering conditions for the specific postpositional constructions with *kug-*
'top' (which could also be treated as a two-place nominal predicate): other
locative relations could have been specified (Dik 1980a would rather have
'copula-support' introduced by predicate formation rules - though *a-* is a full
verb in Aleut associated with an ordinary predicate frame). The expression rule
that triggers anaphoric agreement in these sentences is once again (22) (in
(23a-b) the subject is omitted so of course the subject-marking part of the rule
is irrelevant). In these sentences we see clearly that the anaphoric system of
Aleut is independent of transitivity relations. Observe that no constituent has
been displaced.

What happens when the subject as well as the object are omitted as anaphoric?

The following predications suggest themselves for our next two sentences:

(25) a. (= 9a) $(A1x_j)_{Th}$ Pres kidu-$_V$ $(mx_i: $ asxinu-$_N(x_i))_{Ag}$ $(A1x_j)_{Go}$

    b. (= 9b) $(A1x_j)_{Th}$ Pres kidu-$_V$ $(Amx_i)_{Ag}$ $(A1x_j)_{Go}$

Whereas rule (22) will at once produce the correct agreement for (25a) an
additional rule is required to produce (25b):

(26) $(Amx_i)_{subj}$ V $\rightarrow$ V_{pl} in the context of $(x_j)_{Th}$

Notice that this rule - the ultimate version of which will again refer to 'Top'
rather than 'subj' - only applies when the subject is plural - it could easily be
expanded to allow for dual subject. It applies whatever the number of the Theme.
An analogous rule must apply within NPs to account for *ukina-ngis* in the sense
'their knife/knives' mentioned as (10b) in section 1.[12]

    Sentences (11) and (12) no longer seem so 'illogical', the following predi-
cations accounting for them again without displacement being involved:

(27)   (= 11) $(Amx_j)_{Th}$ Pres awa-$_V$ $(x_i: $ ada-$_N(x_i)(Amx_j))_\emptyset$

(28)   (= 12) $(A1x_k)_{Th}$ Pres kidu-$_V$ $(1x_i: $ 1p$(x_i))_{Ag}$ $(mx_j: $ huyu-$_N(x_j)(A1x_k))_{Go}$

Sentence (11) does not involve anaphoric agreement at all, though it has an anaphoric possessor: this is a reflection of the constraint mentioned in the Introduction whereby it is only anaphoric objects (of semantically transitive verbs)
or their possessors - or the possessor of a locational term - that trigger such
agreement, not anaphoric subjects or their possessors (recall that subjects
cannot be Themes). However, possessors of subjects clearly can be Themes, as
illustrated in footnote 3. It is as if rule (26) - suitably extended to any
subject with anaphoric *possessor*[13] - has overridden rule (22). In itself rule
(26) merely assigns the required plural marking to the verb, regardless of
whether the inflection is anaphoric or not. The blocking of anaphoric agreement
is rather a matter of an adjustment needed on rule (22) and need not entail
rule-ordering. This could be done by adding the feature to the Theme term trigger:

(29)   obj/Poss(obj/Loc)

i.e. object or possessor of object or locative term; the possessor in (27) and (28) should perhaps also be marked 'Poss' to fit this (words like *ada-* do not strictly require such a term). In process terms this would mean that the Theme term's function *in* the predication has to be checked and that predication (27) would trigger (26) but not (22), as we require (there is however a simpler solution suggested in section 3). This addition to (22) represents the one exception to the generalization that all Themes trigger anaphoric agreement: presumably an anaphoric ending on the verb of (27) would suggest an anaphoric *object*. It is precisely a re-analysis in this direction that has led historically to the Eskimo transitivity system.

In the case of (28), agreement is already accounted for by rule (22) (extended for all person subjects): it simply illustrates that it is the number of the Theme itself rather than that of its possessum which triggers agreement - as is also the case with non-anaphoric agreement in (27). Rule (26) is not involved at all. Note that in Aleut 1st and 2nd person subjects *only* occur as verbal inflections (there are object and postpositional stem forms for them however), the non-anaphoric inflections transparently involving historical fusion of pronominal morphemes. Once again, it is not necessary to introduce the notion of displacement in deriving these sentences.

2.3. *More than one Theme in a sentence*

We must now consider what happens when more than one term is marked as Theme. The following underlying predications are adequate to produce sentences (13) and (14), given the pl > du > sg hierarchy suggested in section 1 (I give the versions with overt subject):

(30) $(Amx_j)_{Th}$ $(A1x_k)_{Th}$ Pres aği-$_V$ $(1x_i:$ Ivaana-$_N(x_i))_{Ag}$ $(Amx_j)_{Go}$ $(A1x_k)_{Loc-in}$

(31) $(A1x_j)_{Th}$ $(Amx_k)_{Th}$ Pres aği-$_V$ $(mx_i:$ hla-$_N(x_i))_{Ag}$ $(A1x_j)_{Go}$ $(Amx_k)_{Rec}$

Again it is rule (22) that is triggered in both sentences, but it is only the Theme highest on the number hierarchy that gets to trigger it. What is needed to capture this is a condition on rule (22); how best to formalize this is not clear to me, but a marker N> meaning the term of similarly marked function with the highest number could be added to the triggering term of (22) such that (29) now becomes (32):

(32) $(N^>x)_{Thobj/Poss(obj/Loc)}$

Finally, the subject term of each sentence can be omitted, but this will not trigger any further rules - e.g. (26) - as we have seen (nor will the presence of inflected demonstratives in the predication). Let me just repeat that subjects are simply not available for Themehood and their omission cannot increase the number of Themes. I shall return in section 3 to the question of how this constraint can be captured - and indeed suggest a more satisfactory characterization of this matter in terms of Topic. It should furthermore be pointed out that normally no more than one Theme per clause can be overt in Aleut, and only two may be anaphoric.[14]

2.4. Agreement across clause-boundaries

There are constraints on when an anaphoric marking can be passed across clause boundaries (to do with coreferentiality conditions and the 'mood' of the subordinate verb), but they are not involved in the analysis of (15):

(33) $(A1x_k)_{Th}$ Fut sihmi-$_V$ $(1x_i: 1p(x_i))_{Ag}$ $(x_j: txin(x_j))_{Go}$

         $(su-_V (x_j)_{Ag} (A1x_k)_{Go})_{Condit}$

I shall not discuss the introduction of *aan* here, nor the formation of the compound future tense; what is relevant is the result of applying rule (22), i.e. the formation of the 1sg 3sg anaphoric inflection on the main verb (not 1sg 2sg as might have been expected). This is another clear example of how the anaphoric system is independent of transitivity relations: the object of the main verb is overt, in normal position, and therefore does not need marking for agreement on the verb. Although Theme-marking is 'suspended' until the final verb of the period there is once again no constituent displacement involved. The domain of (22) must simply be understood as the period sentence rather than the clause.

3. Discussion and summary

Bergsland (1976: 21) has remarked that Aleut is a notably 'iconic' language as regards the ordering of successive clauses, with much less grammatical 'scrambling' than in related Eskimo languages, for instance.[15] This is no doubt facilitated by the anaphoric agreement system which largely (or wholly) does away with the need for constituent displacement: the referential situation is by and large kept track of and marked cumulatively at the end of periods independently of intervening grammatical relations of constituents. The question

which I now wish to address is as to whether there are not alternative analyses
of the data which might be preferable, both within and without the FG framework.
As has been suggested - and with this I agree - a transformational approach is
not likely to have anything revealing to contribute here. This is because such
a treatment, whether of the autonomous syntactic or of a semantic base kind, is
going to require a very complex apparatus of movement processes, whereas in fact
the agreement data we are dealing with does not really involve displacement at
all - indeed the very notion of displacement runs counter to the prevailing
spirit of Aleut, its iconicity. Moreover, rule-ordering is going to be excessively tricky to formulate - consider the complex deletion and movement processes
that would have to be invoked to characterize what happens when more than one
constituent is marked as anaphoric within such a framework. A framework such as
FG which minimizes the importance of displacement and maximalizes the notions of
Predication and Theme (or Topic and Comment) would, on the other hand, seem a
reasonable starting point for the analysis of a language such as Aleut.[16]

   Within the FG framework, there would appear to be two main alternatives to
the analysis presented above, both of which seem feasible and could well have
important consequences within FG theory if adopted. On the one hand one might
want to replace my term Theme by Topic throughout, and on the other hand one
might want to separate matters: Theme when the constituent concerned is overt
(as in sentence (4a)) and anaphoricity when it is covert. Without rejecting
either of these approaches out of hand, let me simply underline some of the consequences of their acceptance. First, what would happen if one did replace
'Theme' with 'Topic' throughout? The principle advantage of doing so would be
the avoidance of having to set up initial constraints on what terms can be
selected as Theme/Topic, since Topic-assignment takes place at the pragmatic
function level: only terms from within the predication will be selected and any
'subjects' will simply be excluded.[17] There is also, presumably, less conceptual
difficulty with assigning more than one Topic than more than one Theme to a
single sentence.

   The trouble is, as I hinted earlier, accounting for the fact that terms thus
selected, when overt, must be in the absolutive case (even when coreferential
with a possessor term - which may also be the case with postposed non-inflected
demonstratives) and when omitted leave a complete predication behind (typical
behaviour of FG Themes rather than Topics). Further, Themes that are overt cannot
simply be taken as given/known to the addressee (rather a matter of anaphoric
omission in Aleut) nor as necessarily definite (see below) as the Topic is taken

to be by Dik (1978: 96). Moreover, when one turns to the practical consequences
of such a term marking - namely the triggering of the anaphoric agreement rules -
it is clear that not all Themes/Topics do this (anaphoric subject possessors do
not) and, on the other hand, that anaphoricity alone is not what triggers the
rules (anaphoric subjects don't do so). Ad hoc rules whereby certain anaphoric
terms and certain Themes/Topics trigger these rules could of course be contrived
- but at the expense of the generalization intuited by Bergsland that not only
do anaphoric terms act very like overt Themes/Topics as regards rule-triggering,
but the omission of an overt Theme/Topic (whether pre- or post-posed) also produces a well-formed anaphoric sentence with no further ado. This is of course
the major drawback attendant upon the second alternative approach suggested
above: if one reserves 'Theme' for overt pre-posed absolutive terms and 'anaphoric' for A-marked terms, the rule for anaphoric agreement not only requires
more complex formulation, but the alternative triggering features (Theme and 'A')
are of diverse categorial nature (a function and an operator respectively).
Nevertheless, the possibility of a 'disjunctive' analysis must be left open in
view of the case of Theme not triggering anaphoric agreement (see footnote 3).

It appears to be an inescapable conclusion that anaphoricity and Theme are
intimately related notions in Aleut, but this is of course quite natural: when
one knows what the Theme or Topic of one's utterance is going to be (as textually
or situationally given) one may either choose to omit reference to it overtly
altogether or - if, for instance, there is a pragmatic need for ensuring that
the listener has the same 'anchor' for interpreting the utterance as the
speaker himself presupposes - of setting it up as a thematic initial constituent.
The involvement of demonstrative terms in the anaphoric system is further indication that (situational) deixis is what lies behind the whole system. The Theme-
anaphoricity link in Aleut is of the essence: if it were broken the anaphoric
agreement system could hardly survive, for once anaphoric inflections began no
longer to imply a thematized, possibly overt term it would seem almost inevitable
that they should begin to be interpreted as a transitivity system. Conflict between this basic principle of Aleut syntax and other syntactic/pragmatic forces
such as that which lies behind the 'oddness' of (11) should not cause surprise.

As regards my own analysis presented in this paper, I would like to be able
to say that Theme (and Tail, if that is what a post-posed demonstrative is) is
assigned *at the pragmatic function level*: this terminological sleight-of-hand
obviates most of the problems discussed above. This would simply mean rewriting
the underlying predications without the Theme terms dislocated - or else one

could interpret them as representing a stage after pragmatic function assignment.[18]
There would still be no need of displacement processes, since the placement
'template' will place any overt term so marked in the correct syntactic slot
(their absolutive case being assigned by an appropriate form rule): there is no
question of constituent copying. In fact, if initial predications are to be regarded as loosely bound (non-ordered) bundles of predicates and terms, etc., it is
difficult in process terms to see the point of envisaging for Aleut loosely associated Theme terms which are always redundant (coreferent with terms already in
the bundle). Anaphoricity markers, on the other hand, clearly do belong at the
basic predication level: in a production model these would constitute the essential link to the foregoing context of discourse. Thematization (like Focus-
assignment) is something the speaker *does* to get his message across, whereas
anaphoricity is something determined for him *by* the situational context within
which he must construct his utterance.

Now it may be argued that Aleut does have a Topic function associated with
the P1 slot, corresponding to what I have been calling the subject of the clause.
This is an attractive possibility since it would do away with the need for a
syntactic-function assignment level for Aleut altogether (what would be 'Object'
always being a Goal term and what would be 'Subject' always Agent or Ø - also
including Dik's Positioner, Processed and Force, but never Goal or Loc). It
would also emphasize the more 'topic-prominent' nature of Aleut as compared to
Eskimo (see footnote 20). Once could then characterize the basic predicational
structure of Aleut as:

(34)   P2$_{(Theme)}$ P1$_{(Topic)}$ X/Loc Loc/X V P3$_{(Tail)}$

where 'X' is any term that is neither Theme, Topic nor Loc (a 'local complement'
expression). The relative ordering of X and Loc depends on their definiteness:
X before Loc is definite, after Loc it is indefinite, as in the following, where
X is the object term *kanfiixtas*. *Ivaanax̂ kanfiixtas yaasikam nagan ag̃ikux̂* 'Ivan
puts the sweets into the box', but *Ivaanax̂ yaasikam nagan kanfiixtas ag̃ikux̂*
'Ivan puts (some) sweets into the box' (for the equivalent anaphoric sentences
see sentence (13) and footnote 5). A further 'slot' in the basic template may
be necessary for the 'remote object' of derived causative predicates, e.g. *ngaan*
in the sentence example of footnote 14 (*hlam-aan* 'the boy' would be a corresponding noun - cf. enclitic *aan* 'to him').

This solution has the further advantage (pointed out to me by Lachlan

Mackenzie) that it would clarify the constraint that prohibits 'subjects' or
their possessors from triggering anaphoric agreement. Pre-/post-posed Theme and
Tail may thus be less directly instrumental in triggering the anaphoric agreement
rules: it is rather the anaphoric 'slots' within the predicate to which they
refer which trigger the rules (recall that overt Theme and Tail terms may always
be deleted without changing anything). Any anaphoric term apart from those
associated with P1(Topic) would then trigger the rules: this would presumably
simplify the tentative expanded form of rule (22) in section 2.3. The fixed
position of the Topic/Subject term in Aleut further suggests the former rather
than the latter designation (see Dik 1978: 75); moreover, the Topic analysis
meshes nicely with the definite/indefinite distinction in Aleut, where only
definite terms may appear in the P1 slot. Thus compare sentence (7) (with the
'subject' *qalgadam* in the relative case as expected in the anaphoric construction) with (35):

(35)   qalgada-x̂   kug-an   a-ku-u
        food-abs sg top-3sg Loc   be-pres-3sg anaph
        'There is food on it'

Here the indefinite subject is in the absolutive case despite the anaphoric construction and therefore must be regarded as Theme, outside the predication
proper. This term needs to be marked with an Indefinite operator (this is more
efficient for Aleut than using a Definite operator - which would have to be
applied to by far the majority of all terms). Topic, as opposed to Theme, is
always definite - though indefinite Themes seem to be limited to the construction
in (35), where there is an anaphoric (therefore definite) term within the predicate already triggering anaphoric agreement (the only case of an overt and a
covert Theme in one sentence?).

   The only problem with this analysis concerns the relative ordering of 'subject'
and postpositional (local) expressions when both are overt (or overtly possessed).
Compare the sentence in the text following (7) (where *qalgadax̂* stands first) with:

(36)   stuuluĝim kug-an   qalgada-x̂   a-ku-x̂
        table   top-3sg Loc   food-abs sg   be-pres-3sg
        'There is food on the table'

Here the subject is indefinite since it follows the postpositional expression
parallel to the case of object and local expression discussed above, and is not
thematized in P2 as in (35). One reasonable solution that suggests itself here

is that 'X' can indeed be either subject or object, but only when a subject is
indefinite will it appear under 'X' rather than in the normal position for subjects, P1. The remaining question as to why an indefinite subject is thematized
in P2 when and only when the possessor of the postpositional expression is anaphoric may well be to do with the oddity of an absolutive subject coming to
stand between an anaphoric local expression and an anaphorically agreeing verb:
such a term would tend to be understood as object (the usual absolutive case
filler of 'X'). It may simply be that fully specified postpositional expressions
may be positioned in P2 as Theme when there is no definite subject, as in (36),
although the anaphoric postpositional expression in (35) appears to fill its
usual Loc slot (definiteness is irrelevant since such an expression is always
definite, whatever its position). I favour at all events a solution which reserves *P1* for subjects since a conjunctive mood clause is always coreferential
with the Topic of the main clause, but never with a 'local complement' expression.

Here I would like to hazard a generalization based on the above argument:
might it not be the case that languages with rich verbal agreement systems (for
subject plus object or subject plus anaphoric terms) that render the overt
presence of subject and object terms always optional are unlikely to make systematic use of all three functions Topic, Theme and Subject? Aleut, with its strict
word-order most naturally chooses Theme plus Topic (if this is how one analyses
it) - it is always clear from position and/or anaphoricity what constitutes such
terms - whereas Eskimo, for example, with its labile word-order, appears to
choose Topic and Subject only, since there is no obvious way a term selected as
Theme and placed in initial position could be distinguished from a Topic (both
if dropped would leave grammatically complete predications).[19] As a pendant to
this suggestion, I would still wish to maintain that Aleut is more 'topic-
prominent' than Eskimo, if by that we mean 'Theme-prominent' (see footnote 6).[20]
Eskimo has no way of dislocating or otherwise severing from its predication a
term in first position, nor does it have an anaphoric agreement system sensitive
to such a term's presence.

In sum, it would appear that Aleut is a language where Theme is assigned at
the pragmatic function level (as opposed to others, such as Japanese, where it
needs to be present from the outset). The answer to Dik's question (1978: 133ff)
as to whether Theme is to be 'extracted' from the predication at this level or
not may thus be yes *or* no - dependent upon the syntactic and morphological
options available to the particular language. By 'extraction' I mean here assignment of a term marked 'Theme' at the pragmatic function level to P2 or P3 position

(or anaphorically simply dropped) leaving a pronominal/agreement marker behind
within the predication. In Aleut the close link between Theme and anaphoric
agreement is the decisive factor. As discussed in this paper, at least the communicative functions of indicating 'given' information and focus (on non-Theme
constituents) are also involved here.

NOTES

[1]   For Bergsland's own discussion of problems of a transformational nature here
      see Bergsland (1969), in particular p. 35 where he suggests the possibility
      at least of a 'referential transformation'.

[2]   All examples are taken from Bergsland and Dirks (1981) or other of Bergsland's
      articles referred to (with minor permutations). They are all for Atkan Aleut
      (Eastern Aleut differing somewhat in details). Aleut has (or rather had) a
      dual number also, the last regular users of which have recently died. Some of
      the example sentences may have a somewhat archaic ring today. Aleut repre-
      sents a remote branch of the Eskimo-Aleut family with rather little internal
      dialect variation and a time depth of around 4000 years separating it from the
      Eskimo branch. It has few young speakers left - rapid anglicization is taking
      place amongst them. The orthography used is that of Bergsland and Dirks,
      where x̂ and x are respectively voiceless uvular and velar fricatives and ĝ and
      g the corresponding voiced fricatives; voiceless laterals and nasals are pre-
      ceded by h, and d is a voiced alveolar fricative, and ch is a palato-alveolar
      affricate.

[3]   A demonstrative *subject* may also appear after the verb, not triggering ana-
      phoric agreement but laying focus on the predicate. We are talking here of
      uninflected demonstrative stems; the corresponding inflected pronominal forms
      not triggering anaphoric agreement may occur within the predication when they
      are focused. A pre-posed Theme may also be coreferential with an anaphoric
      possessor, as in the following sentence:

      (i) itx̂aygi-x̂   chnga-a   usa-ku-x̂
          caribou-abs sg   fur-3sg   fall-pres-3sg
          'The caribou, its fur is falling off'

      Compare this to *itx̂aygim chngaa usakux̂* 'The caribou's fur is falling off'
      with the possessor term, now part of the predication, in the expected relative
      case. See my analysis (27) of sentence (11) for the lack of anaphoric agree-
      ment in either of these sentences. It should be mentioned that at least in
      modern Aleut pre-posed Theme is not common. Bergsland (1969) characterizes
      the difference between sentences with and without a Theme as respectively
      'relational' and 'fully explicit'. In the same paper (p. 38) he points out
      that the initial PS rule S → NP + VP is not suitable for Aleut.

[4]   *ng* indicates a 1sg subject-3sg anaphoric term; the 3rd person forms *u* and
      ngis introduced so far presuppose a 3rd person *subject*.

[5]   *nagan aĝikungis* is thus ambiguous between 'they (or they two) put them into
      it' and 'they put it into it'. Compare *(Ivaanam) kanfiixtas nagan aĝikuu*
      '(I.) puts sweets in it' where agreement is with the remaining anaphoric
      referent.

6   Amongst other traits, their 'Topic' refers to a 'universe of discourse' which
     may not have any direct grammatical relationship to the predication it pre-
     cedes. In footnote 3 (p. 486) they cite Kuno (1972), who specifically uses
     the term 'Theme' when referring to such a Topic in Japanese and points out
     that in that language the latter must be either *anaphoric* or generic (and in
     any case Topic must be definite according to Li and Thompson). All of this
     coincides with the use of 'Theme' in FG (note that 'given' anaphoric terms in
     Aleut are simply omitted). Firbas (1966), representing Prague School linguists
     in general, uses Theme in a somewhat different manner: for him every sentence
     has a Theme inferred from the context but not every sentence has a Topic.
     Givón (1976) discusses the close link between Topic and anaphora and verbal
     agreement; certainly Aleut is a clear example of the Topic-verb agreement he
     proposes, however what is 'shifted' in Aleut is not whole pronominals but
     simply 3rd person number markers (plain or 'referential/possessive').

7   This complication is avoided in the reinterpreted version of my analysis
     suggested in section 3 where Theme is assigned at the pragmatic function
     level and there is no redundant duplication of terms. This latter amendment
     is perfectly compatible with sentences such as that in footnote 3, whose
     underlying predication could be captured thus (following Dik (1980a: ch. 4)
     for alienable possession):

(i) Pres usa-$_V$ (1x$_i$: chnga-$_N$(x$_i$): {(1x$_j$: itx̂aygi-$_N$(x$_j$))$_{PossTh}$} (x$_i$)$\emptyset$)$\emptyset$

     The Theme-marking would ensure both the correct placement of the Theme and
     its absolutive case. If Topic is assigned to the final $\emptyset$ (see section 3), it
     is interesting to note that Theme is embedded within it at this stage.

8   As will be argued in section 3, Aleut would appear not to require syntactic
     function assignment. The so-called 'passive' and 'anti-passive' constructions
     both involve derivational extension of the verb, as in *asx̂as-xa-kux̂* 'he has
     been killed' (no agent expressed) and *asx̂at-xa-ĝi-kux̂* 'he has killed some-
     thing' (from pass. part. *xa*, plus *ĝi* 'have'). These constructions merely re-
     duce valency and are not a matter of syntactic 'perspective'.

9   I shall not here go into the question of the desirability of assigning abso-
     lutive case subjects and objects the same underlying $\emptyset$-case marking (see
     Mackenzie 1981) although it may well be the case that Aleut is more simply
     analysed without further breakdown of absolutive terms into various under-
     lying semantic functions according to state-of-affairs typology. Aleut does
     not need a $\emptyset$/Go distinction for syntactic function assignment - though it
     may for Topic-assignment; at all events, state-of-affairs can also be a
     matter of language-specific perspective (see Dik 1978: 41ff for how differ-
     ent languages treat the 'experiencer' function). Maintaining Dik's (1978)
     distinction between $\emptyset$ and Go, as I have done, does not affect the present
     analysis, but as regards that of sentence (11) I see no point in not using $\emptyset$
     for the subject of the intransitive action verb.

10   For a sketch of such a sub-system within a discourse production model see
     Fortescue (1980), and for a version of ATN theory see Thorne, Bratley and
     Dewar (1968).

11   All form features relevant to the operation of the placement template(s)
     must of course be taken as present from the start (e.g. the distinction be-
     tween N and Dem for Aleut). Such general cross-language tendencies bearing
     upon placement as LIPOC (Dik 1978: 21ff), which is formulated as a rule

appearing to require at least some form rules preceding it, can be argued to
be not directly relevant to speech production models (though no doubt it reflects important factors - psychological in origin - behind the particular
ordering 'compromises' individual languages have struck in their grammars).

[12] The connection between this rule and the one for simple number agreement
presented before rule (22) above should be obvious: all that is left behind
by the deleted subject is its ability to trigger ordinary number agreement
on the verb (and then only if not singular - the unmarked number).

[13] i.e. with the following initial term alternates: $(Amx_i)_{subj}/(x_j)_{Poss(x_i)}$,
forming a rule-bundle with two possible input conditions.

[14] More than two Themes per clause (with or without anaphorically omitted subject) are unlikely to occur, though this is just conceivable in certain
cases, according to Bergsland. On the other hand, sequences of chained
clauses may occur, each with its own anaphoric Theme(s), as in the following
'conjoined predicate' construction: *ngaan sux̂tachx̂il asx̂atichx̂ikuu*, interpretable according to Bergsland (p.c.) as 'he$_1$ had him$_2$ hold him$_3$ and kill
him$_3$', where the anaphoric object of the first derived causal verb (conjunctive mood) is coreferential with that of the final full one (only the latter
displays a singular anaphoric inflection, referring to *both* the Themes).

[15] Other ways in which Aleut diverges notably from Eskimo are its strict word-
order and less richly developed system of suffixal derivation (it has only
about 120 productive suffixes compared to between 400 and 500 in any Eskimo
language): nor does Aleut display the controversial overlap between 'internal'
and 'external' syntax of Eskimo. As already mentioned, Eskimo has developed
true transitive verbal paradigms out of an earlier 3rd person anaphoric object
state (still characterizing Aleut) - perhaps by a process of de-emphasising
thematization into neutral object agreement (cf. Givón 1976). Indeed the
thoroughgoing morphological ergativity of Eskimo finds its historical roots
here rather than in anything to do with passive constructions. Hand in hand
with accreting subject-(anaphoric) object inflection in verbs in pre-Eskimo-
Aleut would have come the possibility of omitting a subject or object term
when understood as 'given'. Any such term left behind would need to be
marked somehow to distinguish between subject and object and the relative
case marker would be the obvious candidate (there is not far from the notion
of possessor/controller to that of agent). Cf. Givón (1976) for the origins
of agreement in anaphoric pronominalization. Presumably the situation in
Aleut today arose by extension from an earlier stage where anaphoric agreement was limited to anaphoric objects (Goal terms) - not dissimilar from the
case of Hungarian, for instance - to anaphoric possessors and locative construction controllers.

[16] One potential problem for FG as regards the Aleut data can be dispelled
easily: we have looked at examples of transitive verbs (two-place predicates)
with subject-only inflection and intransitive ones with 'double' subject-
plus-anaphoric-term inflection. Does this mean that individual predicates in
Aleut are not once and for all marked for the number of arguments in their
case frames? It should be clear by now that it does not. Verbal agreement in
Aleut is a 'shallow' matter, and one can state that for example a two-place
predicate is marked for taking two arguments in its frame, either or both of
which may be omitted on the surface, but if there is no overt object term
this must be reflected by an anaphoric inflection on the verb.

[17]   See below for the possibility of treating the subject as 'unmarked' Topic
       but hardly as unmarked Theme (such a Theme would break the absolutive case
       constraint on Themes and would not trigger anaphoric agreement like all
       other Themes apart from subject possessors do).

[18]   Though there is a more economical way of formalizing this stage of course,
       with 'Th' attached directly to the relevant, non-duplicated terms (compare
       footnote 7).

[19]   Unlike in Aleut, any term or satellite may be Topic in Eskimo. Furthermore,
       Eskimo has right-hand dislocation for 'afterthought' material but no left-
       hand dislocation as such (intonation and pause cannot distinguish such a
       Theme from ordinary Topic - including postpositional expressions glossable
       as 'as regards X'). Languages with Themes that may stand outside the predi-
       cation in the sense of not being coreferential with any of its terms may
       well be excluded from Eskimo-Aleut-like 'double inflection' typology (this
       is true of those mentioned by Li and Thompson 1976 at least): such pervasive
       cross-reference would be difficult to 'escape' from. Both Aleut and Eskimo
       contrast with a language like Yukagir, where Focus rather than Theme/Topic
       triggers off different sets of inflectional endings depending on which con-
       stituent - subject, object or predicate - is so marked (see Comrie 1981:
       259ff). It strikes me however that Focus is the most fundamental and uni-
       versal pragmatic function and that Aleut Theme (as well as Focus) has much
       in common with Yukagir Focus (this may even be true historically - see
       Fortescue 1984: 15). Focus in Yukagir appears to have absorbed most avail-
       able means for expressing pragmatic function, whereas Aleut Theme dominates
       over Topic/Subject (which can only be expressed by strict positioning in P1);
       in Eskimo in turn, Topic (alongside and distinct from Subject) predominates
       and there is arguably no systematic use of Theme. My argument reduces essen-
       tially to the FG notion that Subject/Object assignment is only utilized by
       certain languages (plus the possibility that this is also true of Theme
       assignment). It is perhaps of interest for FG theory to note that it is the
       language with the more fixed word-order of the two here treated (Aleut) that
       has no Subject/Object assignment, while that with the freer ordering (Eskimo)
       does require such assignment, contrary to the opposite hypothesis suggested
       by Dik and Gvozdanović (1981: 38).

[20]   The Eskimo-Aleut data also has a bearing on the hypothesis that Subject-
       prominent languages generally derive historically from Topic-prominent ones
       (see Li and Thompson 1976: 484). Aleut, which in most respects has maintained
       a more archaic aspect than Eskimo (partly owing to geographical isolation),
       doubtless reflects an earlier more Topic-prominent stage than Eskimo today
       in both the Theme-prominent sense of Li and Thompson and in the sense of
       not exploiting Subject-assignment - as opposed to Topic-assignment - (which
       Eskimo clearly does in a number of core constructions). One might surmise
       that Eskimo became more Subject-prominent by *only* permitting Ø-Themes (by
       anaphoric omission) as word-order loosened up. Topic-assignment (in my sense
       of the term) could then have developed beyond exclusive association with
       definite subjects to exploit the vacated P2 (now P1) initial position in the
       sentence and the relative case marker of the anaphoric construction has be-
       come associated only with agentive subjects of transitive sentences. If on
       the other hand Theme in P2 and Tail in P3 are specific Aleut developments
       (as is quite likely) we might simply suppose that that language never felt
       the need to isolate a Subject category distinct from Topic - as Eskimo did
       as soon as it became possible for terms other than the Subject (i.e. Agent,
       etc.) to fill the Topic slot and alternative syntactic perspectives began
       to be exploited (e.g. in passive constructions with agent and half-transitive
       ones with instrumental case Objects, not found in Aleut).

Chapter 7

Term operators

D. Richard Brown
Summer Institute of Linguistics, Sudan

0. Introduction

In the formalism of Functional Grammar (FG), semantic representations of natural
language sentences are made using predications built up mostly of lexical
predicates of the language concerned, formed by substituting terms into the
argument slots of a predicate-frame, in so far as the selectional restrictions
allow, and by adding satellite terms with peripheral semantic functions. The
resulting predication may be represented by the schema in (1) below, in which
't_i' stands for a term and the Greek letter pi (π) stands for the predicate
operators:

(1) $\pi \ \phi \ (t_1)_{SF1} \cdot \cdot \cdot (t_i)_{SFi}$

The arguments of these predicates are filled by terms with the following schema-
tic form (Dik 1978: 16):

(2) $(\omega x_i : \phi_1(x_i) : \ldots : \phi_i(x_i))_{SFi}$

Such terms represent expressions with referring potential. The variable 'x_i' may
be called the term variable of term t_i. The open predications in x_i (ie, $\phi(x_i)$)
progressively restrict the reference (within the current universe of discourse)
and so are called 'restrictors'. Let us call the first one the 'term predicate'.
The Greek letter omega (ω) stands for one or more term operators, such as 'i'
for indefinite references and 'd' for definite references and '1' for singular
references. The object of this paper is to inquire into the nature of terms and
term operators and to propose a set-theoretical model for them.

1. A set-theoretic model of terms

The semantics of referential expressions can be represented within Functional
Grammar more satisfactorily, it seems to me, if the following positions are
accepted:

(I)   What is specified by a term is not an individual but a set in the
        Speaker's universe of discourse.

Such a set may be called the term's 'domain', and it may be viewed as discrete
or continuous, depending in part on whether the term predicate is specified to
be count or mass.[1]

(II)   A predicate does not apply directly to an individual or set; rather,
        it applies to the membership of a set specified by its term argument.

Sets to which predicates apply in this way may be called 'collective sets'. The
set of referents to which the Speaker intends a predication to apply may be
called the 'referent set'; it is a subset of the domain.

(III)   A predicate may apply collectively, distributively, or corporately.

By 'corporately' I mean what Dik called 'applying to a set considered as a
totality' (Dik 1975: 10), as opposed to a distributive application. I use
'collective' as did Dik, to mean 'applying to the full range of individuals in a
set' (ibid.). Given the positions presented in (I) and (II) above, however, this
is simply the general (unmarked) kind of predicate application.

(IV)   Terms do not generate sets; rather, they specify properties of sets
        and their contents that already exist in the mind of the Speaker.

By 'mind' I mean the pragmatic information of the Speaker as it is being accessed
or otherwise processed by him for possible use in communication. It may be expected, therefore, that a term will not necessarily determine uniquely the
referent set which the Speaker has in mind, even if it is unique to him, because
the Speaker's description of it might not be definite.

(V)   Term operators specify the sizes of sets and their proportions.

1.1. The appropriateness of set relations for representing term relations

The relations and operations that can be predicated of sets seem to match natural
language usage more satisfactorily than do those relations that apply to individuals.

For one thing, sets can be multiple, so one can refer to more than one entity simultaneously, as in 'They came'. This also allows for ambiguity of number, as in 'The sheep came'. Also, the selectional restrictions for some predicates, such as 'numerous', require a term specifying a multiple set.

Secondly, sets can be empty, so one can refer to non-entities, as in the sentence 'No children came'.

Thirdly, sets can be continuous, and this reflects the linguistic phenomenon of mass nouns. A set theory of terms and term operators allows for a uniform representation of the semantics of both mass and count expressions, and it also allows for the ambiguity in this regard of nouns such as 'grain'.

Fourthly, set inclusion is transitive, whereas the relation of set membership is not, and this matches linguistic usage as well. For example, my son and my daughter can be described as subsets of my children, and my children as a subset of my dependents. My son, therefore, is one of my dependents. With the relation of set membership this is not possible.

Fifthly, sets can be represented in a variety of relationships besides that of membership, and this, too, reflects linguistic usage. For example, they may be stated to be identical (=), as in the expression 'My two children are Daniel and Christina'. They can also be represented with the relation of inclusion ($\subseteq$) as in the sentence 'Christie and Daniel are two children of mine'. This sentence does not indicate whether I have other children. They may also be shown in the relation of proper inclusion ($\subset$), as expressed in the sentence 'Daniel and Christie are two of my children'. Furthermore, these relations are actually applying to the contents of these sets, saying that they are included in more than one set, and this is consistent with our hypothesis that predicates apply to the contents of sets.

Sixthly, sets have sizes, and they can be compared according to size. Discrete sets have cardinal numbers (that is, the number of members), and this, too, reflects natural language in expressions such as 'the five of them' or 'the three bears' or 'the sun' or 'the one last cowboy'. Subsets can also have cardinal numbers, as in 'three dogs' or 'two of the bears'. Continuous (mass) sets have measure, like the measure of a line segment in geometry, and this measure can be described in a relative way, as in 'much water', and may be the basis for comparisons and proportions, as in 'half of my water'.

Seventhly, by adopting this set-theoretic view of reference into the framework of Functional Grammar, it is possible to posit a variety of term operators in a well-defined fashion. With these term operators and the set theory of reference, it is possible to give a good accounting for a variety of semantic phenomena

that have resisted satisfactory analysis within other frameworks, particularly
that of traditional quantificational logic. For example, besides the problems
posed by the phenomena mentioned in the previous points, there is the matter of
'partitive' references, and the different kinds of 'universal' quantifiers. Then
there is the distinction between 'specific' and 'non-specific' references, as in
'a certain book' and 'any book', and the distinction claimed to exist between
'existential' and 'non-existential quantifiers' (McCawley 1981: 425-433). The
ability of a set-theoretic version of Functional Grammar to provide a framework
within which such an accounting can be made - and that without recourse to the
quantifiers of logic - is strong support for the concept of referent sets.

This concept of terms as specifying collective sets can be adopted into the
formalism of Functional Grammar simply by using capital letters for the term
variables, inasmuch as this is a convention for representing variables over sets
in set theory. Thus the schema presented in (2) above would be rewritten as
$'(\omega X_i: \phi_1(X_1)_{SF1} \cdots \phi_i(X_i)_{SFi})'$.[2]

1.2. The representation of collective sets

It will prove useful to distinguish between certain kinds of sets. At least two
distinctions need to be posited: that between collective sets and distributive
sets, and that between discrete sets and continuous sets. Distributive sets are
defined in section 4. As for collective sets, a discrete collective set is a set
of entities, whether these are individuals, as in 'my socks', or sets, as in
'the five teams' or 'my family'. Its members are countable, and so it can be
multiple, singular, or empty. The membership of a continuous collective set, on
the other hand, such as is specified by 'water' or 'grain', is viewed as neither
discrete nor countable, at least not in a practical, finite sense. Thus it cannot
be singleton or multiple, but only empty or non-empty. This distinction, however,
is largely one of perspective, as encoded into a language's predicates, so that
count nouns specify discrete sets and mass nouns specify continuous sets. Sometimes the distinction is left to the Speaker, as in the sentence 'Although God
has counted the *hairs* of my head, I usually think of my *hair* as an unruly mass'.

To illustrate the representation of these kinds of set, let the capital letter
'X' be a variable over sets, let subscript 'm' indicate a mass/measurable predicate, and let subscript 'c' indicate a countable predicate. A set of my socks
would be represented as a discrete collective set as follows:

(3) $(X: sock_{Nc}(X) : my(X))$ or $(X: sock_c : my)$

(where 'my' is an abbreviation for a longer restrictor that indicates possession
by the Speaker). The singularity of 'sock' in the restrictor is insignificant.
It could just as well have been written plural, because the number of members
can only be specified by a term operator. Since there are no term operators in
(3) above, the cardinal number of my socks is not specified. Neither is it
specified whether the set includes all of my socks, some of them, or is empty.
The primitive term operator 'd', however, specifies that a set is a maximal set.
For example, '(dX : sock(X) : my(X))' specifies the set of all of my socks. A
continuous collective set of my clothing would be represented as in (4) below:

(4)   (X: clothing$_m$(X): my(X)) or (X: clothing$_m$: my)

The 'm' on the predicate indicates that the domain of the variable X is viewed
as a continuous set. Since 'X' stands for a variable over sets, the schema
'(X : sock : my)' stands for a set and does not need brace notation. Recall from
(II), however, that the predicate 'sock(X)' applies to the contents of 'X'. Thus
lexemes are predicates whose operands are sets but whose function is the collective ascription of states-of-affairs to the contents of those sets.

A significant difference between discrete sets and mass sets is in the basis
upon which their sizes are compared. For discrete sets this basis is their cardinal number. Let 'card(X)' be the cardinal number function of set theory; its
value is the number of members of the set which is its argument. For example,
the cardinal number of the set of all states of the USA is fifty, as shown in
(5) below:

(5)   card (dX: states of the USA (X)) = 50

A selection restriction on the arguments for this function, however, is that they
be discrete (countable sets). This could be shown by representing this meta-
predicate itself with a predicate-frame such as 'card (X: ϕ_c(X))'.

The size of mass sets, however, is taken with the measure function, which can
be represented with a predicate-frame such as 'm(X: ϕ_m)'. The value of this
function is not directly accessible, so it cannot be used in an absolute way to
specify the size of sets. It can, however, be used in a relative way to specify
the size of a set by explicit comparison to another such set, as in the sentence
'He has twice as much clothing as I have', which could be represented as
'm(dX: clothing$_m$: his) = 2.m(dX: clothing$_m$: mine)'. The Speaker can also make an

implicit comparison to some pragmatic norm, as in the statement 'He has a lot of clothing'. Comparison can also be made to a fixed quantity, as in the expression 'five litres of rice', where the measure of a set of rice is compared to that of a fixed quantity called 'a litre'. Taking 'litre-of' to be a relational (two-place) nominal predicate, the semantics of this latter expression could be represented as follows:

(6) $(5X_1: \text{litre-of}(X_1)(X_2: \text{water}(X_2))$

This is also an example of a collective set of continuous sets. A similar example for a collective set of discrete sets is that below for 'five pairs of my matching socks':

(7) $(5X_1: \text{pair-of}(X_1)\ (X_2: \text{sock}(X_2): \text{mine}(X_2): \text{match}(X_2))$

2. Numerators (Quantitative operators)

The size of a set can be expressed, sometimes absolutely, as in the statement 'Three sheep came'. Sometimes the size is expressed relative to some implicit norm, as in the statement 'Many sheep came'. The semantics of such expressions of quantity is represented in Functional Grammar by term operators called 'numerators'.

2.1. Quantities

By taking the variable 'X' over sets defined above, the cardinal number function 'card(X)', the measure function 'm(X)', and the maximal term operator 'd' as our primitives, it is possible within the framework of Functional Grammar to define a large number of distinctive term operators. Recall the schema for a predication given in (1). We can isolate one of the terms, 't_i', and let its semantic function and the rest of the semantic predication be represented by 'G', so that the predication is represented by '$G(t_i)$'. 't_i', on the other hand, stands for a term which would fit the schema in (2). Let the restrictors of this term all be represented by the predicate letter 'F'. This term, then, can be represented by '$(\omega X: F(X))$' so that the whole semantic representation reduces to '$G(\omega X: F(X))$' The sets to which this predication may 'refer' - or more precisely, which may be specified by it - are delimited not only by the restrictors, but also by the 'universe of discourse'. This universe is determined by a number of pragmatic factors which may be understood to define the universe U of sets in the pragmatic information of the Speaker at a particular moment in a particular situation as affected by the presence of a particular Addressee and perhaps particular Hearers. Our original schema for a predication, therefore, could be more fully represented as 'G(dX ⊂ U : F(X))'.

The set of all Fs in this universe of discourse is the potential referent set, and has been called 'the domain'. It can be defined as below:

(8) $D = (dX \subseteq U : F(X))$

(8')   The domain is the maximal set of Fs in the universe of discourse.

The set of all Fs specified by the Speaker to be G may be defined as follows:

(9) $R = (dX \subseteq U : F(X) : G(X)) = (dX \subseteq D : G(X))$

(9')   The referent set is the maximal set of Fs in U that are G (or did G).

Although the definitions of D and R apply to both count and mass predicates and predications, a distinction is made in defining their size. Let 'F_c' be a count predicate or predication and let 'F_m' be a mass predicate or predication. The size of the domain D and the referent set R which are specified by a predication such as 'G(X: F(X))' may be defined as follows:

(10) $cD = card(dX \subseteq U : F_c(X))$

(11) $mD = m(dX \subseteq U : F_m(X))$

(12) $cR = card(dX \subseteq D : G(X))$

(13) $mR = m(dX \subseteq D : G(X))$

In statements that apply to both discrete sets and mass sets, their sizes may be mentioned simultaneously by writing 'c/mD' and 'c/mR'. For example, since the restrictor G(X) in (12) and (13) cannot increase R, but can limit it further, it follows that D is never a proper subset of R, and that c/mD is never less than c/mR. This can be easily symbolized by writing 'c/mD $\geq$ c/mR'.

2.2. Absolute numerators

Absolute numerators indicate the cardinal number of discrete sets, although not necessarily precisely. The numerator '0', however, seems to be precise, and it also applies to mass terms as well as to those referring to discrete sets. The

numerators '0', '1', '2', 'm', and in general 'n' may be defined as below. Note
that the definition for the numerator 'm' is different for mass terms from what
it is for count terms. If one lets the main predicate 'G(X)' be 'came' and the
term restrictor predicate '$F_c(X)$' be '$boy_c(s)$', then the resulting predications
can be expressed as shown in their glosses.

(14) a. $G(0X: F_c(X))$ iff$_{df}$ $cR = 0$ 'No boys came'

(14) b. $G(0X: F_m(X))$ iff$_{df}$ $mR = 0$ 'No rain came'

(15) $G(1X: F_c(X))$ iff$_{df}$ $cR \geqq 1$ 'A boy came (one at least)'

Although '1' usually indicates that $cR = 1$, it can be used when $cR > 1$. That is
to say, numerators (except for '0') specify minimums; hence the existential interpretation given them in traditional logic. By conversational implicature, however, the Speaker is expected to specify cR fairly precisely if at all.

(16) a. $G(mX: F_c(X))$ iff$_{df}$ $cR > 1$ '(Some) boys came'

(16) b. $G(mX: F_m(X))$ iff$_{df}$ $mR > 0$ '(Some) rain came'

(17) $G(2X: F_c(X))$ iff$_{df}$ $cR \geqq 2$ 'Two boys came (at least)'

(18) $G(nX: F_c(X))$ iff$_{df}$ $cR \geqq n$ 'n boys came (at least)'

The variable 'n' in (18) can be taken to define an infinite set of numerators
corresponding to the positive integers. The numerator 'm' in (16b) indicates
that the referent mass set is non-empty. The numerator 'm' in (16a), however,
indicates that the referent discrete set is multiple. In the case of (17), the
numerator '2' indicates that the number of boys who came was two and possibly
more than that, since one can say 'Two boys came' even if more than that came.

2.3. Relative numerators

In spite of the infinite number of term operators that have been defined so far,
note that there is no 'cost' involved, because the only primitive is the cardinal
number function. In fact, this ability to readily define more operators as needed,
all in terms of one primitive function, improves the typological adequacy of
Functional Grammar. It also enables one to describe the lexemes of a natural
language which express sets of numerators or relations between them. For example,
'few' and 'many' or 'little' and 'much' fall into this category. Note that the
first pair apply only to count predicates, and the second pair only to mass

predicates. Note also that they cannot be defined absolutely, but only relative
to each other and to zero. Furthermore, even their relative relationship is dependent upon their being in identical terms, predications, and situations. A
phrase like 'many cars' would likely refer to a smaller number with reference to
a village situation than it would with reference to an urban situation, and in
either case it might refer to fewer entities than would a phrase such as 'a few
ants'. This can be shown as in (19) and (20) below, where the same universe
prevails throughout, where 'ω' stands for other term operators (if present),
where '$\ll$' means 'far fewer than', and where the common predication is
'$G(\omega X: F(X))$'.

(19) $0 < card\ (few\ \omega X: F_c(X)\ :\ G(X)) \ll card\ (many\ \omega X: F_c(X)\ :\ G(X))$

(20) $0 < m\ (little\ \omega X: F_m(X)\ :\ G(X)) \ll m\ (much\ \omega X: F_m(X)\ :\ G(X))$

2.4. Numerator modifiers

Consider now sentences such as 'Exactly two children came' and 'More than five
children came'. In these sentences quantities are specified relative to a cardinal number. Such modifications could be represented by a set of modifiers that
modify numerators. Symbols for such modifiers are readily available from mathe-
matics and can be adapted for our use.

Some of these numerator modifiers are formally defined and their English
expression exemplified in what follows

(21) $G(\ =nX: F(X))\ iff_{df}\ cR = n$ 'Exactly five children came'

(22) $G(\ \approx nX: F(X))\ iff_{df}\ cR \approx n$ 'Around five children came'

(23) $G(\ \underset{\approx}{<}nX: F(X))\ iff_{df}\ cR \underset{\approx}{<} n$ 'Almost five children came'

(24) $G(\ \leqq nX: F(X))\ iff_{df}\ cR \leqq n$ 'At most five children came'
                                                              'No more than five children came'

(25) $G(\ <nX: F(X))\ iff_{df}\ cR < n$ 'Fewer than five children came'

(26) $G(\ \ll nX: F(X))\ iff_{df}\ cR \ll n$ 'Far fewer than five children came'

Although '2' can be used facultatively for '$\geqq 2$', note that the modifer '$\geqq$'
can be used to make this explicit, and this is expressed in sentences such as
'At least two children came' and 'Two or more came'.

A few of these numerator modifiers can be used with relative numerators as
well, and hence for both discrete and mass sets, as below:

(27)   G(>few X: $F_c(X)$)   'More than a few children came'

(28)   G(<little X: $F_m(X)$)   'Very little rain fell'

3. Proportions

It is possible to specify, not just the size of the referent set, but the size
of the domain as well. These may be expressed in the form of a proportion, as in
(29) below:

(29)   Three of my five children came

This sentence specifies that the referent set has three members and that its
domain has five. In general, such proportions may be called 'quantified', because
the size of both sets is specified. Proportions may also be unquantified, however, as in the sentences 'Most of my children came' and 'Three fifths of my
children came'. In these examples the ratio of the referent set to its domain is
specified, but the actual size of the sets is not. There are also semi-quantified
proportions, as in the sentence 'Most of my five children came'.

    The proportion of numerators in (29) above can be represented by using a slash
'/', with the numerator for the referent set on the left and the numerator for
the domain on the right, such as '3/5'. (Keep in mind from 2.1 that c/mR $\leq$ c/mD.)
This formalism can be defined as follows:

(30) $G(n_1/n_2$ X: F(X)) iff$_{df}$ c/mD = n_2 & c/mR $\geq$ n_1

(30')   By definition, n_1 of the n_2 Fs are G if and only if the size of the
        set of all Fs in U is n_2 and the size of the subset of these which
        are also G is at least n_1

The numerator for either set may be modified, as in

(31) $G(=n_1/>n_2$ X: $F_c(X)$)   'Just 3 of the more than 20 children
                                                are girls'

    In general, proportions may be said to be 'partitive' or 'exhaustive', depend-
ing on whether the referent set R is specified to be a proper subset of the
domain D (c/mR < c/mD) or to equal it (c/mR = c/mD), respectively. There are
also what might be called 'differential proportions', which specify neither the
ratio nor the quantity of these sets, but only the difference in their sizes. An
example of this latter is 'All but two of my children came'.

3.1. *Partitive proportions*

3.1.1. *Unquantified partitive proportions*

The sentences in (29) and (31) above exemplify quantified partitive proportions. Unquantified proportions specify the size of neither set, but only their ratio. Ratios can be specified by what we may call 'proportional operators'. These may be precise, as is expressed by the word 'half', or relative, as is 'most of the', or very general, as is 'some of the'. The precise proportional operators may be called 'rational operators'.

3.1.1.1. *Rational operators*

Let 'f' stand for a rational number between 0.0 and 1.0, exclusively: that is f $\in$ { x $\in$ Z : 0 < x < 1 }. An infinite number of rational term operators 'f' corresponding to these numbers can be defined as in (32) below:

(32)   G(f X: F(X)) iff$_{df}$ c/mR $\geq$ f.c/mD

Just as with other numerators, these may be modified. For example,

(33)   G($\underset{\sim}{\leq}$half X: F(X)) or G($\underset{\sim}{\leq}\frac{1}{2}$X: F(X))
         'Almost half of my children came' 'Almost half of my rice is milled'

As can be seen in the examples above, rational operators can be used with regard to both discrete sets and mass sets.

When a rational operator is to be expressed as a fraction, such as 'two thirds', and a slash must be used, then it can be represented within parentheses as '(2/3)', or with '/' or '/m' following as '1/2/m', to show that it is a rational operator and not a proportion meaning 'two of the three'.

3.1.1.2. *Relative proportional operators*

Other rational operators are less precise, and some of them must be described in reference to a range of ratios, as with those below:

(34)   0.0 $<$ minority of $<$ 0.5 $<$ majority of $\leq$ most of $\leq$ 1.0

Note that words like 'most of (the)' express a relative proportion, whereas words like 'many' express a relative quantity. The same distinction exists between 'some of (the)' and 'some', although these are more general than relative.[3] A phrase such as 'many of (the)', on the other hand, expresses a semi-quantified proportion, and these are discussed further below.

3.1.1.3. *The partitive operator*

Since a partitive term is any which specifies that $c/mD > c/mR$, any rational term operator whose value is less than 1.0 may be called partitive. It is common, however, for languages to encode a partitive operator which is very imprecise, in that it only indicates that a ratio is less than 1.0. A mass example of this is 'some of my rice'. To represent this we could use the modified operator '<1.0'. However, in order to capture the heavy functional load on this operator and to render its representation more lucid, it seems warranted to provide it with an independent symbol and definition, as below:

(35) $G(iX: F(X))$ iff$_{df}$ $c/mD > c/mR$ iff $G(<1.0 \ X: F(X))$
         'Not all of my rice is milled'

This 'i', of course, is the term operator proposed by Dik for 'indefinite' references (1978: 58). Note, however, that according to the definition of 'i' in (35) above, c/mR could be zero. It remains, then, for a numerator to specify something about the size of c/mR.

3.1.2. *Semi-quantified proportions*

For mass sets, the numerator represented by 'm' specifies that a set is not empty, so that '$G(mX: F_m(X))$' could represent a sentence like 'Some rice of mine is milled'. The phrase 'some of my rice' mentioned above, however, specifies that the referent set is both non-empty and partitive. This is like the distinction between 'some boys' and 'some of the boys', and could be represented by using a proportion such as 'm/>m' for the term operators. An alternative would be to let the term operator 'i' combine with numerators to indicate that a partitive proportion is specified. This notation could be defined as below:

(36) $G(inX: F(X))$ iff$_{df}$ $c/mD > c/mR \geq n$

Thus 'some of' in the example above could be represented as follows:

(37) $G(imX: F_m(X))$ iff $mD > cR > 0$ 'Some of my rice is milled'

Recall that for discrete sets, '1' indicates that a set is singleton, 'm' indicates that it is multiple, and so on. These are exemplified below:

(38)   G(i1X: F(X)) iff cD > cR $\geq$ 1   'One of my children came'
(39)   G(imX: F(X)) iff cD > cR > 1   'Some of my children came'
(40)   G(i3X: F(X)) iff cD > cR $\geq$ 3   'Three of my children came'
(41)   G(i0X: F(X)) iff cD > cR = 0   'None of my children came'

Contrast (41) with the non-proportional term below with just a numerator:

(42)   G(0X: F(X)) iff cR = 0   'No children of mine came'

   The relative numerators can also be combined with 'i':

(43)   G(many iX: F_c(X))   'Many of my children came'

(44)   G(little iX: F_m(X))   'A little of my rice is milled'

3.2. Exhaustive proportions

If the ratio cR/cD equals 1.0, then the referent set may be said to exhaust its domain, and such references may be called 'exhaustive'.

3.2.1. Unquantified exhaustive proportions

Consider the sentence 'All of the rice in this shop is milled' or just 'The rice in this shop is milled'. These two sentences may be considered to be semantically equivalent, even though pragmatically they are not equivalent. They indicate nothing about the quantity of rice in that shop, only the ratio of milled rice to total rice, which is 1.0. The underlying term operator can be represented by '1.0', but recall that this indicates that the referent set exhausts its domain, which is a maximal set. Therefore the maximal operator 'd' which specifies the domain can be used instead of '1.0', in order to provide a more lucid representation and one which captures more of the significance of this operator, as shown below:

(45)   G(dX: F(X)) iff G(1.0 X: F(X)) iff c/mD = c/mR
        'The sheep came'

When used this way the operator 'd' may be called 'the exhaustive operator'.

3.2.2. *Quantified exhaustive proportions*

If c/mD = c/mR and the size of these sets is specified, then the proportion is both exhaustive and quantified, as exemplified below:

(46) $G(5/5 X: F_c(X))$ 'Five of my five children came'

Such expressions, however, are rare. One would usually say something like 'All of my five children' or 'All five of my children'. These quantified proportions may be represented by '$(d/5X: F_c(X))$' and '$(d5/X: F_c(X))$', respectively, and this latter may be further simplified by removing the slash, so that it is just like the standard FG representation: 'd5X'. Note that this latter could also be expressed as 'my five children' if the term operator is without Focus. This notation may be defined as follows, where 'n' stands for any numerator:

(47) $G(dnX: F(X))$ iff$_{df}$ $G(n/nX: F(X))$ iff c/mD = c/mR

4. *Term operators involving distributive referent sets*

Let '{Rn}' be a distributive referent set, the size of whose member sets are all specified by 'n'. The distributive referent set for a predication such as that represented by '$G(X: F(X))$' may be defined as follows:

(48) a. $\{Rn\} = \{X \subseteq U : F_c(X) : card(X) = n : G(X)\}$ or

(48) b. $\{Rn\} = \{X \subseteq U : F_m(X) :   m(X) = n : G(X)\}$

The braces indicate a maximal distributive set, the intersection of whose members is null. Let 'c{Rn}' stand for the cardinal number of this set. There are certain additional term operators that specify something regarding c{Rn}. For example, given a predication 'The children came', a distributive referent set where n = 1 is the set of singleton sets of children who came.

Through the following discussion it should be borne in mind that term operators and terms do not generate sets; rather, they specify properties of sets and their members in the pragmatic information of the Speaker.

4.1. The distributive and corporate operators

Consider the following sentences:

(49)   My cousin and I are each married   (My cousin and I are both married)

(50)   My cousin and I are married

(51)   My cousin and I are married together

In the first example (49), the word 'each' may be said to express an underlying term operator which specifies a distributive application of the predicate;
let us call this operator 'each'. In the third sentence (51), the word 'together',
as Dik has noted (1975: 9), specifies that the predicate is to be applied corporately; let the term operator specifying this be called 'corp'. Of course, the
sense of 'be married' differs in these cases, and presumably there would be a
different predicate-frame for each of these two senses, one requiring a distributive referent set, and the other requiring a corporate referent set of two.
This could be indicated by the different term operators in each predicate-frame.
In the second sentence (50), the predicate application is unmarked, and so it is
just the usual collective application.

These operators may be defined as follows:

(52) $G(\text{each } X: F(X)) \text{ iff}_{df} c\{R1\} = cR$

(53) $G(\text{corp } X: F(X)) \text{ iff}_{df} c\{R1\} = 0$

In the sentence above, the referent set consists of my cousin and me, and so
$cR = 2$. In the distributive case (49) the predicate could apply to each of us
individually and the resulting distributive referent set would have two members,
so that $c\{R1\} = cR$. In the corporate case, the term operator 'corp' would specify
that the predicate is not to be applied individually. The predicate-frame for the
intended sense of 'be married' would in fact preclude its application to singleton referent sets, so $c\{R1\}$ would equal zero.

For many or most predicates, their mode of application is specified in the
predicate-frame and the corresponding term operator need not be expressed.
Examples include 'numerous', 'unanimous', and 'elect'. For example, given the
statement 'The people elected John to be their president', it is not necessarily
the case that everyone voted for John, and anyway, an individual person cannot
usually elect someone; only a group of people can do that. Part of a predicate-
frame for 'elect', therefore, might be as follows:

(54) elect_V (corp mX: human(X))$_{Ag}$ (X: human(X))$_{Go}$

These operators may combine with quantitative and proportional term operators, as shown below:

(55)   G(each n_1/n_2 X: F(X)) iff$_{df}$ c{R1} = cR & cR $\geq n_1$ & cD = n_2

(55')   Three of my five children each brought a present

(56)   G(corp n_1/n_2 X: F(X)) iff$_{df}$ c{R1} = 0 & cR $\geq n_1$ & cD = n_2

(56')   Three of my five children are similar

4.2. *The universal operator*

Distributions are not always one-to-one, however, as seen below:

(57)   John gave one bag of candy to every 3 of the 15 boys in the park

Since 'every' specifies every set of three, then it is referring to a set of sets of three. In fact, it is referring to its distributive referent set, whose member sets have three members each, specifying that it exhausts its domain as much as possible. The '3' in (57) does not specify cR but rather the 'n' in {Rn}; that is, it specifies the cardinal of the member sets of the distributive referent set, rather than the size of the normal referent set. This operation is different from the distributive one in 4.1, therefore, both in its exhaustiveness and in its different use of numerators. A different term operator is therefore required. Dik originally proposed 'every' as a term operator distinct from 'all' and 'd' (1978: 61), so let this be it. It can be defined as follows:

(58)   G(every nX : F(X)) iff$_{df}$ c{Rn} $\approx$ cD/n

(58')   By definition *every* set of n Fs is G if and only if the number of
         sets of n Fs in U which are G is approximately equal to the number
         of sets of n Fs in U, which is cD divided by n.

This definition could be expanded to include a numerator for the domain:

(58'')   G(every n_1/n_2 X: F(X)) iff c{Rn_1} $\approx$ cD/n & cD = n_2

For example, the term operators for (57) would be 'every 3/15 X'. The distributive referent set would be specified to have member sets of cardinal number 3. The cardinal number of the distributive set would be $c\{R3\}$, which is specified to approximately equal cD divided by 3, which is 15/3, which is 5. Note that 'every $1/n_2$ X' can be expressed in English as 'each of the n_2', as in 'John gave a bag of candy to each of the fifteen boys in the park'. This 'each of', however, is different from the operator 'each' in 4.1 above.

4.3. The specific and random operators

Consider the sentences below:

(59)   John sent Bill to buy a certain two books of the many available

(60)   John sent Bill to buy   two books of the many available

(61)   John sent Bill to buy   any two books of the many available

Sentence (59) informs us that there are only two books that John sent Bill to buy. Sentence (61) informs us that there are not two particular books which Bill is supposed to buy, but that any two (or more) books may be purchased. Sentence (60) is ambiguous; it can be interpreted like (59) or like (61). References such as that in (59) are usually referred to as 'specific', and those such as in (61) as 'non-specific'. All three sentences, however, make a partitive dual reference with regard to the books, and the term operators for this are 'i2'. The '2' indicates that John is to buy two books (at least), and the 'i' indicates that these books are to be selected from a larger set. The term operators so far discussed, then, are inadequate to distinguish between (59) and (61).

To appreciate the difference between these two kinds of reference, consider the difference in regard to the distributive set of books to be bought. The distributive set for the specific term in (59) will have just one member set, which will contain one pair of books. These are the two books which Bill was sent to buy. The other pairs of books are not to be bought. Thus $c\{R2\} = 1$. Since Bill was sent to buy two books, the cardinal of the collective set of books to be bought is specified to be two. Thus cR = 2. In the case of the random term in (61), there is no way to distinguish between pairs of books in regard to whether Bill was sent to buy a particular pair or not. Either the description fits none of the pairs, as in (61), or it fits all of them, as in (62) below:

(62)   Bill can buy any two of the books

In no case, then, will a random (partitive) term specify a distributive set of just one member set. In the case of random terms, then, $c\{R\} \neq 1$. However, although the books to be bought are not specified, their number is. Thus the cardinal (cR) of the collective set of books to be bought is specified in (61) and (62) to be 2, and in general to be n. In general we can say that specific terms specify that $c\{Rn\} = 1$ & $cR = n$, and that random terms specify that $c\{Rn\} \neq 1$ & $cR = n$. In the case of sentences like (60), the value of $c\{R\}$ is not specified.

Let 'cert' be the term operator for specific references, and let 'any' or '-cert' be the term operator for non-specific references. These operators can be respectively defined as follows, where the definition of 'every' is included for comparison, as is that for a general proportional term:

(63) $G(\text{ cert } n_1/n_2 \text{ X: F(X)}) \text{ iff}_{df} c\{Rn_1\} = 1 \;\&\; cR = n_1 \;\&\; cD = n_2$

(64) $G(\text{ any } \; n_1/n_2 \text{ X: F(X)}) \text{ iff}_{df} c\{Rn_1\} \neq 1 \;\&\; cR = n_1 \;\&\; cD = n_2$

(58) $G(\text{every } n_1/n_2 \text{ X: F(X)}) \text{ iff}_{df} c\{Rn_1\} \approx cD/n_1 \qquad \;\&\; cD = n_2$

(30, 31) $G(\qquad =n_1/n_2 \text{ X: F(X)}) \text{ iff}_{df} \qquad\qquad cR = n_1 \;\&\; cD = n_2$

Thus the terms in (59) and (61) could be represented as '(cert i2/many X: book)' and '(any i2/many X: book)', respectively. Of course, n_2 is optional.

5. Conclusion

When Dik proposed that 'quantifiers should be regarded as elements internal to terms,' he noted the 'many difficulties concerning quantification' and wondered whether there would be 'any undesirable consequences of this suggestion from the point of view of logic' (1978: 61). The consequences, it would seem now, show his FG system to be more felicitous than that of quantificational logic for representing the semantics of natural language.

NOTES

[1]   I am grateful to Simon Dik for reviewing an earlier draft of this paper and for making several valuable criticisms. He raised the question of why I did not use Bunt's theory of ensembles (1976, etc.). In fact, the 'collective sets' posited for terms in this paper could be called 'ensembles', since they include both discrete and continuous sets. The rationale for Bunt's theory of ensembles, however, seems to be to give an accounting of the distributive properties of mass predicates. Not all properties of mass sets are distributive, however. For example, one could say 'The dry cement I carried

was heavy, but the small bits of it were as light as dust'. In the final
analysis, therefore, distributivity might be seen to be a property of predicates and of the Speaker's intent, as indicated by term operators, rather
than a property of mass sets as against discrete sets. In the theory presented here, distributivity is encoded into term operators and into predicate-
frames, an option for those working within FG. This theory has in common with
Bunt, however, the application of predicates to the contents of sets (ensembles) rather than directly to entities.

[2]   For the purposes of this discussion, labels describing kinds of states-of-
affairs, pragmatic functions, syntactic functions, and sometimes syntactic
category and semantic function, will be omitted. Redundant repetitions of
term variables will also be omitted from restrictors on occasion.

[3]   One might be inclined to consider 'some of' to be a relative proportion less
than 'most of', and 'some' to be a relative numerator less than 'many' and
greater than 'few'. Although 'some' is often to be used for moderate quantifiers for which 'many' and 'few' are inappropriate, this may be attributed
to the use of a general word for lack of a more specific one. The quantity
specified by 'some' is actually no more specific than to mark a mass set as
non-empty and a discrete set as multiple. Say that a meeting was called for
my linguistic society and only one per cent of the members attended. If I
asked the chairman whether *some of the* members attended, he would say yes.
If I asked him whether *many of the* members attended, he would say no. If, on
the other hand, ninety-nine per cent of the members attended, and I asked
him whether *some of the* members attended, he would still say yes. The case
with 'some' is similar. These expressions, therefore, express operators which
are relative only in the most general way. For this reason a representation
using 'm' seems appropriate.

Chapter 8

On the notion 'relator' and the expression of the genitive relation

Machiel J. Limburg
Institute of General Linguistics, Free University of Amsterdam

0. Introduction*

This paper discusses the notion 'Relator' as it was introduced in Functional
Grammar by Dik (1983d), and the predictions made by the typological ordering
principles concerning Relators. It will be seen that different definitions of
'Relator' lead to different consequences of the ordering principles. Two such
definitions will be proposed (section 1). In section 2, data on genitival constructions from a sample of thirty languages will be presented. These seem to
suggest that one of the proposed definitions leads to the correct predictions.
However, in section 3 a different interpretation of the facts is discussed which
accounts for some problematic cases.

1. On defining 'Relator'

In Dik (1983d) the notion of 'Relator' was defined as (a) an Adposition, (b) a
case marker, or (c) a subordinating device (i.e. an independent subordinator or
a subordinating affix such as occurs in nominalized and participialized constructions). It was stated that 'functionally, Relators have in common that they link
one constituent to another, that they establish a relationship between two relata.
At the same time, the Relator forms one constituent with one of its relata'
(1983d: 273-274).[1] Two ordering principles are proposed that together predict
that the possible positions of Relators in (1) are preferred to the positions
shown in (2):

(1) a.   (relatum)   ((R) relatum)
    b.   (relatum (R))   (relatum)
(2) a.   ((R) relatum)   (relatum)
    b.   (relatum)   (relatum (R))

In Dik (1983d), Limburg (1983), and Kahrel (this volume) numerous facts are
adduced showing the correctness of the above predictions, and, furthermore,
showing that in languages where the effect of other ordering principles would
lead to systematic violations of the Relator principles, measures are taken to
restore the preferred patterning of (1).

However, the usefulness of the notion 'Relator' for typological research is hampered, in my view, by the fact that it is sometimes difficult to make out if a particular morpheme is to be considered as such or not. Firstly, note that while it is said that 'the Relator forms one constituent with one of its relata', it is not said which relatum that is. For instance, in genitival constructions the relata are the term referring to the Possessor and the term referring to the Possessed item. From (1), it is not clear whether the Relator is an element marking the Possessor, the Possessed, or if both possibilities obtain. The listing of categories as 'Adposition', 'case marker', etc., is of no help here since particular morphemes in particular languages are not easy to classify in these terms (note the frequent use by authors of grammars of the term 'particle' as a waste-paper basket).

More fundamentally, in syntactic and morphological typological research, one needs a semantic-functional definition of the phenomenon to be studied in order to identify and compare the relevant constructions. Since languages vary widely in the means used to perform similar functions and express similar meanings, the functions and meanings should be taken as the starting-point.[2]

Lastly, the disadvantage of a listing definition as in Dik (1983d) is that one is obliged to go on adding categories to be considered Relators every time one encounters constructions in which elements seem to function as such. Several languages, for instance, have general 'linking' or 'associative' morphemes whose function seems to be to connect constituents of the noun phrase (Adjectives, Genitives) to each other or to the head noun (this obtains in Bantu languages, Sino-Tibetan and Iranian languages). For another example, consider particles marking Theme or marking special Topic and Focus constituents placed in P1 (as in Japanese, Lisu or Yoruba). These might be said to establish a link between the pragmatically marked constituents and the predication (or rest of the predication) and therefore predicted to be positioned as in (1b). In these and similar cases, one might want to add new categories to the list of Relators, but this decision would be taken on the basis of the function of the elements involved.

One might therefore propose a purely functional definition of 'Relator', as follows:

Definition I. A Relator is any element that links one constituent to another, that establishes a relationship between two relata.

As we will see below, this definition is certainly too broad and will have to be
restricted in some way. Specifically, in genitival constructions Definition I
would imply that all elements apart from the terms referring to Possessor and
Possessed are to be considered Relators, since they can all be said to establish
a relationship between these terms. The italicized elements in (3)-(5) would
then be predicted to occur typically in the positions characterized by (1) but
only rarely in those specified by (2) (the Hungarian example (5) would then show
an exceptional ordering):

(3)   Standard Dutch:

   a.   Jan -*s*   boek
        John-Gen book
        'John's book'

   b.   boek *van* mij
        book of   me
        'my book'

(4)   Colloquial Dutch:

   a.   Jan *z'n* boek
        John his book
        'John's book'

   b.   hem *z'n* boek
        him his book
        'his book'

(5)   Hungarian (Uralic; Casper de Groot p.c.):

   a.   János kabát-*ja*
        John coat -3sg
        'John's coat'

   b.   az én kabát-*om*
        the me coat -1sg
        'my coat'

However, note that there is at least one important difference in function between
the italicized elements in (3) on the one hand, and those in (4)-(5) on the other:
the presence of the former is dependent on the presence of the Possessor term with
which they form one constituent, but this is not so in the case of the latter.
Leaving out *Jan* and *hem* in (4) leads to a well-formed expression meaning 'his
book', and similarly Hungarian *kabát-ja* and *kabát-om* are well-formed expressions
meaning 'his/her coat' and 'my coat' respectively.[3] The difference is one between
Possessor-marking and Possessed-marking, or, in more general terms, between
Dependent-marking and Head-marking. A more restrictive definition of Relator could
make use of this distinction as follows (cf. Limburg 1983):

> *Definition II.* In any construction in which a constituent B is dependent on a constituent A ('the head'), a Relator is an element marking the dependent constituent B for this relation.[4]

Given this definition, the ordering principles of Dik (1983d) now predict the patterns in (6) to be preferred to those in (7), where (6)-(7) are identical to (1)-(2) except that the nature of the relata is now specified.

(6) a.   (Head)   ((R) Dependent)
   b.   (Dependent (R))   (Head)
(7) a.   ((R) Dependent)   (Head)
   b.   (Head)   (Dependent (R))

This definition makes explicit claims as to which elements in particular languages are constrained in their positioning by the ordering principles concerning Relators, and which elements are not so constrained (though different ordering principles may apply to them). It is superior to a simple listing of categories, since now it is a general relationship, namely dependency, that provides the criterion, rather than specific characteristics of the elements in the languages in question, or the terminology used by the author of the grammar. (8) lists some of the categories included by Definition II that were found in the sample presented in section 2 below, and the categories excluded by the definition. Thus, the elements in (4)-(5) are excluded, as are affixes (such as occur in some languages) which indicate that a term is a possessed item without specifying the Possessor.

(8)   Genitival constructions:
       Head   = Possessed Item
       Dependent = Possessor
       Relator   = Prepositions,Possessive Particles, Connectives, etc.
                     Postpositions,Genitive Suffixes, Possessive Particles
                  ≠ Weak Possessive Pronouns, Pronominal Affixes, Possessed
                     Item Affixes

Before turning to the data on genitival constructions, it is interesting to have a brief look at the consequences that Definition II has for other types of constructions. We will discuss here only the constructions mentioned by Dik (1983d) and Limburg (1983).

Firstly, all types of case-marking within the predication would be included but agreement affixes and pronominal affixes (see for examples section 3) would be excluded since these mark the verb, i.e. the head:

(9)   Predication:

         Head   = (Verbal) Predicate
         Dependent = Arguments, Satellites[5]
         Relator   = Prepositions, Preclitic Case Markers, Case Prefixes
                       Postpositions, Postclitic Case Markers, Case Suffixes
                    ≠ Agreement Affixes, Pronominal Affixes

Within such comparative constructions as 'bigger than John' the elements marking
the standard 'John' are Relators by Definition II, but the comparative suffix -er
or an adverb like *more* in 'more difficult than ...' are not:

(10)   Comparative constructions:

         Head   = Comparative Adjective
         Dependent = Standard of Comparison
         Relator   = Adpositions, Case Affixes
                    ≠ Comparative Affixes, Comparative Adverbs

Thirdly, in relative clause constructions the elements marking the subordinate
clause as such are to be considered Relators according to Definition II (some
examples of the relevant categories are mentioned in (11)), but elements marking
the antecedent as such are excluded. Examples of the latter would be the Persian
suffix -*i* marking the antecedent of restrictive relative clauses, and the italicized element in constructions like (12) and (13).

(11)   Relative Clause constructions:

         Head   = Antecedent
         Dependent = Relative Clause
         Relator   = Relative Pronouns, Subordinators
                       Particles, Postclitic Particles, Participial Suffixes
                    ≠ Antecedent Markers

(12)   Bambara (Mande; Bird 1966, quoted in Keenan & Comrie 1977):

         Tye ye   ne ye   so   *min*   ye san
         man Past I Past horse which see buy
         'The man bought the horse that I saw'

(13)   John always reads *whatever* book I read

As a final example, consider adverbial clauses. These may be marked by categories
such as those mentioned in (14) which are then predicted to occur in the positions
indicated in (6). However, there may also be elements in the main clause signalling
the presence of such an adverbial clause such as *dan* in (15) and *jiù* in (16). Their
presence may be regarded as a therapeutic measure in cases where the Relators are
in non-preferred positions, but their positioning is not constrained by the ordering principles, if Definition II is accepted.

(14)   Adverbial Clause constructions:

       Head   = Main Clause
       Dependent = Adverbial Clause
       Relators   = Subordinators, Conjunctions
                     Conjunctions, Participial Suffixes
               ≠ 'Dummy' Adverbs

(15)   Dutch (Dik 1983d):

       Als hij geld heeft, *dan* kan de jongen boeken kopen
       if he money has, then can the boy   books buy
       'If he has money, the boy can buy books'

(16)   Mandarin Chinese (Li & Thompson 1978, quoted in Dik 1983d):

       (Yàoshi) ni qù, wo *jiù* qù
       If   you go, I   then go
       'If you go, I will go'

More examples of constructions could be adduced where Definition II, taken together with the ordering principles of Dik (1983d), makes predictions as to the
preferred ordering of some categories of elements and where other categories are
specifically excluded (cf. the particles marking pragmatic functions mentioned
above). We will now, however, turn to typological data concerning genitival constructions to see if the predictions made by (8) above are correct.

2. The typology of genitival constructions

In this section data from thirty languages will be presented. The construction
under consideration is heuristically defined as 'that construction within the
term that includes among its meanings the meaning that can be paraphrased as
"the X that Y possesses"'. That is, we are concerned here only with attributively
used genitive expressions, and only with those that can be used to express alienable possession. Constructions used *only* for inalienable possession or part-
whole relations are therefore excluded. Similarly excluded are constructions involving relative clauses (which would be included by the definition), since these
would be more relevant to a discussion of relative clause constructions in general and no language seemed to have this as the only option for expressing possession attributively.[6]

  Subsection 2.1 discusses the method of sampling and justifies the genetic and
typological representativeness of the sample. Subsection 2.2 shows how the constructions found were classified into different construction types.

2.1. The sample

The selection of languages in this sample has been done according to the method
outlined by Bell (1978). Bell has grouped the languages of the world into 16 large
genetic-areal 'stocks' and has estimated the genetic diversity within each in
terms of the number of distinct groups. He counts groups as distinct if they are
separated by a time-depth of at least 3,500 years. In this way, he arrives at a
total number of 478 distinct groups.

Any sample should be representative of the number of groups within each stock.
That is, a stock with a large number of distinct groups should be represented by
more languages than a stock with fewer. Table 1 shows the individual languages
that were chosen and refers to the sources used for them.

TABLE 1. Genetic representativeness according to Bell (1978)

Stocks	Groups (Bell 1978)	Languages, sources
Dravidian	1	1: Tamil (Asher 1982)
Eurasiatic	13	1: Hungarian (Casper de Groot p.c.)
Indo-European	12	2: Spanish (Else Schat p.c.)
		Welsh (Jones & Thomas 1977)
Niger-Kordofanian	44	3: Swahili (Welmers 1973)
		Vai (Welmers 1976)
		Yoruba (Welmers 1973; Ogunbowale 1970)
Nilo-Saharan	18	1: Turkana (Dimmendaal 1983)
Afroasiatic	23	1: ECCArabic (Gary & Gamal-Eldin 1982)
Khoisan	5	0
Amerind	150	8: Guaraní (Gregores & Suárez 1967)
		Hixkaryana (Derbyshire 1979)
		Jacaltec (Craig 1977)
		Lakhota (Van Valin 1977)
		Tetelcingo Nahuatl (Langacker 1979)
		Imbabura Quechua (Cole 1982)
		Resígaro (Allin 1976)
		Squamish (Kuipers 1967)
Na-Dene	4	0
Austric	55	4: Banoni (Lincoln 1976)
		Chrau (Thomas 1971)
		Tagalog (Schachter & Otanes 1972)
		Wolio (Anceaux 1952)
Indo-Pacific	100	5: Abelam (Laycock 1965)
		Daga (Murane 1974)
		Hua (Haiman 1980)
		Kobon (Davies 1981)
		Siroi (Wells 1979)
Australian	27	2: Mangarayi (Merlan 1982)
		Maranungku (Tryon 1970)
Sino-Tibetan	20	1: Lisu (Hope 1974)
Ibero-Caucasian	4	1: Abkhaz (Hewitt 1979)
Ket	1	0
Burushaski	1	0
Total	478	30

Care was taken not to select two languages drawn from the same group or spoken in the same general area.

The typological word order characteristics of the languages thus selected turn out to be not very different from what one would expect on the basis of current samples (e.g. Greenberg 1963, Mallinson & Blake 1981, Hawkins 1983). There is only one striking divergence, in that the order NA (i.e. the adjective following the noun) is strongly preferred, even in SOV languages (of these, five have the order AN and seven have NA).[7] Table 2 shows the word order characteristics of the languages in the sample.

TABLE 2. Typological representativeness of the sample

Total no. V-1 languages	6	Total no. of languages having	
SVO "	8	Prepositions	13
SOV "	12	Postpositions	16
OVS "	2	Neither/unknown	1
mixed/free	2		30
	30		

Total no. of languages having		Total no. of languages having	
Order GN	15	Order AN	7
NG	14	NA	21
Both	1	Both/neither	2
	30		30

2.2. Genitival constructions

In word order typology, linguists generally try to establish a basic or unmarked order for each language in the sample. In the present sample, this was possible in most cases since the grammars used contained explicit statements on order or provided examples in which only one order was manifested (Table 3 shows the word order characteristics that were found in this way). However, the situation is quite different when one looks at constructions and construction types. It is quite common for languages to have different constructions according to the syntactic category or subcategory of the Possessor. In Abelam for instance, the pronominal possessor is marked with a suffix -*kw* in the third person only (cf. (17)), while nominal possessors are marked with a suffix only if animate (Laycock 1965, p. 57).

(17)   Abelam (Indo-Pacific; Laycock 1965):

   a. dʌy-kw   balə
       3pl-poss pig
       'their pig'

   b. wnə apʌ
       1sg father
       'my father'

In situations like these, it is impossible to point to either construction as the unmarked one, according to the usual criteria for (un-)markedness. Therefore, the different constructions were simply noted for each language. The statistical observations in the remainder of this paper all refer to the number of constructions found in the languages of the sample, not to the number of languages displaying a certain construction.

Decisions about the categorization of constructions found in a particular language were taken on the basis of three types of criteria, viz. (a) marking, (b) order, and (c) pronominal versus nominal possession. As to the marking, it will be obvious from the discussion in section 1 that a major point of interest was the question whether the Possessor was marked, the Possessed, both or neither. Constructions were also considered distinct if the order of Possessor and Possessed differed, even if no difference in marking was involved. Lastly, since some of the research questions (not discussed here) concerned the correlation between constructions having pronominal possessors (the translation equivalents of 'my book', 'your book', etc.) and those having nominal possessors ('John's book', 'that man's book', etc.), the two types were also distinguished. Every language in the sample had at least two constructions, one for pronominal and one for nominal possession. The maximum number of constructions found in one language by the above mentioned criteria was six.

Table 3 shows the results for each individual language. A construction was classified as construction type 1 or I if there was no marking of either Possessor or Possessed. For pronominal possession, this meant that the pronoun expressing the possessor was identical to the pronoun used as argument of the verb or at least some form used this way. However, if there were special possessive pronouns (like English 'my', 'your', etc.), these were considered to be (inherently) marked. Construction type 2 therefore includes both special possessive pronouns and pronouns marked by an adposition, case suffix, etc. Constructions were classified as type 3 if the Possessed was marked, regardless of whether a free pronoun referring to Possessor could be added or not. Thus, this type includes both the Hungarian construction exemplified by (5b) and one like (18b), while (18a) was classified as type 1:

TABLE 3. Languages, language types, constructions classified for construction types

Language	Type	Construction types	
Abelam (Indo-Pacific)	SOV/--/GN/AN	1, 2,	I, II
Abkhaz (Caucasian)	SOV/Po/GN/NA	3	III
Arabic (ECCA; Semitic)	SVO/Pr/NG/NA	2, 3	I, II
Banoni (Austronesian)	SVO/Pr/NG/NA	2^2	III(II)*
Chrau (Mon-Khmer)	SVO/Pr/NG/NA	1	II
Daga (Indo-Pacific)	SOV/Po/GN/NA	3(2)*	III(II)*
Guaraní (Amerind)	SVO/Po/GN/NA	3	I
Hixkaryana (Amerind)	OVS/Po/GN/--	1 3	I
Hua (Indo-Pacific)	SOV/Po/GN/AN	2, 3, 2+3	II II+III
Hungarian (Uralic)	---/Po/GN/AN	3	III, II+III
Jacaltec (Mayan)	V-1/Pr/NG/NA	3^2	III
Kobon (Indo-Pacific)	SOV/Pr/GN/NA	1	I III
Lakhota (Amerind)	SOV/Po/GN/NA	2, 3	III
Lisu (Tibeto-Burman)	---/Po/GN/NA	1	I
Mangarayi (Australian)	OVS/Pr/NG/NA	3^2	II^2 $II+III^2$
Maranungku (Australian)	SOV/Po/--/NA	1, 2	II^2
Nahuatl (Tetelcingo; Amerind)	SVO/Po/NG/NA	3	III, II+III
Quechua (Imbabura; Amerind)	SOV/Po/GN/AN	1, 2	II
Resígaro (Amerind)	SOV/Po/GN/AN	1, 3	I
Siroi (Indo-Pacific)	SOV/Po/GN/NA	2^2	II
Spanish (Romance)	SVO/Pr/NG/NA	2	II
Squamish (Amerind)	V-1/Pr/NG/AN	3^3	II, III
Swahili (Bantu)	SVO/Pr/NG/NA	2, 3	II
Tagalog (Austronesian)	V-1/Pr/NG/--	2^2	II
Tamil (Dravidian)	SOV/Po/GN/AN	1, 2	I, II
Turkana (Nilo-Saharan)	V-1/Pr/NG/NA	2^2	II
Vai (Mande)	SOV/Po/GN/NA	2	II
Welsh (Celtic)	V-1/Pr/NG/NA	1 3	I
Wolio (Austronesian)	V-1/Pr/NG/NA	3	III
Yoruba (Kwa)	SVO/Pr/NG/NA	2	II

1 = pronominal possession, no marking; e.g. Chrau *ier ǎnh,* 'chicken me'
2 = pronominal possession, dependent marked; e.g. *my book,* Dutch *boek van mij*
3 = pronominal possession, head marked; e.g. Abkhaz (*sarà*) *sə-yºnè,* '(me) my house'
2+3 = pronominal possession, both dependent and head marked; Hua *dgai' fu-di,* 'my pig-my'

I   = nominal possession, no marking; e.g. Lisu *ása ámu,* 'Asa horse'
II = nominal possession, dependent marked; e.g. English *John's house*
III = nominal possession, head marked; e.g. Abkaz *à-c'kº'ən yə-yºnè,* 'the-boy his-house'
II+III = nominal possession, both dependent and head marked; see (20).
n^2, n^3, N^2, N^3 = two or three constructions respectively of the relevant type

(18)   Resígaro (Andean-Equatorial; Allin 1976):

a. n̄a hanígí
   3pl father
   'their father'

b. n̄anígí
   'their father'

The constructions in Table 3 marked with an asterisk are of type 3/III since the
Possessed is marked with a possessive pronoun as in the Dutch examples in (4).
However, since the possessive pronoun itself consists of the free pronoun followed by a case suffix, the construction is relevant to the statistics concerning the ordering of Relators (to be discussed in section 3) and was therefore
counted as type 2/II for that purpose. This construction is exemplified by (19):

(19)   Daga (Indo-Pacific; Murane 1974):

a. dugup mu -ga
   house 3pl-Gen
   'their house'

b. pumpuni-wa   dugup mu-ga
   black   -Subst house their
   'the house of the black (ones)'

We will now turn to the results concerning the ordering of Relators and other
devices marking Possessor and Possessed.

3. Results and discussion

In subsection 3.1. the results concerning the ordering of elements in genitival
constructions are presented. It will be seen that these argue against a broad
definition of 'Relator' as in Definition I and in favour of some more restricted
version such as Definition II. However, there is another possibility for re-
stricting the notion of 'Relator'; this is discussed in 3.2. Some of the consequences of this possibility will be discussed in the conclusion (section 4).

3.1. Results

Table 4 presents the data on the ordering of the two kinds of elements discussed
in section 2.

TABLE 4. Head marking, dependent marking constructions and their ordering

Constructions having the order

(Pr REL) Pd	16	Pr (PRO Pd)	2
Pd (REL Pr)	16	(Pd PRO) Pr	4
Subtotal	32	Subtotal	6
(REL Pr) Pd	3	(PRO Pd) Pr	4
Pd (REL Pr)	5	Pr (Pd PRO)	10
Subtotal	8	Subtotal	14
All orders	40	All orders	20
Internally marked	6	Clitics and others	16
Total	46	Total	36
Neither Possessor nor Possessed marked			19

The first column shows the results for those constructions in which the Possessor was marked as such by an adposition, a case suffix, a general linking morpheme, etc. That is, all constructions of types 2 and II were included, as were those constructions in which both Possessor and Possessed are marked (i.e. types 2+3 and II+III). For instance, though Hungarian has constructions of type 3 and III, as exemplified by (5), it also has a construction in which the Possessor is marked by a case suffix:

(20)   Hungarian (Uralic; Casper de Groot p.c.):
         Peter-nek   a   könyv-e
         Peter-Gen/Dat the book -3sg
         'Peter's book'

The second column shows the results for those constructions in which the Possessed was marked, i.e. constructions of types 3 and II as well as 2+3 and II+III. In nearly all cases, the elements involved were pronominal in nature (i.e. indicating the person, number, and sometimes gender of the possessor) and are therefore called PRO in the table. The constructions not relevant for the discussion are mostly of the type exemplified by the Resígaro example in (18), i.e. constructions in which the Possessed is marked for Possessor but no free Possessor expression could be added.

It will be clear that the data presented in the first column of Table 4 present strong evidence for the ordering principles concerning Relators proposed by Dik (1983d). Of 40 constructions that are relevant in this respect, 32 (80%) show the expected patterning and only 8 (20%) deviate. Compared to the well-known

correlations between Verb-Object ordering, Preposition/Postposition, Genitive/
Noun, and Adjective-Noun ordering, the percentage of Relators in the expected
pattern comes out as one of the higher ones. In Limburg (1983) the statistics
concerning the strength of these correlations was presented (using the sample of
Hawkins 1983). The correlations between Adposition ordering and Genitive-Noun
ordering on the one hand, and those between Adposition and Verb-Object order on
the other, proved to be the strongest (both c. 90%, as expected). The correlation
between Noun-Genitive and Verb-Object was c. 80% as expected, and the three
correlations concerning Adjectives were much weaker (around 65%). The above
results therefore establish the Relator principles as important universals.

The results presented in the second column of Table 4 are quite different.
Here, fourteen of the twenty constructions would be counterexamples to the Relator
principles, if the elements involved were Relators. It seems that in particular
the patterning in which the Possessed is marked for Possessor by a suffix is preferred. In most cases the free NP form expressing the Possessor then precedes
(the Hungarian examples are typical in this respect). If the figures of column two
were added to those of the first column, there would be twenty-two counterexamples
from a total of sixty relevant constructions. The Relator principles would still be
upheld, but they would be among the weaker universals (c. 63%). Furthermore, most
of the counterexamples on the wide definition of Relators would fall into one
specifiable class: the constructions in which the Possessed is marked for Possessor.

These data clearly argue for a more restricted view of Relators. The Definition
II proposed in Limburg (1983) and discussed in section 2 does exclude the class of
counter-examples mentioned above, since it excludes Head-marking devices. But
since in the present sample the Head-marking devices are pronominal in nature, it
could be argued that it is their pronominal nature that makes them exceptional.
We now turn to the discussion of this possibility.

3.2. Pronominal forms

Languages displaying the construction type in which the Possessed is marked for
Possessor and a free NP form is co-referential to the marking affix share a number
of characteristics that other languages do not typically or always have. For
instance, these languages not only use pronominal affixes on nouns to refer to
the Possessor, but also use them either on verbs to refer to Subject, Direct
Object, or Indirect Object, or on Adpositions to refer to the Object of the
Adposition, or on both. Sometimes there are two or three different paradigms of

affixes with these functions, but usually there is much overlap or complete
identity. In Hungarian for instance, the same suffixes used on nouns to refer to
the Possessor are used on postpositions (cf. (5) and (20)):

(21) a. az   (én) kabát-om
         the (me) coat -1sg
         'my coat'

      b. (én-)alatt-om
         (me) under-1sg
         'under me'

Furthermore, the free NP form can always be left out, whether it is pronominal
or nominal. For this reason, De Groot & Limburg (in prep.) conclude that the
affixes in these constructions are not a form of agreement but are alternative
expressions of terms, i.e. they are potentially referring expressions.

   De Groot & Limburg (in prep.) propose a formalization that captures the
specific characteristics of these constructions, as well as the diachronic
process by which we argue that they arise. In this view, a term in these languages can consist of two parts. The first part is a specification in terms of
±Speaker, ±Hearer, and ±Other (cf. (22a)). This specification has the form of a
term built from an abstract predicate and is expressed as a bound form. A term
built from a nominal predicate can then be added if the speaker wants to give
more information as to the nature of the referent of a +Other (i.e. third person)
term. A term consisting of a free pronoun can be added for pragmatic reasons,
such as the expression of Focus in the Hungarian examples (cf. (22b)):

(22) a.
$$(d1x_i: \begin{bmatrix} +S \\ -H \\ -O \end{bmatrix} \ (x_i)_\emptyset)_{Poss/Loc}$$

    b.
$$((d1x_i: \begin{bmatrix} +S \\ -H \\ -O \end{bmatrix} \ (x_i)_\emptyset) \ , \ (d1x_i: \ én \ (x_i)_\emptyset))_{Poss/LocFoc}$$

We do not wish to discuss the pros and cons of this formalization here, but will
simply point out that there may be a connection between the exceptional ordering
of Head-marking devices in genitival constructions and the pronominal character
of most of these. That is, the question is whether the restriction on the broad
Definition I should be made in terms of Head-marking versus Dependent-marking or,
alternatively, in terms of the referentiality versus non-referentiality of the
markers. In the latter case, one could still maintain the broad Definition I

(repeated here as (23a) with the very plausible proviso (23b):

(23) a. *Definition I.* A Relator is any element that links one constituent
        to another, that establishes a relationship between two relata.

   b. *Proviso.* Referential (e.g. pronominal) elements do not primarily
        serve to link one constituent to another.

This option has the advantage of not relying on a notion of 'dependency' that
has to be defined derivatively in Functional Grammar. Furthermore, it can deal
with such a construction as in (24b). On the basis of (24a) one might think that
the possessive pronoun for third person singular male, *nawany*, was a Head-marking
device comparable to the Dutch construction in (4). However, in Maranungku the
Possessor can also follow the Possessed giving (24b):

(24)   Maranungku (Australian; Tryon 1970):

   a. Micky nawany mi
      Micky his   dog
      'Micky's dog'

   b. mi   Micky nawany
      dog Micky his

The latter construction looks bizarre in a Head-marking/Dependent-marking dichotomy, since it is the Possessor, not the Possessed, which seems to be marked for
Possessor. Examples like the above are too rare to form the basis for a definitive
decision on how to define 'Relator', especially since such a decision has important empirical consequences. Some of these are discussed in the next section.

4. Conclusion

In section 1 we discussed the notion of 'Relator' in the form in which it was
introduced into Functional Grammar by Dik (1983d). We saw there that a number of
conceptual problems arise concerning this original formulation, notably an indeterminacy concerning the constituency of the Relator. This indeterminacy is
solved by the definition in Limburg (1983), in which 'Relator' is defined as the
element marking the dependent constituent in any construction in which one constituent is dependent on another (Definition II).

   It was shown in section 2 that this second definition fits better with the
typological data on genitival constructions presented there. That is, elements
marking the Possessor (the dependent constituent) generally adhere to the ordering constraints for Relators, but there is a class of constructions in which the

Possessed (the Head) is marked by elements that do not adhere to these ordering constraints. The Hungarian examples in (5), here repeated as (25), are typical in this respect:

(25)   Hungarian (Uralic; Casper de Groot p.c.):

   a. János kabát-*ja*
      John coat -3sg
      John's coat

   b. az   én kabát-*om*
      the me coat -1sg
      'my coat'

The important issue raised in section 3 is whether it is the Head-marking nature, or the pronominal nature, of these elements that makes the principles governing their ordering different from those governing the ordering of Relators. On the basis of the evidence now available, it is impossible to decide the issue. But note that empirical consequences follow from this theoretical issue. For instance, there are languages in which nouns have special forms when possessed. The affixes on these Possesseds do not specify the Possessor, are therefore non-pronominal in nature, but nonetheless Head-marking devices. On the basis of their non-pronominal nature one might expect them to pattern like Relators, but if Definition II is correct, they should not do so. The same goes for agreement affixes on verbs. Again, these are included in the set of Relators by Definition I, but excluded by Definition II. They could be said to establish a link between two relata, and be expected to be ordered like the other Relators, or they could be excluded as Head-marking devices. Further typological data on the ordering of such elements are needed to decide on how to define 'Relator', and, more funda-mentally, to judge the necessity of recognizing the notion of Dependency in Functional Grammar.

NOTES

*   I would like to thank Simon Dik for several discussions on Relators that
     helped me to clarify my ideas; further, thanks are due to the editors of
     this volume and to Geert Booij for their helpful comments and criticism.
     The final responsibility for the paper remains mine.

[1] In Tagmemics, the term 'Relator' has been used as a cover-term for Sentence-
     Subordinators, Clause-Subordinators, Prepositions, and Inflection, i.e.
     those elements that are added to a structure to 'fit (...) it for use in
     higher level structures' (Cook 1969: 33; see also Longacre 1964). The prob-
     lems that arise with this formulation are the same as those discussed in
     this paper.

2   For instance, Keenan & Comrie (1977) give a 'largely syntax-free' definition
     of 'relative clause', which in fact is very close to the definition of
     'restrictor' in Functional Grammar. Their definition is not entirely syntax-
     free since it refers to 'sentence'. In general, starting out from a semantic-
     functional definition, one usually comes across classes of elements or con-
     structions that behave differently syntactically. If one succeeds in showing
     that these special syntactic characteristics correlate with special semantic-
     functional properties, one is justified in singling them out. This harmlessly
     circular approach is taken in this paper.

3   In fact, in both the Dutch and Hungarian constructions the full pronouns are
     used only when in Focus. De Groot & Limburg (in prep.) assume that in this
     and similar construction types (see section 3.2) it is always the case that
     the full pronouns are left out unless focal.

4   The notion of dependency is not a primitive in Functional Grammar, but can be
     formulated.

5   In fact, a distinction should be made between elements marking arguments, and
     those marking satellites, since in the latter case the dependency relation is
     really between the nuclear predication and the satellite constituent. However,
     if the satellite is ordered among the other constituents of the nuclear predi-
     cation (e.g. in the position X in a functional pattern S O X V), no particular
     prediction concerning Relators is made. If it is ordered outside the nuclear
     predication (in patterns such as X S O V or S O V X), the same predictions are
     made as for the elements marking arguments.

6   Some difficult decisions had to be made regarding constructions that could be
     described as reduced relative clauses. However, these were rare enough not to
     bias the results.

7   It is unclear what the reason for this discrepancy is. It may be due to
     chance, or to the fact that most samples are not genetically representative
     (this point is argued by Bell 1978). In the latter case, the above findings
     are clear evidence for Dik's ordering principle (VII) (1983d: 272).

Chapter 9
Indirect questions and relators

Peter Kahrel
Institute for General Linguistics, University of Amsterdam

*0. Introduction**

In Dik (1983d) the principles governing word order that were proposed earlier
(Dik 1978, 1980a) are expanded so as to account for cross-categorial correlations
of constituent ordering. Some of the principles that Dik introduces are laid out
in the following paragraphs.

The Head of a construction is called the *Centre*, i.e. the verb in a verbal
predication, the noun in a term phrase and the adjective in an adjectival phrase.
The area in front of the Centre is called the *Prefield* and the area after the
Centre the *Postfield*. The field opposite a given field is called the *Counterfield*.
Schematically this may be shown as follows (Dik 1983d: 271):

(1)   Prefield   Centre   Postfield

                          ⎧ Predicate (V) ⎫
            --------   ⎨ Head Noun   ⎬   ---------
                          ⎩ Adjective   ⎭

Another notion introduced by Dik is that of *Relator*. Relators are defined as
(a) adpositions, (b) case markers or (c) subordinating devices. The latter are to
include both independent subordinators such as English *that* in e.g. relative
clauses, and subordinating affixes as they occur in nominalised and participial-
ised constructions. Functionally, Relators link constituents to one another and
establish a relationship between these constituents. According to Dik constructions in which a Relator occurs have the following preferred patterns:

(2) a.   (relatum(R)) (relatum)
    b.   (relatum) ((R)relatum)

where *R* is to be read as 'Relator' and *relatum* should be taken as 'constituent',
e.g. an embedded predication.

The two Relator principles that Dik formulates are as follows (1983d: 274):

(3)   Principle I: The preferred position of a Relator is at the periphery of
                       its immediate relatum
        Principle II: The preferred position of a Relator is in between its two
                       relata.

The first principle entails that a Relator prefers a position at the beginning
or the end of an embedded clause, and not *in* such a clause. Whether a Relator is
found at the beginning or the end of a clause depends on the type a language
belongs to; Prefield languages place their Relators at the end of a clause, while
Postfield languages place them at the beginning. The second principle states that
a Relator is preferably placed in one of the positions given in patterns (2a-b),
while the positions in (4) are not preferred:

(4) a. *((R)relatum) (relatum)
    b. *(relatum) (relatum(R))

In the sample on which this article is based, only the unpreferred pattern (4b)
occurs, i.e. only in Prefield languages are indirect questions placed in the
Counterfield. This may be accounted for with reference to two further principles.
In the first place there is LIPOC - the Language Independent Preferred Order of
Constituents - that says that terms are placed in order of increased complexity.
Secondly, Dik (1983d: 272) formulates a Principle V that says that the Prefield
is less hospitable to complex material than the Postfield, so that it is to be
expected that Prefield languages will take measures to 'relieve the Prefield of
excessively complex material'. This explains among other things 'leaking' in the
sense of Ross (1973b), and the placement of embedded predications in some
Prefield languages. Postfield languages, on the other hand, do not place embedded
questions in the Prefield, i.e. there are no mirror principles to LIPOC and
Principle V.[1]
    The aim of this paper is to test the validity of the two Relator principles
quoted in (3) with respect to indirect yes-no questions (henceforth IndYN) and
indirect question word questions (IndQW), and to see what happens in terms of
'Relatorship' when an unpreferred pattern like (4b) occurs. The data are drawn
from a stratified sample that consists of 30 languages (see Table 1). The two
types of indirect questions discussed here are exemplified in (5) (Relators will
be underlined in all examples):

(5) a.   IndYN: I asked Mary <u>if</u> she had seen my lighter

    b.   IndQW: I asked Mary <u>what</u> she had bought

Section 1 discusses the notions Prefield and Postfield, and the classification
of some of the languages included in the sample. Section 2 discusses Relators in
indirect questions; section 3 summarises the results of this investigation.

1. Preliminary remarks

1.1. Prefield and Postfield

The first principle of Dik's (1983d) theory of constituent ordering is that languages make a basic choice between Prefield and Postfield ordering. The order of
Subject, Object and Verb is thus a consequence of a language being of the Prefield or the Postfield type; it will be clear that SOV languages are Prefield,
and VSO languages Postfield. The distinction between Prefield and Postfield cuts
through the usual three-fold distinction SOV/SVO/VSO; SVO languages can be classified as either Prefield or Postfield on the basis of further criteria. In the
sample I have used it was in each case possible to do so, although such a classification is not always self-evident.

    Mandarin, for example, is described by Li and Thompson (1981) as having SVO
and SOV features, i.e. in terms of FG both Prefield and Postfield features. I
have classified Mandarin as a Prefield language, since the strongest word order
correlates indicate Prefield characteristics. These are as follows: (a) Relative
clause precedes the Head noun, (b) in comparative constructions the Standard
precedes the adjective, (c) in nominal phrases the adjective precedes the noun
and (d) in possessive constructions the possessor precedes the possessed. The
only problem would seem to be that Mandarin is analysed as having prepositions,
which are the strongest correlate with Postfield ordering (cf. also Limburg
1983). However, Chao (1961: 38, 49) prefers to speak of 'verbs in series'; what
are currently called 'prepositions' are in fact verbs. The fact that verbs in
Mandarin parallel prepositions in e.g. the Germanic languages seems poor motivation for the claim that Mandarin has prepositions.

    Another difficult case is Ojibwa. In the literature, word order in Ojibwa is
described in several ways. Bloomfield (1957) says it is rather free. There are
curious contradictions in that Fuller (1981) claims Theme-Rheme order, while
Tomlin and Rhodes (1979) claim Rheme-Theme. Fuller notes that several word orders
are possible, but that SVO is by far the most frequent. It seems, however, that
word order in Ojibwa is determined by pragmatics rather than by rigid functional

patterns with fixed positions for terms carrying syntactic functions. Nevertheless word order across categories justifies the classification of Ojibwa as
Prefield: (a) relative clauses may precede or follow the Head noun, (b) Ojibwa
has Locative suffixes, (c) in comparative constructions the order is Standard-
Marker-Adjective, (d) in nominal phrases the adjective precedes the noun; and
(e) Ojibwa has sentence final question particles in yes-no questions, which is
a strong correlate with V-final languages (see Greenberg 1963: 81, Universal 9).

An advantage of the Prefield/Postfield distinction is that it goes beyond the
categories Subject and Object, so that it is not dependent on a definition of
these categories. Several authors (Mallinson and Blake 1981, see also references
therein) have demonstrated that it does not make much sense to classify a language as e.g. SVO if Subject and Object are not uniformly defined. Such a classification makes even less sense, especially in terms of FG, when the notions
Subject and Object, or either of them, are not relevant for a given language.
Dik (1980a) has argued that Object is not relevant for Hixkaryana; Van Schaaik
(1983) has argued that Subject and Object are not relevant in Turkish. A classification in terms of Pre/Postfield gets around such difficulties.

Table I, which lists the languages in the sample, divides into two parts. The
upper section contains the Prefield languages, the lower section the Postfield
languages. Besides this classification I have added the word order patterns in
terms of S, V and O, based on the judgement of the author, or on the authority
of an expert.

Besides the principles that languages classify as either Prefield or Postfield, there are other principles that exert influence on word order. Two principles that are relevant for this paper are 'Principle V' (Dik 1983d: 272) which
says that in general the Prefield is not very hospitable to complex terms.
Another principle is LIPOC - Language Independent Order of Constituents (Dik
1978: ch. 9). This principle says that constituents tend to be ordered in order
of increased complexity. Coordinate terms and relative clauses, for example, are
predicted to be ordered after less complex terms. Table 1 shows that 5 out of 16
Prefield languages place the relative clause after the Head noun. The effect of
these two principles in connection with the position of the Relator - if there
is one - will be discussed below.

Table 1: The sample and some basic ordering principles

	Word order	Prep/Postp	NG/GN	NA/AN	NRc/RcN	AdjMS/SMAdj
Abkhaz	SOV	+	+	+	+	+
Basque	SOV	+	+	+	+	+
Nama Hottentot	SOV	+	+	+	+	
Kobon	SOV	+	+	+	+	−
Quechua	SOV	+	+	+	+	
Tamil	SOV	+	+	+	+	+
Turkish	SOV	+	+	+	+	+
Urdu	SOV	+	+	+		+
Japanese	SOV	+	+	+	+	+
Ngiyambaa	SOV	+	+	+	+	+
Navaho	SOV	+	+	+	+	+
Luiseño	SOV	+	+	+	+ +	+
Mandarin	SVO/SOV	?	+	+	+	+*
Ojibwa	SVO/SOV	+	+	+	+ +	+
Mohave	SVO	+	+	+	+	
Finnish	SVO	+	+	+	+	+ +
Hixkaryana	OVS	+	+	−**	−	+
Yoruba	SVO	+	+	+	+	+
Chichewa	SVO	+	+	+	+	
Bahasa	SVO	+	+	+	+	+
Egyptian	SVO	+	+	+	+	+
Dutch	SVO	+	+ +	+	+	+
Vietnamese	SVO	+	+	+	+	+
Italian	SVO	+	+	+	+	+
Niuean	VSO	+	+	+	+	
Jacaltec	VSO	+	+	+	+	+
Squamish	VSO	+	+ +	+	+	
Nootka	VSO	+	+	−***	+	
Zapotec	VSO	+	+	+	+	+
Turkana	VSO	+	+	+	+	+

Key: *Prep* = Preposition, *Postp* = Postposition, *N* = Noun, *G* = Genitive (Possessor)
A = Adjective, *Rc* = Relative clause, *AdjMS* = Adjective Marker Standard
(order of constituents in comparative constructions).

  * Strictly speaking, Mandarin has no 'Marker' in the comparative construction.
Nevertheless, the Standard precedes the Adjective.

 ** Derbyshire (1979) argues that Hixkaryana has no adjectives, and hence, no
relative clauses.

*** In Nootka, adjectives are incorporated into the verbal complex (Sapir and
Swadesh 1939).

1.2. *The sample*

Following Bell's (1978) recommendations on the compilation of language samples, I used the following sampling method. On the basis of Voegelin & Voegelin (1977) a list was drawn up of all the languages of the world, divided into families and sub-families. From each family a language was chosen, until the number of 30 languages was reached. This number was determined by what could reasonably be handled in a year, while at the same time it is large enough to be represent-ative: all major language families are represented in the sample. The choice of a particular language from a family was determined by the availability of bibliographical material and of information from native speakers and specialists (cf. also introductory note). A relatively large family that is not represented is Macro-Chibchan; no reliable information on embedded questions in a Macro-Chibchan language could be obtained.

In three cases more than one language was chosen from one family. Due to the absence of bibliographical material on some of the smaller language families, I chose two languages from the two largest families, viz. Bahasa Indonesian and Niuean from Austronesian, Chichewa and Yoruba from Niger-Kordofanian. In select-ing the languages from these families Bell's recommendations about geographical and genetic spread were again taken into account. Finally, three languages were chosen from Indo-European phylum; Italian (Romance), Urdu (Iranian) and Dutch (Germanic).

A note is in order about the data that this paper is based on. The material is fairly heterogeneous due to the diversity of the sources. In some cases the data are based on isolated examples provided by a grammar. In other cases, e.g. Nootka, all examples were taken from texts that are transcripts of spoken texts. Optimal results were of course obtained when a native speaker or a specialist in a given language could be consulted. However, I do not have the impression that the results have been significantly influenced by these circumstances.

2. *Relators in indirect questions*

Dik's definition of Relators will initially be maintained, that they may be an adposition, a case marker or a subordinating device, and that they link two con-stituents to one another and establish a relationship between these constituents. Although Dik did not specifically discuss indirect questions in his (1983d) article, the notion Relator is valid for this construction as well. Compare the following examples:

(6)   Turkish (Prefield, Gerjan van Schaaik, p.c.)

        Ahmed ben-im   kitap al- dɨǧ- ɨm-ɨ   sor-du
        Ahmed I- gen book buy-nomr-my-A̲c̲c̲ ask-Past
        'Ahmed asked if I had bought a book'

Turkish, a Prefield language, places the embedded question in the Prefield, and
it is a suffixing language. The Relator, the Accusative marker -ɨ, is in preferred position.

(7)   Nootka (Postfield, Sapir and Swadesh 1939)

        ?a?a:to-?at- we?in qʷa-wo:si   wikýo nac- o?aɬ
        ask-   Pass-3Quot R̲e̲l̲-3RelDub not   look-see
        'He was asked whether he had not yet seen him'

In (7) the embedded question is introduced by the particle q^wa-, which introduces
embedded predications. -wo:si is a '3rd person Relative Dubitative' particle,
which is used in indirect yes-no questions. In (7) q^wa- is in preferred position.
   Dik (1983d: 287) notes that 'if these principles [i.e. the Relator principles]
have any use at all, then one would expect there to be a certain pressure on
violations [...] to undergo restructuring, so as to come into line with the
principles again'. Basically such violations are due to the conflict between
principles. On the one hand there is principle V, which says that complex material (such as embedded predications) should be placed in the Postfield, and there
is LIPOC, which says that complex constituents should be placed in order of increased complexity. On the other hand there is the second Relator principle which
says that a Relator is preferably placed between its two relata. The conflict may
be illustrated with reference to the following pattern (= 4b):

(8)   *(relatum) (relatum(R))

In (8) a situation is represented that occurs when a Prefield language places
its indirect questions in the Postfield. The Relator is now in unpreferred position, on the assumption that Prefield languages have final Relators. What is of
special interest is what happens in terms of Relators when a Prefield language
systematically places its indirect questions in the Postfield. Dik (1983d: 296)
speculates that when a situation such as represented in (8) occurs systematically, the violation of the second Relator principle may be compensated for by
the introduction of a new Relator in preferred position, and that the final

Relator in unpreferred position drops out.

This prediction is only partially confirmed by the data found in the sample. There are instances, which will be discussed below, of the introduction of a new Relator with the Relator in unpreferred position being retained. This may be explained as follows. On the level of predication a Relator is a subordinator (or very often so), which is a syntactic device to mark subordination. The desire to retain a syntactic Relator as the marker of subordination may help to explain why it is maintained, even in unpreferred position.

As an example of the introduction of a 'new' Relator, take the following sentence from Basque (J.C. Ruiz-Antón, p.c.):

(9)   Janek galdetu du   (ea) liburu bat   erori zue-   n
       Janek ask   he=has=it (Rel) book one=Abs buy   you=had=it-Rel
       atzo
       yesterday
       'Janek asked whether you bought a book yesterday'

In Basque, a Prefield language, embedded questions are marked by the suffix -*n* on the auxiliary of the embedded question (Ruiz-Antón, De Rijk 1977). Besides this affix, which qualifies as a Relator under Dik's definition, there is also the optional particle *ea*, which can only be used in embedded yes-no questions. It seems, then, that there are two relators in (9): -*n* as a syntactic Relator, and *ea* as a Relator that links the main and the embedded predication to one another. The latter I will call the 'secondary' Relator; it takes over from the syntactic Relator the function of linking the two constituents - i.e. the main and the embedded predication - to one another.

An 'element' that occurs 9 times in the sample as a linking element is a Quote particle. It occurs 9 times in the sample, both in direct quotes (see (10)) and as a subordinator, as in (11). 'Quote particle' is used here to cover 'particle' in the strict sense of the word, i.e. an uninflectible particle. The term is also used here to cover the equivalents of the verb 'say', which may or may not be inflected, depending on the language in question. Two examples will illustrate the point. The first is from Quechua, in which *ni* 'say' plus a cross-referential adverb *shpa* is used as a Quote particle:

(10)   nuka wawki- ta riku-rka- ngui-chu ni- shpa tapu-wa-rka
       my   brother-acc see- Past-you- Q say-Adv ask- me-Past=he
       '"Did you see my brother?", he asked me'

Another example is from Chichewa. In Chichewa, the relative pronoun is based on the verb stem *kutí* 'say' (Trithart 1979), and so is *ngatí*, in the following example (J.M. Schoffeleers, p.c.):

(11)   Ndi-na- m- funs-a   Jóni ngatí a-na- nyanuul-a
        I- Past-Dir-ask- Ind John what 3-Past-carry- Ind
        'I asked John what he carried'

Quote particles will often be used in Direct Quotes, as in (10), but this is not necessarily so, witness (11). Compare also Lord (1976), who argues that in the Kwa languages subordinators derive from verbs, among others from verbs of saying.

Typical Relators that emerge from the sample are the following. Secondary and syntactic relators are not distinguished:

(12) a. IndYN   Prefield   Postfield

        Quote particle   9   0

        case affix   3   0

        Conditional particle 0   5

        Dubitative particle   2   2

        relative clause   0   1

        other   1   2

     b. IndQW

        Quote particle   6   0

        case affix   3   0

        question word   1   10

        other   1   4

In (12) question words are included as Relators. This can be motivated as follows. In the first place Keenan and Hull (1973) observe that indirect questions more often than not pattern as relative clauses, or clefts.[2] This may be seen as a strategy to front the question word in indirect questions. The second and stronger motivation derives from those languages that have two alternative ways of forming (direct) questions, viz. (a) placing the question word in pattern position or (b) placing the question word in P1, while the question word is normally placed in P1 in indirect questions. Take the following examples from Egyptian (Postfield, Samir Gaafar, p.c.):

(13)   inte iʃtareet-hu eeh?
         you bought- it what
         'What did you buy?'

(14)   eeh illi inte iʃtareet-hu?
         what RM   you bought- it   (RM = relative marker)
         'What did you buy?'

(15)   Muniib sa?al- it eeh illi enne iʃtareet-hu
         Muniib ask=Past-Fem what RM I   bought- it
         'Muneeb asked what I had bought'

(13) and (14) are direct questions; (13), with the question word in pattern
position, is used in unmarked questions. (14), with the question word in P1, is
used in marked questions to indicate disbelief, anger, etc. (15), however, is
the unmarked form for indirect questions. Other languages that place the
question word in P1 in indirect questions, are Luiseño (R.W. Langacker 1977 and
p.c.), Yoruba (Emmanuel Ayodele, p.c.), Indonesian (Sie Ing Djiang, p.c.).[3]

   The category 'other' in (12) covers such Relators as can only be used in
indirect questions. A Basque example was given in (9); another example is from
Dutch (Postfield):

(16)   Jan vroeg   of ik een ander book wilde
         Jan ask=Past if I a   other book want=Past
         'John asked if I wanted another book'

of is a disjunctive particle 'or', and as a subordinator can only be used in
indirect questions.

   Typical Relators in IndYN questions, in Prefield languages, are Quote particles and case affixes. In Postfield languages conditional particles, or 'conditional mood markers' and dubitative particles prevail. A revealing example from
Luiseño seems to suggest that it is not so much the type a language belongs to,
i.e. Prefield or Postfield, that determines whether a conditional particle may
be used, but rather the position of the embedded question. In Luiseño - a Prefield language - IndYN questions in the Prefield can be Direct Quotes, with a
Quote particle in preferred Relator position. There are also examples of embedded
questions in the Postfield in Luiseño, which have the conditional particle tee
'if' in preferred position. Compare (17) (Langacker 1977):

(17)   no-kaamay ney tuvyuni-q tee waxaam   po- xili-vo-y
         my-son   me ask- Tns if yesterday its-rain-R- Acc
         'My son asked me if it rained yesterday'.

         (R = 'realised aspect')

Notice again that (17) has two Relators, tee 'if' as a secondary Relator, and -y
as a syntactic Relator.

Table 2. Position of indirect question and Relator

	Indirect Yes-No Question						Indirect QW Question					
	Pref	Postf	Y	N	y	n	Pref	Postf	Y	N	y	n
Abkhaz	+			+	+		+			+	+	
Basque		+		+	+		+	+				
Kobon	no data						o	+				
Quechua		+	+				+			+	+	
Tamil	o			+			o					+
Turkish	+		+				+	+				
Japanese	+		+	+			+					+
Ngiyambaa		+		+	+		no data					
Nama Hottentot		+		+	+		+			+	+	
Urdu	o			+			o					+
Navaho	o			−	−		o			−	−	
Luiseño		+		+	+		+			+	+	
Mandarin	o		−	−	−	−	o			−	−	
Mohave	no data						+	+				
Ojibwa		+		−	−		+					+
Finnish	o		−	−		+	o		−	−		+
Hixkaryana	+		+	−	−		+	+				
Yoruba		+	+					+	+			
Chichewa		+	+					+	+			
Bahasa		+	+					+	+			
Egyptian		+	+					+	+			
Dutch		+	+					+	+			
Vietnamese	o	−					o	−				
Italian		+	+					+	+			
Niuean	no data							+	+			
Jacaltec		+	+					+	+			
Squamish		+	+					+	+			
Nootka		+	+					+	+			
Zapotec	no data							+	+			
Turkana	no data							+	+			

Key: + = embedded question   Y = syntactic Rel in preferred position
     o = direct quote   N = syntactic Rel not in pref. pos.
     − = no Relator   y = pragmatic Rel in preferred position
     n = pragmatic Rel not in pref. pos.

3. Results

3.1. Indirect yes-no questions

In (18) below the position of the syntactic and the secondary Relator are sum-
marised; 'OK' means 'Relator in preferred position'.[4]

(18)   SYNTACTIC   SECONDARY
    a. Prefield languages   OK: 6/15   OK: 4/15

                                      not OK: 6/15   not OK: 2/15

                                      no Rel: 3/15

    b. Postfield languages: OK: 9/10

                                      not OK: -

                                      no Rel: 1/10

In 6 out of 15 Prefield languages the syntactic Relator is in unpreferred position (Abkhaz, Basque, Quechua, Ngiyambaa, Nama, Luiseño). In 4 of these 6 languages the violation of the Relator principles, due to the placement of the
indirect question in the Postfield, is compensated for by a secondary Relator in
preferred position. These 4 instances will be discussed below.

   The first example is from Ngiyambaa (Donaldson 1979):

(19)   naya:ma-nhi=dji:=lu yama-ga: dhuru   mingha-dhi guruga-nha-ba
        ask-Past=me=3Erg   Dub-Ign snake(Abs) burrow-Circ be=in-Pres-Sub
        'He asked me whether there was a snake in the burrow'
        [Dub-Ign = 'dubitative-ignorative']

The final subordinator -ba is used to embed the complements of verbs of saying,
asking, thinking. This subordinator is in unpreferred position, but notice the
dubitative particle yama, which is in preferred position, and which I regard as
a secondary Relator.

   The following is from Nama Hottentot (Hagman 1973):

(20)   tií-ta   ke   kè   'úú   'ií !úu-ts ta   !xái'è
        I- 1SgMasc Decl Past not=know PTC go -you Impf 'whether'
        'I didn't know whether you were going'

        (PTC = Past Tense Copula)

The 'Past Tense Copula' is described by Hagman as occurring in those clauses
that lack a Tense or an Aspect marker. Notice however that there is an Aspect

marker in the embedded clause, but not a Tense marker. *'ií* is not just a 'dummy Tense marker'; compare for example the following example of a relative clause:

(21)   //naá !hùúpá xuú kè   /xií hàa 'ií kxòeṅ
         that land   from RemPast come Perf PTC people
         'The people who had come from that land'

'ií, then, seems to have grammaticalised as a Relator, and the unpreferred position of *!xai'è* in (20) seems to be compensated for by *'ií*.

   The following is from Luiseño (Langacker 1977):

(22)   no-kaamay ney tuvyuni-q   tee waxaam   po- xili-vo-y   (= (17))
         my-son   me ask-   Tns if yesterday its-rain-R- Acc
         'My son asked me if it rained yesterday'

In (22) the embedded question is marked by a final Relator, the accusative marker *-y*, which is in unpreferred position. Notice however the conditional particle *tee* 'if'. which is also used in conditional clauses, and which is in preferred position.

   In (9) an example from Basque was given, repeated here as (23):

(23)   Janek galdetu du   (ea) liburu bat   erori zuen   atzo
         Janek ask   he-has-it   book   one-Abs buy   you-had-it yesterday
         'Janek asked whether you bought a book yesterday'

In (23) the embedded predication is in the Postfield, and the particle *ea* may optionally be placed between the main and the embedded clause, i.e. in preferred position.

   The following example, of the failure to introduce a secondary Relator, is from Quechua (Cole 1982):

(24)   Jozi tapu-rka   Marya shamu-shka-ta
         José ask- Past=3 Maria come- Nomr-Acc
         'José asked if Maria had come'

In (24) the syntactic Relator *-ta* is in unpreferred position, while in the several examples of such Quechua sentences there is no Relator between the main and the embedded clause.[4] However, embedded clauses are not systematically placed in the Postfield, so that the introduction of a 'new' Relator is not expected under the circumstances. Recall that the introduction of a 'new' Relator was expected just in those cases when an embedded predication is systematically placed in the Counterfield.

3.2. *Indirect question word questions*

In (25) below the position of the syntactic and the secondary Relator in IndQW
questions is given:

(25) [5]		SYNTACTIC	SECONDARY
a. Prefield languages		OK: 10/16	OK: 2/16
		not OK: 3/16	not OK: 1/16
		no Rel: 3/16	
b. Postfield languages		OK: 11/12	
		not OK: -	
		no Rel: 1/12	

In 3 out of 16 languages the syntactic Relator is in unpreferred position, (Nama
Hottentot, Luiseño, Kobon), while in only one of these (Kobon) the secondary
Relator is not in preferred position. The relevant examples will be discussed
below.

Consider first Nama Hottentot (Hagman 1973)[6]

(26)   sií-kxm̀   ke   //'iiku tsiíñà miipa tama kè   hàa   'if maápa-kxm̀
       we- 1DualMasc Decl them   either tell not Past Indef PTC where-we

       ta   !úu !xáisà
       Impf go Sub
       'We didn't tell them either where we were going'

The subordinator *!xáisà* is in unpreferred position when the embedded question is
placed in the Postfield. As was argued under (20), the 'Past Tense Copula' *'if*
is considered to be a possible relief-measure to compensate for the unpreferred
Relator position of *!xáisà*.

The following example is from Luiseño (R.W. Langacker, p.c.),

(27)   no-n 'ayaali-q   'axíy-i o-   téetela-qala-y
       I- I know-   Tns who- Acc your-speak- Dur- Acc
       'I know who you are speaking of'

The syntactic Relator *-y* is in unpreferred position; as was noted above, in
Luiseño there is a tendency to prepose question words in embedded questions,
more than in direct questions. This tendency may be regarded as a relief-measure
to compensate for the unpreferred position of *-y*, as was argued above.

Davies (1981: 27) gives the following example of an indirect question from Kobon:

(28)   nipe ip hag nŏn-a   ne   gai   ar-ab- ŏn   a   g-a
        he   me say perceive-RemPast=3sg you where go-Pres-2sg Quote do-RemPast=3sg
        'He asked me, "Where are you going?"'
        'He asked me where I was going'

Davies notes that Kobon does not have embedded questions. Kobon seems to represent a counterexample, in that what I have called a secondary Relator, the Quote-particle *a* is not between the main clause and the direct quote. Note however that (28) has a 'discontinuous' main clause, so to speak. The main clause in (28) is *nipe ip hag nŏn-a* [...] *g-a*. It could be argued the secondary Relator *a* is in preferred position whether it precedes or follows the reported question; however, since *a* is not between the reported question and that part of the main clause that contains the verb 'ask', *a* is considered to be in unpreferred position.

3.3. Apparent counterexamples

Apparent counterexamples to the claim that question words are Relators can be found in languages that do not have embedded questions, but which express indirect questions as reported speech. First an example from Mandarin (Pow Chee Chen, p.c.):

(29)   Máo wèn nǐ   qǐng   shéi chī-fàn
        M. ask you invite who eat-food
        'Mao asked whom you invited for dinner'

And from Vietnamese (Truc Ha, p.c.):

(30)   Sòn hôi họ   họ   cho ai tiền
        John ask them they give who money
        'John asked them who they gave money to'

However, I assume that the notion Relator is not relevant in reported quotes, since they do not involve subordination.

4. Conclusions

In IndYN questions 6 languages out of 25 (24%) were found to have the syntactic Relator in unpreferred position. In 4 of these 6 cases the violation of the unpreferred position is compensated for by a Relator that was defined as a secondary Relator, and which is in preferred position. In IndQW questions, 3 languages out of 29 (10.4%) were found to have the syntactic Relator in unpreferred position, while in 2 of these cases the violation of the Relator principles is compensated for by a secondary Relator. The result is that in IndYN questions there are 8% counterexamples (2 languages out of 25); In IndQW questions 3.5% counterexamples (1 language out of 29). These figures show that Relators are among the strongest word order correlates (cf. also Limburg 1983 and this volume). Furthermore the compensatory introduction of the so-called secondary Relator goes a long way to demonstrating the descriptive adequacy of the Relator principles.

NOTES

*   I would like to thank the following people: Prof. Simon Dik for discussions in general; and for their helpful information on particular languages, Mrs Lili Ahonen (Finnish), Mr Emmanuel Ayodele (Yoruba), Miss Pow Chee Chen (Mandarin), Dr G. Dimmendaal (Turkana), Mr Samir Gaafar (Egyptian), Miss Patrizia Gentile (Italian), Prof. Kenneth Hale (Navaho), Mr Ahmed Khurshid (Urdu), Prof. Ronald Langacker (Luiseño), Dr Pieter Muysken (Quechua), Mr J.C. Ruiz-Antón (Basque), Mr Gerjan van Schaaik (Turkish), Mr Sie Ing Djiang (Bahasa, Mandarin), Prof. J.M. Schoffeleers (Chichewa) and Mrs Truc Ha (Vietnamese).

[1]   There may be independent reasons for the placement in the counterfield of a particular type of embedded predication. For example, 'before' clauses and conditional clauses have an independent preference for the Prefield, so that such clauses are found in the Prefield even in Postfield languages (see Greenberg 1963: 111, Universal 14, and Dik et al. in preparation).

[2]   Keenan and Hull (1973) claim that direct questions are formed as either Cleft or relative clauses. This is only partially true, and their observation applies best to Postfield languages. Their claim is based on a sample consisting of 10 languages, which includes 2 Prefield and 8 Postfield languages. They note that their generalisation does not hold for Finnish, one of their two Prefield languages. My data show that Keenan and Hull's observations hold in Postfield languages, and in SVO languages that are either of the Prefield or the Postfield type.

[3]   This tendency is probably more widespread than can at present be attested; data from native speakers may show this.

[4]   Nearly all Quechua examples I have collected have the embedded question in the Postfield. Pieter Muysken suggests that this may be due to the fact that the Quechua examples are translations from Spanish. Embedded predications in Quechua usually precede the main clause.

5   (25) does not entirely match (18). In the first place information on one
     language was available for IndQW but not IndYN. Secondly, in a given lan-
     guage a Relator position may be OK in IndYN and not in IndQW. For details
     cf. Table 2.

6   Hagman (1973: 258) states that the complements of 'say', 'ask' and 'don't
     know' are formally identical.

Chapter 10

Two types of resultative construction in Basque and their non-aspectual meanings

Noriko Shiratsuki
Department of Linguistics, Kyoto University

0. Introduction*

In this paper I will discuss two morphologically related constructions in Basque, which have been interpreted by linguists in considerably divergent ways.[1] These divergent interpretations mainly come from the so-called (pure) formal approaches such as Transformational Grammar (TG) or Relational Grammar (RG). The aim of this paper is to re-examine and clarify the structural and functional properties of the two constructions within the framework of FG. And it will be shown that with the aid of a functional view of language we can shed light on the mechanisms underlying the two constructions.

The structure of this paper is as follows. In section 1, after the introduction of the relevant data, three existing explanations for the two constructions will be discussed. Although two of them, the pseudo-cleft and the passive approaches, are rejected, this should not be taken to mean that the two corresponding interpretations are impossible. With respect to the third, the aspectual approach, a distinction is proposed between Inner Aspect (IA) and Outer Aspect (OA) to account for the notion of resultativeness, and the constructions under consideration are identified as Resultative Aspect constructions. In section 2, after a brief discussion of non-verbal predicates in Basque, one type of Resultative Aspect construction will be analyzed as having a one-place predicate. And it will be shown that this construction may also be interpreted as what we shall provisionally call 'pseudo-pseudo-cleft' under specific conditions. A brief comment on its 'passive-expressibility' will also be included in passing. In section 3 the other type will be analyzed as having a two-place predicate. Here it will be argued that, depending upon whether the embedded predication contains a two-place predicate or a one-place impersonal predicate, the construction can express either Resultativeness or some sort of 'possession'. Throughout, the framework of FG will permit us to give a precise overall picture of the two constructions.

1. Preliminary remarks

1.1. Case-marking and verbal agreement in Basque

As can be observed in the following two sentences, the Basque case-marking system
obeys an ergative/absolutive pattern:

```
(1)    Ni-Ø   Kyoto-ra    joan      n-aiz
       I-abs  Kyoto-dir   gone(pf)  1sg abs-izan(Aux)
       'I have gone to Kyoto'
```

```
(2)    Ni-k   zu-ri    liburu  hori       eman       d-izu-t
       I-erg  you-dat  book    that(abs)  given(pf)  3sg abs-2sg dat-1sg erg
                                                     (ukan(Aux))
       'I have given the book to you'
```

What Wilbur (1979) calls the 'verb complex' consists of a participle (*joan*, etc.)
and an auxiliary verb (*naiz*, etc.) which indicates tense, mood and agreement.
Some verbs in Basque including *izan* 'be', *egon* 'stay', Spanish *estar*, *ukan* 'have',
eduki 'have', etc. have what is called a 'synthetic' or 'simple' form which in-
corporates all the elements of Aux into a verb. All Basque verbs (except *ukan*)
enter into a 'verb complex'. As an auxiliary verb, synthetic *izan* is used with
one-place verbs (cf. (1)) and synthetic *ukan* is used with two or three-place
verbs (cf. (2)). The auxiliary always agrees with the abs (-Ø), erg (-k) and dat
(-(r)i) terms. There are three kinds of participle in Basque: two of these indicate the distinction between Perfective (*joan*, *eman*) and Imperfective (*joa-ten*,
ema-ten) aspect. With respect to tense and mood, the Present (which indicates
the Near Past when used with the Perfective) and Indicative form is used throughout this paper.[2]

1.2. The relevant data

1.2.1. Type I

The grammatical status of sentence (3a) has been attracting Bascologists' attention for a long time:

```
(3) a.  Liburu  hori       ni-k    irakurri-a        d-a
        book    that(abs)  I-erg   read(pf)-def sg    3sg abs-izan(be)
```

Note that the abs term alone causes agreement and that the participle has a
suffix -*a*(*k*) which agrees with the abs term in number (the suffix becomes -*ak*
(def pl) when an abs term is definite and plural).

As far as verbal morphology is concerned, two more forms could be added to

(3a), because in many cases they are interchangeable:

```
(3) b.  Liburu  hori       ni-k    irakurri-a          d-ago
        book    that(abs)  I-erg   read(pf)-def sg     3sg abs-egon(stay)
    c.  Liburu  hori       ni-k    irakurri-rik(or -ta)  d-ago
        book    that(abs)  I-erg   read(pf)-part(-and)   3sg abs-egon(stay)
```

(-(r)ik is originally the partitive marker (part); -ta(or -da after l and n) derives from <eta(= and)).

Here it must be mentioned, however, that little attention has been paid so far to the existence of the following sentence-type, perhaps because of its statistical scarcity in Basque texts:

```
(4)     Ni-∅    liburu  ugari-∅    irakurri-a          n-aiz
        I-abs   book    many-abs   read(pf)-def sg     1sg abs-izan(be)
```

This sentence-type is found almost only when the Goal term is indefinite as in (4). In (4) too, the other two morphological combinations found in (3b-c) are possible.

All three morphological devices are also possible in intransitive verbal predications:

```
(5)     Ni-∅    Kyoto-ra    joan-a           n-aiz
        I-abs   Kyoto-dir   gone(pf)-def sg  1sg abs-izan(be)
```

Note that all the above sentences are characterized by their agreement as having one-place predicates even if there are two participants as in (3) or (4). When used independently, *izan* and *egon* are generally both one-place verbs. For the time being we will refer to the morphological combination of the verb suffixes (-a(k), -(r)ik, -ta) and *izan/egon* as Type I.

1.2.2. Type II

The same suffixes can also combine with *ukan/eduki* 'have', both of which are two-place verbs when used independently:[3]

```
(6) a.  Ni-k   liburu  hori       irakurri-a       d-u-t
        I-erg  book    that(abs)  read(pf)-def sg  3sg abs-ukan(have)-1sg erg
    b.  Ni-k   liburu  hori       irakurri-a       d-auka-t
        I-erg  book    that(abs)  read(pf)-def sg  3sg abs-eduki(have)-1sg erg
```

c. Ni-k   liburu hori   irakurri-rik(or -ta)   d-auka-t
   I-erg   book   that(abs)   read(pf)-part(-and)   3sg abs-eduki(have)-1sg erg

Note that this time both the erg and the abs terms cause agreement on the aux.
And the suffix -a(k) agrees with the abs term in number.[4] We will refer to the
morphological combination of the three verb suffixes with *ukan/eduki* as Type II,
which is characterized by two-place predicates.

   In what follows three approaches to the semantics of Type I and Type II are
re-examined.

1.3. The semantics of Type I and Type II

1.3.1. The pseudo-cleft approach

With respect to Type I, when the suffix is -a(k) and the verb is *izan*(be), one
possible translation of (3a), for instance, is 'That book is what I have read',
i.e. the pseudo-cleft construction in English. All previous discussions dealing
with the pseudo-cleft interpretation found in Type I agree with the view that
(3a) is derived from (7) (Bouda 1973, Goenaga 1978 and p.c., De Rijk 1978 and
p.c., Eguzkitza 1981, etc.):

(7)   Liburu hori   ni-k   irakurri d-u-da-n-a   d-a[5]
       book   that(abs)   I-erg   read(pf) 3sg abs-ukan(Aux)-   3sg abs-izan(be)
                                             1sg erg-rel-def sg

In FG, this amounts to the claim that *nik irakurria* (in 3a) as wel as *nik
irakurri dudana* (in 7) is analyzed as a term: $(d1x_i: \text{Perf irakurri}_V(\text{ni})_{Ag} (x_i)_{Go})$.
(For further details on cleft and pseudo-cleft constructions, see Dik 1980a:
ch. 10, Mackenzie & Hannay 1982 and Hannay 1983).

   In FG, terms are defined as 'expressions with referential potential, i.e.
expressions which can be used to refer to entities in some world' (Dik 1980a: 9).
However, observe that, unlike *nik irakurri dudana*, the phrase *nik irakurria* can
function as a referring expression only if its referent is given beforehand in
context. In (8) the phrases *Ameriketara joana* and *etxean gelditua* can function
as referring expressions because their referents have already been mentioned in
the sentence (*bi seme*) and this helps these two phrases to refer to entities:

(8)   Bi   seme-∅   d-it-u-∅   Ameriketa-ra joan-a
      two   sons-abs 3abs-pl-ukan(have)-3sg erg   America-to   gone-def sg

      eta   etxe-a-n   gelditu-a   (De Rijk to appear: ch. 21)
      and   house-def sg-in   stayed-def sg

      (He has two sons, the one who has gone to America and the one who has
      stayed in the house)

But if this condition is not satisfied, phrases like *nik irakurria* fail to
function as referring expressions, which explains why *nik irakurria* is not
acceptable to many informants when introduced into the discourse for the first
time with Topic function, whereas Topic assignment to *nik irakurri dudana*, which
is always a referring expression, is not problematic:

(9) a.??(Nik irakurria)_{Top}   (liburu hori)_{Foc} da

    b. (Nik irakurria dudana)_{Top}   (liburu hori)_{Foc} da

    c. 'What I have read is that book'

The above observations suggest that phrases like *nik irakurria* are not expressions with referential potential, because their ability to refer to entities is
not inherent but derived through the context. Therefore, my conclusion is that
phrases like *nik irakurria* are not terms and that only when the condition mentioned above is satisfied do they behave like terms. Although both (3a) and (7)
express some sort of relation of identification, it will be shown in section 2.3
that they have different semantic structures and that (7) is a pseudo-cleft
construction, but (3) is not. It is in this sense that the pseudo-cleft approach,
which treats (3a) and (7) alike, must be rejected.

1.3.2. The passive approach

Another well-known approach to sentences like (3a-c) (but not (4) and (5)) is in
terms of passive. (For discussions pro and con, see Lafitte 1962, Bollenbacher
1977, Brettschneider 1979, Villasante 1980, Eguzkitza 1981, etc..) The motivation
for this approach is perhaps that in order to translate the passive sentences of
French or Spanish into Basque, in addition to the so-called impersonal sentences,
sentences like (3a-c) have also been used repeatedly because of their morphological affinity with the passive. (In fact, (3a-c) obey the universal characterization of passive in RG at least superficially, cf. Perlmutter & Postal 1977.)
    If (3a-c) is simply a passive construction, its predication will be represented
as follows in FG:

(10)   Perf irakurri$_V$ (ni)$_{Ag}$ (liburu hori)$_{GoSubj}$

Note that (10) represents an Action state of affairs (SoA). Normally, Action predications can occur with the progressive aspect.[6] However, no form of Type I, i.e. including (4) and (5) as well as (3a-c), can express an Action SoA, as is shown by the fact that the Progressive *ari izan* (literally, 'be engaged') is not permitted in Type I, which means that (10) does not correctly represent the predication of (3a-c):

(11)   *Liburu hori   ni-k   irakurri-a   iza-ten
        book that(abs) I-erg   read(pf)-def sg   izan(be)(impf)

        ari   d-a
        prog   3sg abs-izan(be)

The above observation indicates that the analysis which regards sentences like (3a-c) as passive *constructions* must be rejected. However, it will be shown in section 2 that an FG analysis will give a much more precise explanation of their 'passive-expressibility'.

1.3.3. The aspectual approach

Although little systematic work has yet been done on aspect in Basque, some traditional grammarians of Basque have noticed the existence of expressions indicating a kind of completion (cf. Lafitte 1962, Arotçarena 1951, both of whom use the term *Parfait* for the constructions named here Type I & II).

As almost all linguists who discuss aspect recognize, the definitions of aspect and the methods used to analyse it are too divergent to permit any brief survey. Let me then make it clear that by *aspect* I mean (the speaker's subjective) different choices as to the 'internal temporal constituency' (Comrie 1976c: 3) or the 'temporally distinct phases' (Marion 1981: 152) of a SoA. The temporal phase of a SoA, which I understand in a slightly different way from Marion, ranges from before t_1 (= beginning point) through the overall process to after t_2 (= terminal point) as far as there is some temporal relevance to the SoA involved.

Here it will be useful to introduce another aspectual distinction, between Inner Aspect (IA) (between t_1 and t_2) and Outer Aspect (OA) (before t_1/after t_2). The aspectual categories of the 'internal temporal constituency' (perfective, imperfective, progressive, habitual, iterative, etc.) and some of the phasal

aspects (ingressive, etc.) will belong to IA. And the phasal aspects such as
prospective, resultative will belong to OA. As will be justified below, what is
relevant here is the resultative.

To clarify the meaning of the resultative, I will begin by comparing it with
the perfect, since both are concerned with the notion of completion in some way
or other. Although there is not enough space to discuss at full length the grammatical status of the perfect, suffice it to say that, assuming Reichenbach's
famous definition of the perfect, i.e. E-R (the event time is anterior to the
reference time), the perfect *can* indicate or express a nuance of completion (or
more precisely, completedness) by locating a SoA anterior to the reference time.[7]
But the way in which the resultative implies some sort of completion or completedness is different. Unlike the perfect which contains an element belonging to the
realm of tense, the resultative is a purely aspectual notion referring to the
situation which follows the successful completion of the preceding SoA. To put
it another way, the resultative's reference to the temporal area posterior to
t_2 suggests the termination, hence, completedness, of the SoA involved. Another
important feature of the resultative is that the SoA designated by the resultative
form and the SoA before t_2 are not one and the same SoA, although they are temporally sequential. In terms of FG, this means that, unlike the perfective, imperfective, progressive, etc., the resultative aspect cannot be analysed as a
predicate-operator.

Let us now return to the Type I & II constructions of Basque. A close investigation of these leads us to conclude that the term resultative is preferable
to the term perfect (indeed, Brettschneider 1979 and Rebuschi 1982 also choose
the term resultative). Firstly, unlike the perfect forms, neither Type I nor
Type II combines with the Progressive form *ari izan*, which explains the non-
dynamic property of the Type I & II sentences:

(12) a.* Liburu hori ni-k irakurri-a iza-ten ari d-a   (= (11))

    b.* Liburu hori ni-k irakurri-a ego-ten ari d-a   (cf. (3b))

    c.* Liburi hori ni-k irakurri-rik(or -ta) ego-ten ari d-a (cf. (3c))

    d.* Ni-Ø liburu ugari-Ø irakurri-a iza-ten ari n-aiz   (cf. (4))

    e.* Ni-Ø Kyoto-ra joan-a iza-ten ari n-aiz   (cf. (5))

    f.* Ni-Ø liburu hori irakurri-rik(or -ta)   eduki-tzen ari n-aiz

                                                              (cf. (6c))

Secondly, the Type I & II forms entail their corresponding perfective forms.
There is no such entailment relation between the perfect and the perfective.

Thus, (3a-c) and (6a-c) entail (13), and (4) and (5) entail (14) and (15) respectively:

(13)   Ni-k   liburu hori   irakurri d-u-t(Pres)/n-uen(Past)
        I-erg   book   that(abs)   read(pf) 3sg abs-ukan(Aux)-1sg erg/1sg erg-
        'I have read/read that book'   ukan(Aux)

(14)   Ni-k   liburu ugari-∅ irakurri d-u-t(Pres)/n-uen(Past)
        I-erg   book   many-abs read(pf) 3sg abs-ukan(Aux)-1sg erg/1sg erg-
        'I have read/read many books'   ukan(Aux)

(15)   Ni-∅   Kyoto-ra joan   n-aiz(Pres)/n-intzen(Past)
        I-abs   Kyoto-to gone(pf) 1sg abs-izan(Aux)/1sg abs-izan(Aux)
        'I have gone/went to Kyoto'

Recall that in the case of the Perfective the Present and the Past forms refer to the Near Past and the Remote Past respectively (see also note 2). And unlike the perfect (as found in English), there is no selectional restriction of temporal adverbials peculiar to the resultative. Any temporal adverbial permitted in the Near or Remote Past Perfective sentences can also occur with the Type I & II sentences in the Present (e.g., *gaur* 'today', *atzo* 'yesterday', *bietan* 'at 2 o'clock', *bere gazte denboran* 'in one's youth', etc.).[8]

Thirdly, t_2 plays an important role in the analysis of the Type I & II sentences. The terminal point (t_2) links the preceding SoA and the subsequent SoA. The aspectual meaning of (3a-c), for example, can be brought out by translating them as something like 'That book is in the state that I have read/read it'. Note that in the case of (3a-c), t_2 is quite clear, because the preceding SoA is characterized as telic, i.e. having a natural terminal point. In general, it can be said that a nuance of resultativeness comes from the implication that at t_2 the preceding SoA is over. The Resultative, applied to a telic SoA, describes the subsequent SoA with the implication that the telic SoA is no longer ongoing; this is shown graphically in (16):

(16)

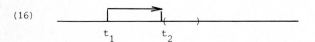

$$t_1 \qquad t_2$$

But what happens when the preceding SoA is atelic? In an atelic SoA, one can make an arbitrary pause at any moment, so there is no well-defined natural terminal point. Type I & II forms may be used for such an atelic SoA, but without any implication of the completion of the SoA before t_2 as found in (3a-c). But, as can be shown by the following examples and diagrams, they refer to the SoA pos-

terior to the pause that can be inferred from adverbials such as *bi ordu* 'for
two hours', *bi aldiz* 'twice', etc. or from temporal deictic information, regardless of whether the atelic SoA involved stops there or not:[9]

(17) a. Ni-Ø   jadanik bi   ordu   ibili-a   n-aiz
        I-abs   already two   hours   walked(pf)-def sg   1sg abs-izan(be)
        'I am already in the state that I have walked/walked for two hours'

     b. Ni-Ø   liburu ugari-Ø   irakurri-a n-aiz   (= (4))
        'I am in the state that (now) I have read many books'

(18) a.

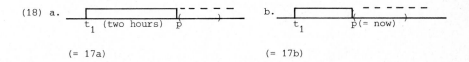

(= 17a)   (= 17b)

In an atelic SoA, t_2 is replaced by the pause established arbitrarily.

   So far, no explanation for the distinction between Type I and Type II has been
given in this paper. As will be recalled, the distinction was based on the difference in valency (i.e. one-place vs. two-place predicates). However, the following observation is worth mentioning here. In the case of Type I sentences,
there are cases in which, *as a natural reading*, the SoA referred to is described
with no nuance of resultativeness. For various reasons the existence of the preceding SoA becomes vague or even disappears from the perspective of the speaker's
cognition, with the result that these Type I sentences are interpreted as describing a simple stative SoA. (Recall that the SoA described by Type I & II
sentences are always -dynamic, cf. (12).) I will give two examples, suggesting
in each case the factor suppressing the resultative interpretation:

(19)   Ni-Ø   hemen   eseri-ta   n-ago[10]
        I-abs   here   sit(pf)-and   1sg abs-egon(stay)
        'I am sitting here'

        [The subsequent SoA is visible and lasting]

(20)   Eskutitz hau   ondo idatzi-a   d-ago
        letter   this(abs)   well written(pf)-def sg 3sg abs-egon(stay)
        'This letter is written well'

        [The preceding SoA is conceptualized impersonally]

Both examples may be represented graphically as follows:

(21)

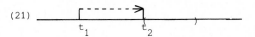

However, with Type II sentences, there is no such possibility, because their two-place predicate forces the speaker to perceive the relationship between the participants in the preceding SoA and as a result, the cognition of the preceding SoA never disappears.

In summary, from the above observations it can be confirmed that both Type I and II constructions refer to the one-place (in the former) or two-place (in the latter) non-dynamic SoA posterior to t_2 or some arbitrarily established pause, i.e. belonging to the OA area except when some special conditions preclude it, and then only in the case of Type I. It follows from this that the term 'resultative' is preferred and the validity of the distinction between Type I and Type II is justified. Now the remaining task is to clarify the structural properties of both constructions.

2. The structural properties of the Type I construction

Of the three possible approaches to the Type I construction discussed in section 1, two, the pseudo-cleft approach (1.3.1.) and the aspectual approach (1.3.3.) involve non-verbal predicates. Thus, before discussing the Type I construction as such, I will say something about the non-verbal predicates of Basque in general.

2.1. Non-verbal predicates in Basque

The following sentences contain relevant examples of non-verbal predicates:

(22)   Koldo-Ø   irakesle-a-Ø   d-a (*d-ago)
        Koldo-abs teacher-def sg-abs 3sg abs-izan(be)(*3sg abs-egon(stay))
        'Koldo is the/a teacher'

(23) a. Koldo-Ø   handi-a   d-a (*d-ago)
        Koldo-abs big-def sg   3sg abs-izan(be)(*3sg abs-egon(stay))
        'Koldo is big'

     b.*Koldo-Ø handi d-a (or d-ago)

(24) a. Koldo-Ø   triste d-ago (*d-a)
        Koldo-abs sad   3sg abs-egon(stay)(*3sg abs-izan(be))
        'Koldo is sad'

     b.*Koldo-Ø triste-a d-ago (or d-a)

In both (22) and (23) *izan*(be) functions as a linking verb for identification, but the difference between the sentences is parallel to the one discussed in 1.3.1. Observe:

(25) a. Bi   seme-Ø   d-it-u-Ø   handi-a   eta txiki-a
          two   sons-abs 3abs-pl-ukan(have)-3sg erg big-def sg and small-def sg
          'He has two sons, the big one and the small one'

   b.*Handi-a$_{Top}$ Koldo$_{Foc}$ d-a

It is clear that *handia* is not a term. Therefore, my analysis is that in (22)
two terms are linked by the relation of Equality-Identification, whereas in (23)
handia functions as a property expression and its relation to *Koldo* is that of
Property-Identification. In fact, as to (22), there are two alternative representations in FG, i.e. with or without term predicate formation. I shall assume
that at least in Basque the analysis by term predicate formation makes it possible to treat both types of identification relation in a unified way and propose the following underlying predications for (22) and (23) respectively; both
require *izan*-support:[11]

(26)   Pres $\{(d1x_j: irakasle_N (x_j)_\emptyset)\}$ $(d1x_i: Koldo_N (x_i)_\emptyset)_\emptyset$

(27)   Pres handi$_A$ $(d1x_i: Koldo_N (x_i)_\emptyset)_\emptyset$

(24), rather than involving Property-Identification (having a property of), indicates a Property-State (i.e. the referent of the term is in a state of ...) and
the verb *egon* is used in place of *izan*. Here the verb *egon* is no mere linking
verb, but, in company with an adjectival element which specifies the semantic
content of the property, constitutes a one-place complex property predicate and
occupies the predicate slot from the very start:[12]

(28)   Pres $[triste_A egon_V]_A$ $(d1x_i: Koldo (x_i)_\emptyset)_\emptyset$

2.2. Type I interpreted as resultative

Type I, when interpreted as resultative, can be regarded as a kind of Property-
State construction like (24a). Its semantic content is such that in the OA
(after t_2) area an entity chosen from the participants of the IA SoA is in the
state of having completely experienced as a participant the overall process of
the IA SoA. In FG, this can be formulated by putting the predication of the IA
SoA with the Perfective predicate operator into the property-predicate position
alongside *izan/egon* (see note 10 for a relevant comment on the three morphological combinations of the Type I), i.e. as in (29):

(29) $[[[\text{Perf } \varphi_V \ldots (x_1)_S \ldots]_{\text{Action/Process}} \text{ izan/egon}] (x_1)_\emptyset]_{\text{State}}$ [13, 14]

   condition: S = Ag, Fo, Proc, Go, $^?$Rec (this is due to the semantic

     function recoverability constraint) [15]

Note that the general schema given in (29) is used to refer to the OA area. The
semantic function of the chosen argument is constantly Zero ($\emptyset$), which means
that the SoA in the OA area is in fact devoid of any substance *per se*. Thus, for
instance, the underlying predication of (3a) will be:

(30) $\text{Pres}[[\text{Perf irakurri}_V \text{(ni)}_{Ag} (x_i)_{Go}]\text{izan}_V] (\text{d-p1}x_i: \text{liburu}_N (x_i)_\emptyset)_\emptyset$ [16]

However, as mentioned in 1.3.3., when the Type I Resultative form expresses a
simple stative (-dynamic) SoA, the schema is used to refer to the SoA reinterpreted as belonging to the IA area. In this case, the semantic function of the
argument varies with the feature Control. In the case of (19), we have the
following representation:

(31) $\text{Pres}[[\text{Perf eseri}_V (x_i)_{Ag} \text{(hemen)}_{Loc} \text{egon}_V] (\text{d1}x_i: \text{ni}_{PRO} (x_i)_\emptyset)_{Po}$

One strong argument in favour of the analysis in (29) is that Manner adverbials
used with +dynamic SoA can also occur with the -dynamic Type I predications:

(32)   Eskutitz   hau   ni-k   presaz   idatzi-a   d-a
         letter   this(abs)   I-erg   in a hurry   written(pf)-def sg   3sg abs-izan(be)
         'This letter is in the state that I have written/wrote it in a hurry'

This apparent contradiction, however, is due to the fact that Manner satellites
can be freely added to the predication embedded in the property-assigning predicate
which in fact is a +dynamic predication.

2.3. Type I interpreted as pseudo-pseudo-cleft

We have already seen in 1.3.1. that the Type I construction with the morphological combination of the suffix -a(k) and the verb *izan* cannot be equivalent to
the pseudo-cleft construction which expresses the relation of Equality-
Identification between two definite terms. However, recall that *izan*(be) indicates the relation of Property-Identification when used with adjectives in
Basque (see (23a)). As far as the morphological combination of -a(k) and *izan* is

concerned, if the whole 'property-predication' is regarded as one adjective, such a morpho-syntactic parallelism makes it possible to regard, for example, (3a) as expressing the relation of Property-Identification just like (23a). This might be called 'pseudo-pseudo-cleft' as opposed to the real pseudo-cleft construction as in (7), the difference between them being that between Equality-Identification and Property-Identification respectively. The general schema and its application to (3a) will be as in (33) and (34) to which *izan*-support is applied:

(33) $[\text{Perf } \varphi_V \ldots (x_1)_S \ldots]_A \ (x_1)_\emptyset$

(34) $\text{Pres}[\text{Perf irakurri}_V(\text{ni})_{Ag} \ (x_i)_{Go}]_A \ (\text{d-plx}_i: \text{liburu}_N \ (x_i)_\emptyset)_\emptyset$

2.4. The 'passive expressibility' of Type I

Given that theoretically the single argument of a one-place predicate automatically has Subj function, if in the structure of (29) the Goal entity is chosen as the $\emptyset$-argument, the connection between the Subj and the Goal easily gives rise to an extension of Type I to translate the passive sentence of foreign languages albeit under restricted conditions (e.g., the progressive passive is impossible):

(35) $[[\text{Perf } \varphi_V \ldots (x_2)_{Go} \ldots \text{izan/egon}_V] \ (x_2)_{\emptyset \text{Subj}}$

3. The structural properties of the Type II construction

3.1. Type II interpreted as resultative[17]

We saw in section 1 that in Basque there are two kinds of constructions for the resultative aspect: the one-place one and the two-place one.[18] Here we will deal with the latter. Both constructions refer to the OA (after t_2) SoA respectively, but they present different conceptualizations of the SoA.

The SoA designated by the Type II construction like that designed by Type I, is characterized as -dynamic. But, what about the parameter of control? If it is possible to regard the notion of control as containing two elements: potential domination (over the other co-participants) and control of the realization (of the SoA involved), then only the former is relevant here. Tentatively we might refer to 'potential domination' as 'reduced control', in the sense that the range of control is restricted to the entities involved. The notion of reduced control

is not relevant to the typology of states of affairs. Indeed, the SoA designated
by the Type II construction is always characterized as a State, because in the
OA area, where the event is already over, there can be no choice as to whether
or not that event will obtain. Thus, in the State SoA in the OA area, which is
in fact devoid of any concrete substance, the ergative/absolutive case-marking
pattern merely shows the trace of the domination relationship between the two
arguments involved, and not any kind of semantic relationship. Assuming that
this kind of domination relationship will be described by the two quasi-semantic
functions, reduced Positioner (rPo) and reduced Goal (rGo), the general schema
for the Type II Resultative construction and its application to (6a), for
instance, will be as in (36) and (37) respectively:

(36) $[[[\text{Perf } \varphi_V(x_1)_{Ag} \ (x_2)_{Go} \cdots]_{Action/Process} \text{ukan/eduki}_V] (x_1)_{rPo} (x_2)_{rGo}]_{State}$
        Fo

(37) $\text{Pres}[[\text{Perf irakurri}_V(x_i)_{Ag}(x_j)_{Go}] \text{ukan}_V] (d1x_i:\text{ni}_{PRO}(x_i)_{\emptyset})_{rPo}$
        $(\text{d-plx}_j: \text{liburu}_N(x_j)_{\emptyset})_{rGo}$

The three morphological combinations allowed in the type II are quite interchangeable. And note that here the verbs *ukan/eduki* merely indicate the domination relationship between the two arguments. However, as will be mentioned below,
there are cases in which these verbs function as expressing some sort of possession.

3.2. Type II interpreted as indicating possession

The prototypical possessive construction in Basque makes use of the synthetic
form of *ukan/eduki* (to have) with the ergative/absolutive pattern:[19]

(38)   Ni-k   liburu hori   d-u-t (or d-auka-t)
        I-erg   book   that(abs) 3sg abs-ukan(have)-1sg erg (or 3sg abs-eduki
        'I have that book'   (have)-1sg erg)

Now, alongside its resultative reading, the Type II construction can also be
interpreted as expressing the idea that *I have that book as having read it*, if
we take (6a-c) as an example.[20] Although there is little work on the possessive-
like reading of Type II and there is no room in this paper to discuss it in
detail, I will just mention two points concerning the source of the ambiguity of
this kind found in (6a-c). The first point is that in the 'possessive' reading

the Type II construction refers to the SoA in the IA area. In this case, it designates a Position SoA just like (38). The second point concerns the first argument. In the 'possessive' reading, it is conceptualized as a possessor rather than an Agent of, for instance, the action of reading. Now we can give (39) as the schema for this linguistic phenomenon and (40) as its application to (6a):

(39) $[[[\text{Perf } \varphi_V (x_2)_{Go} \ldots]\text{ukan/eduki}_V](x_1)_{Po}(x_2)_{Go}]_{\text{Position}}{}^{21}$

(40) $\text{Pres}[[\text{Perf irakurri}_V(x_j)_{Go}]\text{ukan}_V](d1x_i: \text{ni}_{PRO}(x_i)_{\emptyset})_{Po}(d\text{-plx}_j:\text{liburu}_N(x_j)_{\emptyset})_{Go}$

The non-occurrence of the first argument in the embedded predication may explain why such a temporally sequential connection as found in the resultative reading is precluded and the verbs *ukan/eduki* regain their original possessive meaning.[22]

4. Concluding remarks

I hope I have been able to show that the analysis developed in this paper gives a persuasive explanation for the overall picture that the Type I & II construc-tions display - i.e. the structural and semantic difference between the Type I & II Resultative constructions on the one hand,[23] and the structural ambiguity of Type I (the resultative versus the 'pseudo-pseudo-cleft') and that of Type II (the resultative versus the 'possessive') on the other. With respect to Type I, a brief explanation for its 'passive expressibility' was also included.

NOTES

*   I am extremely grateful to Casper de Groot who sent me many valuable and instructive comments on an earlier version of this paper. Without his gen-erous advice, I could not have completed the paper in its present form. I also would like to thank the other editors of this volume for their sug-gestions and encouragement, Simon Dik and Tatsuo Nishida for their constant encouragement, Patxi Goenaga for his patience and willingness to answer my many questions, and Rudolf de Rijk and Terence Wilbur for discussions of the constructions treated here. And I feel deeply indebted to my informants for their willingness to teach me Basque. However, all errors and inadequacies are, of course, my own.

[1]   The data in this paper are based on the Guipuzcoan dialect. Some informants also know *euskara batua* (Unified Basque, which was established by the Real Academia de la Lengua Vasca in the 1970s). The orthography and the verbal inflections adopted here are also those of *euskara batua*.

2 Present Perfective sentences, which indicate the Near Past, co-occur with
such temporal adverbials as *gaur* 'today', *lehentxeago* 'some time ago',
whereas Past Perfective ones, which indicate the Remote past, co-occur with
atzo 'yesterday', etc. In all other cases, the Present form is related to
the 'now' time. The notions of perfective, imperfective are used in line
with Comrie's (1976c) definitions. And I use an initial capital for the
language-particular forms.

3 In fact, the semantic difference between *ukan* and *eduki* is very subtle so I
don't go into a discussion of it, because it does not affect the issues
treated here.

4 This is shown in (i):

(i) Ni-k   liburu horik   irakurri-ak   d-it-u-t
    I-erg   book   those(abs)   read(pf)-def pl   3abs-pl-ukan(have)-1sg erg

5 *-n* is the relative clause marker:

(i) ni-k   irakurri d-u-da-n   liburu-a
    I-erg   read(pf) 3sg abs-ukan(Aux)-1sg erg-rel   book-def sg
    'the book which I have read'

6 I agree with the view defended in De Groot (this vol.) in which *predications*
are taken as a point of departure for establishing a typology of SoAs, and
not *predicates*.

7 For a discussion of the notions 'complete' and 'completed' see De Groot
(1984).

8 Here, by adding examples of Past and Future, I will illustrate the five
possible combinations of preceding and subsequent SoA with respect to tense:

(i) Near Past/Present

IA: Ni-k   liburu hori   gaur   irakurri   d-u-t(Pres)
    I-erg   book   that(abs)   today   read(pf)   3sg abs-ukan(Aux)-1sg erg
    'I have read that book today'

OA: Liburu hori   ni-k   gaur   irakurri-a   d-a(Pres)
    book   that(abs)   I-erg today   read(pf)-def sg 3sg abs-izan(be)
    'That book is in the state that I have read it today'

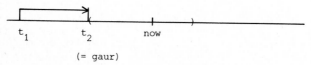

(= gaur)

(ii) Remote Past/Present

IA: Ni-k liburu hori atzo (= yesterday) irakurri n-uen(Past)
    'I read that book yesterday'
OA: Liburu hori ni-k atzo irakurri-a d-a(Pres)
    'That book is in the state that I read it yesterday'

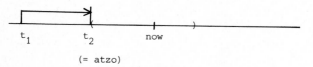

(= atzo)

(iii) Near Past/Past

IA: Ni-k liburu hori gaur irakurri d-u-t(Pres)
    'I have read that book today'

OA: Liburu hori ni-k gaur irakurri-a z-en(Past)(3sg abs-izan(be))
    'That book was in the state that I had read it today'

(= gaur)

However, this combination is ungrammatical when the adverbial *orain* 'now' is used, in which case t_2 becomes 'now' and the Present form is chosen for the OA sentence.

(iv) Remote Past/Past

IA: Ni-k liburu hori atzo irakurri n-uen(Past)
    'I read that book yesterday'

OA: Liburu hori ni-k atzo irakurri-a z-en(Past)
    'That book was in the state that I read it yesterday'

(= atzo)

(v) Future/Future

IA: Ni-k   liburu hori   bihar   irakurri-ko   d-u-t(Fut)
    I-erg   book   that(abs) tomorrow   read(pf)-fut 3sg abs-ukan(Aux)-1sg erg
    'I will read that book tomorrow'

OA: Liburu hori   ni-k   bihar   irakurri-a   izan-go d-a(Fut)
    book   that(abs) I-erg tomorrow read(pf)-def   sg be-fut 3sg abs-izan(be)
    'That book will be in the state that I will have read it tomorrow'

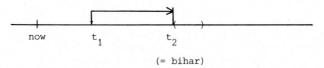

(= bihar)

The following two combinations are impossible, because in (vi) there is no Perfective form which indicates the time of 'now' and in (vii) the two SoA involved are not sequential in time:

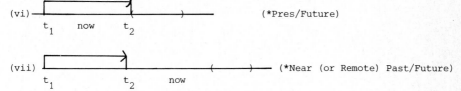

(vi)   (*Pres/Future)

(vii)   (*Near (or Remote) Past/Future)

Lastly, note that the subsequent SoA is conceptualized imperfectively. Their Present tense indicates the time of 'now'.

[9] If there is no information available to establish a pause, the time of speaking will fulfil this role.

[10] As far as the morphology of Type I is concerned, the combination of *-rik* (or *-ta*) and *egon* 'to stay' is most likely to indicate a simple stative. This may be related to the fact that, as will be shown in section 2.1, in non-verbal predicates *-a(k)* 'the' and *izan* 'be' are both connected with expressions of the relation of identification, whereas *egon* is used for expressing Property-State. But, when Type I explicitly indicates the resultative meaning, the three morphological devices are equally possible. This also holds true for the Type II morphological devices, because they are quite interchangeable.

[11] For a series of discussions of this matter, see Dik (1978, 1980a), Junger (1981a), Mackenzie & Hannay (1982), Bolkestein (1983), De Groot (1983b), Mackenzie (1983) and Vet (1983).

[12] Some problems arise from regarding this type of complex property-predicate as the output of predicate formation. First, it is difficult to find its corresponding input predicate(s). In Basque there is no predicate-frame like $triste_A(x_1)_\emptyset$ nor $egon_V(x_1)_\emptyset$. The adjective *triste* is never used for expressing Property Identification and the verb *egon* is obligatorily accompanied by a locative expression when used as a verbal predicate:

```
(i)    *Koldo-Ø    triste-a      d-a
        Koldo-abs   sad-def sg    3sg abs-izan(be)
(ii)    Koldo-Ø     etxe-a-n              d-ago
        Koldo-abs   house-def sg-in       3sg abs-egon(stay)
        'Koldo is in the house'
(iii)  *Koldo-Ø     d-ago
        Koldo-abs    3sg abs-egon(stay)
```

Thus, rather than look for a predicate formation rule, I would like to propose that the basic predicate $[\varphi_A egon_V]_A (x_1)_\emptyset$ is included in the lexicon.

[13] As mentioned in note 10 too, *izan* is here no mere linking verb, but, just like *egon* takes part in the formation of resultative state sentences.

[14] There is no need to specify the tense operator of the embedded 'property predication', becuase in this construction it functions as a property of the Ø-argument and does not designate a SoA to which the category of tense is related. Note also that, unlike the case of subordination which involves a full predication being inserted in a term position, the embedded predication discussed here always ends up with an open predication (see (30), for instance), due to which the expression rule of verbal agreement which is possible in Basque only for full predications does not occur on the level of this embedded predication (observe the non-occurrence of agreement with *ni-k* in (3a-c), *liburu ugari-Ø* in (4) or *zu-ri* in note 18).

[15] Statistically the Recipient is rarely chosen as the Ø-argument position. Unless the erg term appears in the surface, such expressions are not acceptable:

```
(i)    Amaia-Ø     Koldo-k      liburu hori      eman-a            d-a
        Amaia-abs   Koldo-erg    book    that(abs) given(pf)-def sg  3sg abs-izan(be)
        'Amaia is in the state that Koldo has given/gave that book to her'
```

    (ii) Amaia-∅   liburu hori   eman-a   d-a
          Amaia-abs book   that(abs) given(pf)-def sg 3sg abs-izan(be)
          'Amaia is in the state that she has given/gave that book to someone'
          '*Amaia is in the state that someone has given/gave that book to her'

[16]   -p indicates non-Proximate (cf. Dik 1978: 62).

[17]   As it is rather difficult to translate into English the exact meaning of the
Type II Resultative construction, I'll cite the following equivalent construction from Spanish:

    (i)   Tengo   leído   ese   libro
         I have read (pp masc sg) that book (masc sg)
    (ii) Tengo   escritas   dos   cartas
         I have written (pp fem pl) two letters (fem pl)

[18]   It should be noted that even if a Recipient term exists, normally it causes
no agreement in the Type II construction, which demonstrates the two-place
status of the construction:

    (i) ?Ni-k   liburu hori   zu-ri   eman-a   d-izu-t
         I-erg   book   that(abs) you-dat given(pf)-def sg 3sg abs-2sg dat-
                                                       1sg erg(ukan)

    (ii) Ni-k   liburu hori   zu-ri   eman-a   d-u-t
         I-erg   book   that(abs) you-dat given(pf)-def sg 3sg abs-ukan-1sg-erg

However, some examples with dative agreement are also found.

[19]   See note 3.

[20]   Paying attention to the fact that in the Type II construction the suffix
-a(k) agrees with the abs term in number, it can be said that the 'possessive'
structure reflects this morpho-syntactic characteristic better than the resultative one.

[21]   Following the view defended in note 12, all the predicate-frames containing
an embedded predication in the predicate position could also be included in
the lexicon in the forms of (29), (33), (36) and (39).

[22]   Two rather different sentences expressing this sort of possession might be
useful to clarify the structural and semantic properties of the construction
involved:

    (i)   Ni-k   Koldo-∅   seme-a-∅   d-u-t
         I-erg   Koldo-abs son-def sg-abs 3sg abs-ukan(have)-1sg erg
         'I have Koldo as a son/Koldo is my son'

    (ii) Ni-k   zango-a-∅   gaixo-a   d-u-t
         I-erg   leg-def sg-abs bad-def sg 3sg abs-ukan(have)-1sg erg
         'I have a leg as being bad/My leg is bad'

In (i) and (ii), the position of an embedded predication is occupied by the
Equality-Identification nominal predication and the Property-Identification
adjectival predication respectively, and as a result they have the following
structures:

(iii) $\text{Pres}[[\{(\text{d1x}_k: \text{seme}_N(x_k)_\emptyset)\} (x_j)_\emptyset] \text{ukan}_V]$

$$(\text{d1x}_i: \text{ni}_{\text{PRO}}(x_i)_\emptyset)_{\text{Po}} \ (\text{d1x}_j: \text{Koldo}_N(x_j)_\emptyset)_{\text{Go}}$$

(iv) $\text{Pres}[[\text{gaixo}_A(x_j)_\emptyset] \text{ukan}_V]$

$$(\text{d1x}_i: \text{ni}_{\text{PRO}}(x_i)_\emptyset)_{\text{Po}} \ (\text{d1x}_j: \text{zango}_N(x_j)_\emptyset)_{\text{Go}}$$

Observe that in (iii), (iv) and (40) the first argument does not appear in the embedded predications. But this first argument has to satisfy one important condition, i.e. it must have some connection with the SoA described by the embedded predication (e.g., as an Agent (in (40)), as related by family (in (iii)), as an inalienable Possessor (in (iv)), etc.).

[23] As other languages which have a resultative expression corresponding to Type I, we may mention Japanese and Modern Armenian (cf. Comrie 1981b), both of which form the resultative with the aid of the verb 'be'. As an example of the Type II resultative form, I have already mentioned the case of Spanish, which uses the verb *tener* 'have'.

Modality and the models: a problem for functional grammar

Louis Goossens
Department of Germanic Philology, University of Antwerp

0. Introduction*

By way of introduction let me clarify the title of this paper. It implies that modality and the modals are an inescapable subject for FG. Modality in all its aspects is an important meaning component of language and the modals are an important way of expressing various dimensions of it in a great many languages of the world.[1] English, for one, is a language which extensively illustrates the use that languages make of modal verbs.

Another implication of the title is that FG has so far not been centrally preoccupied to locate modality and the modals within its framework. We find a brief but useful proposal to deal with epistemic modals in Vet (1981a), a general consideration of the place of modality in a full-scale functional framework in De Schutter and Nuyts (1983) (which, however, does not go into any detail and, moreover, presents us with an 'integrated model of a functional grammar' which differs in several respects from Dikkian FG), and a number of interesting and, as will be found, workable proposals in Machtelt Bolkestein's insightful study of a number of Latin modal verbs/constructions (Bolkestein 1980), but again her treatment can hardly qualify as full-scale attempt to integrate modality and the modals into FG.

This paper does not claim to be a full-scale proposal either. For one thing it focuses almost exclusively on the modals of English, for another it will have to leave several questions unanswered or come up with suggestions which will have to be worked out (and perhaps rejected on further investigation). It is hoped, though, that it will amply illustrate that an integration of modality and the modals into FG is possible, that it requires elaborations of the model and that such elaborations are bound to contribute to our understanding of what human language is like.

1. Modality and the English modals

1.1. Three dimensions of modality

Modality, as I understand it here, is multidimensional. The three dimensions I want to concentrate on are as follows:

(a) *Epistemic* (or inferential) modality, which expresses the speaker's subject-
    ive qualification of a given State of Affairs as *possible, probable, certain*
    (we find it in sentences like *It may/will/must be true,* paraphrasable as
    It is possible/probable/certain that it is true).
(b) *Deontic* modality, which is concerned with the expression of the notions
    permission and obligation. Unlike Palmer (1979), I do not reserve the term
    for 'discourse oriented' instances (Palmer, 2.4.3.), typically expressed in
    English by *must* (and often *may*), but I also include non-discourse-oriented
    cases, usually (but not uniquely) associated with *have to, be allowed to.*
(c) *Facultative* modality (the term has been taken over from De Schutter 1983)
    deals with the capacity- and volition-meanings, exemplified by *He can swim*
    and *She won't come* (= 'refuses to').

Types (b) and (c) are often referred to as *root*-modality, because diachronically
(and to some extent synchronically) they can be shown to be prior to epistemic
modality.[2] Other types of modality, which will only be dealt with in passing or
not at all, are *objective inferential* modality (as in *This can be the jawbone of
a dinosaur*) and *existential* (in Palmer's terminology) or *presentative* (De
Schutter's label) modality, which we get in e.g. *She can be catty* (= 'she
occasionally is'), *Boys will be boys* (= 'tend to behave like').

1.2. Use of the English modals

The modals of English (*can, could, may, might, will, would, shall, should, must
ought*) are the favoured, though not exclusive[3] expression of the different dimensions of modality outlined in the preceding section, though only some figure in
all of them. The picture is as follows:

(a) epistemic modality: all modals, but *can* cannot be used to express subjective
    inferential modality in positive, affirmative sentences; *shall* is restricted
    in an epistemic sense.
(b) deontic modality: all modals (though some modals require somewhat specific
    contexts to function deontically).
(c) facultative modality: especially *can, could, will, would.*

Obviously, a treatment of the modals in terms of just these three types of modality does not cover them exhaustively.

First, there is the important contribution of *will* (in standard British English *shall* and *will*) to the formation of the future tense, and of *would* (*should* and *would*) to the formation of the 'past future' and the conditional tenses. Second, the use of *should* in certain specific types of subclauses (often, though not always, alternating with subjunctives in written American English). Thirdly, the use of *may* to express a wish and its related use in certain sub- clauses. Furthermore, there are the additional modality dimensions mentioned in 1.1 (*objective inferential* and *presentative modality*) and the uses of the modals in a number of stereotyped contextualizations and in numerous contexts where more or less conventionalized implicatures are generated.

In what follows only the first two of these additional uses will receive some further attention.

2. Morpho-syntactic preliminaries

My main concern in what follows will be with the ways in which the modals can be integrated into the construction of predications in FG. Before presenting my proposals let me mention three other points (one morphological one, but with im- portant syntactic consequences, the other two syntactic) which FG will also have to account for:

(a) The defective character of the English modals. This will have to be listed in the lexicon as a feature shared by the modals and marginally also by a few other verbs. On the basis of this feature all modals which would have to be realized by non-finite forms will have to be replaced by the appropri- ate periphrastic modal (*have to, be allowed, be possible*, etc.) at the level of the expression rules.

(b) Another feature to be listed in the lexicon is the specification that verbal predicates that are combined with modals will have to be given expression by means of plain infinitives.

(c) A third feature specification in the lexicon will take care of the behaviour of modals as *anomalous finites*. It accounts for the fact that they exhibit the so-called NICE-properties (see Huddleston 1976) regulating their behav- iour in negative, interrogative (etc.) contexts. Reference will have to be made here to clause negation and to basic speech act types (in the sense of Van der Auwera (1984b)), which I suppose can be taken care of in FG by means of predicate operators.

An elaboration of these issues will bring to light a host of related issues
which I have glossed over here. To mention only two of them: there is the exceptional behaviour of *ought* in more than one respect; and the question of weak
and strong forms of the modals. At present it is sufficient to note that such an
undertaking seems feasible, but will entail enriching the model in several
respects.

3. Three possible analyses

3.1. Independent predicates, predicate formation and predicate operators

Three possibilities offer themselves which we can use to integrate the English
modals into the construction of predications.

We may treat them as predicates in their own right, which implies that they
are listed in the lexicon as such, that they will have their particular argument
structure and that we will have to account for the subject assignment features
which they exhibit.

We can also deal with them as resulting from predicate formation. We then
claim that they are not independent predicates, but that as a result of predicate formation rules certain classes of predicates can be combined with them to
yield derived predicates in which they figure.

The third possibility views them as resulting from the combination of a given
predication with an operator of the type of those that take care of Tense or
Aspect.

3.2. A scale of grammaticalization

One way to look at these three possibilities is to consider them as presenting
us with three points on a grammaticalization scale. On this view predicate
operators can be said to deal with fully grammaticalized meanings, predicates in
their own right are in no way grammaticalized, predicate formation gives us a
position in between. The transition from one position to another is best thought
of as gradual, which may make it difficult to offer precise criteria to arrive
at clear-cut distinctions.[4]

In the following sections we argue that the most auxiliarized uses of the
English modals should be dealt with in terms of predicate operators (section 4).
Less auxiliarized uses, i.e. where one of the three modality types introduced in
section 1.1 is involved, can be taken care of either by predicate formation or
as instances where the modals are considered to be predicates in their own right.
How this can be done will be outlined in sections 5 and 6. Arguments for either

position will be given in the course of this outline. At present I prefer to
leave it undecided which is the best solution. Perhaps the complex nature of the
English modals will not permit a one-sided decision, though there are syntactic
arguments to view them as at least shifting away from a status as independent
predicates.

4. The modals as predicate operators

Predicate operators seem to me to be the most adequate way to deal with those
uses of the English modals where they combine with other predications to indicate
meaning dimensions coming under the heading tense or mood.[5] Whereas in (more)
synthetic languages these are usually expressed by verb morphology, we find that
an analytical language like English mainly uses periphrastic conjugational forms
to express them. Dik (1983c), for one, proposes predicate operators for Tense
and Aspect, in cases where English uses analytical as well as synthetic forms at
the expression level.

The following categories are the prime candidates for a treatment of this
kind.

4.1. Future modals

Although I am aware that the existence of a *future tense* in English is question-
able (see e.g. Quirk et al. 1972: 87), there are sufficient grounds in my opinion
to consider separately the combination of *shall/will* + infinitive which are
purely predictive and cannot be classified as epistemic, deontic or facultative.
Instances such as (1) and (2) are cases in point:

(1)   We shall all die one day
(2)   If he comes, he will tell you about it

To deal with them I propose to make use of a predicate operator *Fut*, to be added
to the Tense operators *Pres* and *Past* in Dik (1983c). Postulating it for English
brings the language in line with languages where a *Fut*-operator is needed to
arrive at a synthetic future tense (e.g. Latin or French, to name just two).
Note, however, that combinations with *shall* or *will* for which there is a dis-
cernible modality component, will have to be taken care of along the lines suggested in sections 5 or 6.

4.2. 'Hypothetical' modals

A similar treatment can be proposed for the combination of *should/would* + infinitive which typically functions in conditional main clauses of the 'hypothetical'
as opposed to the 'open' type, as in (3):

(3)   If she came, she would have fun

As far as I can see this use of *should/would* is not reducible to one of the
modality dimensions either. A mood operator *Cond(itional)* could deal with it.
Again a *Cond*-operator is required to deal with synthetic forms in languages
with richer verb morphology such as Latin, French, etc. Notice that cases of the
type exemplified in (4) will have to be dealt with as instances of a *future tense*
which comes within the scope of a *Past Tense*-operator in a higher predication:

(4)   He said that they would all die one day

4.3. Modals in subclauses

It is beyond the scope of this paper to give an exhaustive treatment of the
modals which occur in a number of specific types of subclauses. What I have in
mind in the first place are the uses of *should* in instances like (5), (6) and (7):

(5)   If you should be interested, I have several books on the subject
       (in conditional subclauses)
(6)   They demand that there should be a vote (after a main clause with a main
       verb reporting a directive, like *demand, suggest, order*)
(7)   It is odd that they should mention it (after a matrix clause like
       it is odd/surprising, etc.)

Each of these will have to be studied separately. At present it seems to me that,
although some of these uses are diachronically relatable to deontic modality,
they are too distinct from it synchronically to be treated as instances of the
basic modality types. At least those exemplified by (6) could be considered as
realizations of a *mood*-operator *Subju(nctive)*: they alternate with subjunctives
in the older stages of the language and to some extent in present-day written
American English.

The use of *may/might* in subclauses of purpose will have to be taken care of
in a similar way, cf. (8):

(8)   We did it so that you might benefit from it

5. *The modals as independent predicates*

Dealing with the modals as independent predicates means deciding about predicate
type, number and roles of arguments and assignment of nuclear functions (specifically, Subject assignment). Taking inspiration from Bolkestein (1980), I turn
to epistemic modals (5.1), deontic modals (5.2) and facultative modals (5.3.)
successively.

Unless otherwise stated all modals are regarded as *States* with *zero*-role
arguments, in accordance with the name given by Dik (1978) to States of Affairs
which are [-control] and [-dynamic].

The following conventions will be adopted. Superscript arabic numerals will
be added to the modal to mark the modality type, superscript 1 standing for
epistemic, superscript 2 for deontic and superscript 3 for facultative modality
(in the single case where subtypes are considered, viz. for deontic modality,
lower case letters will be added; thus $must^{2a}$ represents a subtype of deontic
modality which differs from the subtype denoted by $must^{2b}$). The second convention
is the use of subscript *mv* to mark the modals as *modal verbs* (e.g. $must_{mv}$).

5.1. *Epistemic modals*

Epistemic modals can be dealt with as one-place predicates taking a predication
as their single argument. There is at least one important restriction on this
argument. It cannot be an *Action*, unless it is further prefixed by a *Progressive,*
Perfective or *Habitual* predicate operator (note that Dik 1983c provides us with
Progr and *Perf* only). Following Steedman (1977), we can posit a hyperclass of
predications ('situations'), which includes States together with other predication types prefixed by *Progr*, *Perf* and *Hab*. Note, however, that, in addition, we
have to allow for (unprefixed) *Positions* and *Processes* as well, witness the
acceptability of (9) and (10). Further investigation is in order here.[6]

(9)   John may stand in the rain now (besides the more usual *John may be*
         standing in the rain now) (a Position)
(10)   She may take fight   (an experiential Process with 'future inter-
         pretation')

The different epistemic contribution of individual modals will have to be
specified in the lexicon. Thus epistemic *must* gets the following predicate frame:

(11)

$$\text{must}^{1}_{mv} \quad (x_1 : \begin{Bmatrix} \text{situation} \\ \text{position} \\ \text{process} \end{Bmatrix} \quad (x_1))_{\emptyset}$$

Subject assignment will be to (one of) the argument(s) in the embedded predication. Hence to arrive at (12) we would get (13) as the underlying predication
after syntactic function assignment:

(12)   Jack must have been fetched by Jill

(13) must^{1}_{mv} (Perf fetch$_V$ (Jill)$_{Ag}$ (Jack)$_{GoSubj})_{\emptyset}$

The fact that the selection restrictions for the argument(s) are entirely determined within the embedded predication is a semantic argument against the treatment of the epistemic modals as full predicates. A further argument may be
derived from the fact that it is hard to pronominalize the underlying predication
as a whole, witness the oddity of (15b) as a reply to (14), whereas (15a) is
fully acceptable.

(14)   Do you think that Jack and Jill will marry?
(15) a. They may
       b.?It may (In Dutch *Het kan* is the rule)

Possible refinements

1. A further subdivision might be adopted to distinguish between subjective
epistemic modality (exemplified by (16)) and objective (theoretical) inferential
modality (as in (17)). If this is done, they might be given two different super-
scripts, 1a and 1b respectively. Subjective epistemic modals should somehow be
relatable to *speaker's judgement*, a dimension to be added to the pragmatic
repertoire of FG.

(16)   It may be true
(17)   It can be true

2. As has often been pointed out in the treatment of English modals (see e.g. Halliday 1970), the correlation between e.g. epistemic *may* and epistemic *might* (*must*: *should/ought*, etc.) is one of increased tentativeness in the second member of these pairs. A similar correlation exists between deontic and also between facultative pairs, at least to the extent that they typically function in hypothetical context. The subject requires further elaboration in an FG context.

5.2. Deontic modals

Deontic modals can also be assigned the status of one-place predicates, though an additional possibility should be considered in which they are also two-place predicates.

The single argument of the one-place predicate or, alternatively, the second argument of the two-place predicate is a full predication. Again an important restriction can be imposed on them: they must be 'events' (also Steedman's terminology), i.e. (roughly) non-progressive, non-perfective, controlled states of affairs in complementary distribution with *situations* (see 5.1). Again further investigation is needed. Observe that the quasi-modal *have to* (which typically expresses so-called 'external obligation') permits combination with *States*, whereas *States* trigger off an epistemic interpretation with *must*, cf. (18) and (19):

(18)   You have to be clever to finish (your studies) in four years' time
(19)   You must be clever to finish (your studies) in four years' time

One-place deontic modals would be assigned predication structure (20):

(20)   must/may (etc.)$_{mv}^{2a}$ $(x_1: \text{event } (x_1))_{\emptyset}$

Again Subject assignment is to one of the arguments in the embedded predication. Hence (21) will be like (22) at the stage where syntactic functions have been assigned:

(21)   Jack may be kissed by Jill
(22)   may$_{mv}^{2a}$ (kiss$_V$ (Jill)$_{Ag}$ (Jack)$_{GoSubj}$)$_{\emptyset}$

The argument for postulating two-place deontic predicates is that often the subject of the modal can be thought of as having a semantic role in relation to the permission or obligation expressed by the modal (it is the entity that has the permission or is under obligation). Probably this is even the rule when we have an animate subject, except when the underlying predication is passivized. What exactly this role is within FG is not clear to me at present. We could say that it should express that the entity concerned is somehow 'affected by the obligation or permission', but within a State-predication there appears to be no other possibility than $\emptyset$ (unless we accept Experiencer-roles there). We therefore propose the following predicate frame:

(23) $\text{must/may}^{2b}_{mv}$ $(x_1: \text{animate } (x_1))_\emptyset$ $(x_2: \{\varphi (x_1) \dots (x_n)\} (x_2): \text{event } (x_2))_\emptyset$

Subject assignment is to the first argument; the x_1-argument in the embedded predication, being identical with the x_1 in the higher predication, remains un-expressed; no Subject assignment takes place in the embedded predication.

The issue whether animate Subjects of deontic modals reflect the role 'affected by the permission/obligation' or not is crucial, not only when it comes to de-ciding about one or two-place predicates, but probably also as regards choosing between predicate formation versus independent predicate status. Rejecting an independent first role should favour the predicate formation position, the more so as it is impossible to pronominalize the second of the two arguments in (23), witness (24):

(24)   - Must Jack and Jill fetch a pail of water?
        - Yes, they must
         *Yes, they must it

The situation in Dutch or French is different;[7] we can say *Dat moeten ze* 'That they must', *Ils le doivent*. (Cf. however, the oddity of (25).)

(25)   - Mag Jack door Jill gezoend worden? 'May Jack be kissed by Jill?'
        - ? Ja, dat mag hij 'Yes, that he may' (Here we would prefer *Ja, het mag* 'Yes, it may' which seems to reflect a one-place predicate)

Further observations

1. The opposition between directive and non-directive cuts across the two types of deontic modals distinguished and is pragmatically determined. To account for it further pragmatic elaborations of FG are required. Both the notions 'speaker-

orientation' and 'discourse-orientation' (see Palmer 1979: 2.4.3.) will have to
be taken into account in this context.

2. Dutch sentences like (26) require a three-place structure, i.e. they have an
addition source-satellite); they have no parallels in English:

(26)   Jan mag van mij niet komen
         John may from me   not   come
         'I do not allow John to come'

5.3. Facultative modals

They are best treated as two-place predicates. I classify them as States, though
at least volitional *will/would* might come out with an Experiencer-role in a refined classification of Dik's class of *State*-predicates (again the problem is
outside the scope of this paper).

The first argument may be given the restriction *animate*, but this is no more
than a strongly preferential feature, given instances like (27):

(27)   This mixture can/won't dissolve in water

Note however, that cases like this could be considered as *shifts* (see 7). The
second argument is again an embedded predication which must be an event (see
5.2). This gives us predications of the type:

(28)   can/will (etc.)$_{mv}^{3}$ $(x_1:$?animate $(x_1))_{\emptyset/?Exp}$

$(x_2: \{\varphi (x_1)...(x_n)\}$ $(x_2:$ event $(x_2))_{\emptyset}$

Subject assignment will be to x_1; in the embedded predication x_1 remains un-
expressed. Note that the combination with passives also produces shifts, away
from purely facultative meanings (as is illustrated by (29) and (30), except
when volitional *will* is combined with the negation (as in (31)), where the facultative meaning *can* be preserved:

(29)   Jack will be met by Jill (predictive or epistemic)
(30)   That weight can't be lifted by anyone (from Palmer 1979, § 5.3.6)[8]
(31)   Jack won't be treated like a child

The main argument for a treatment of facultative modals as two-place predicates is of course semantic. The selection restrictions are not just those of the embedded predication, but also between the first argument (x_1) and the modal (this argument is viewed as being endowed with the given capacity or the volition (willingness)). Pronominalization also seems to bring this out, though x_2 cannot be pronominalized, as illustrated in (32):

(32)   - Can Jill carry a pail of water?
      - Yes, she can
       *Yes, she can it (cf. again Dutch 'Ze kan het' and French 'Elle le peut')

6. Predicate formation

Let me now indicate how the three main modality types can be dealt with in terms of predicate formation within FG. This requires rules of the type (33) (adapted from Vet's (1981a) rule for French epistemic modals):

$$(33) \qquad \varphi \; (x_1) \ldots (x_n) \; \rightarrow \; \left[\begin{Bmatrix} \text{may}_{mv} \\ \text{must}_{mv} \\ \text{etc.} \end{Bmatrix} \varphi \right] (x_1) \ldots (x_n)$$

In this rule φ stands for some predicate with its associated arguments, and *mv* for any modal verb. With respect to the semantic differentiation between *epistemic, deontic* and *facultative* modality we can maintain the distinction between *mv1, mv2* and *mv3* (according to the modality type) and impose parallel restrictions on the predicate which combines with them (roughly, *situations* for *mv1* as opposed to *events* for *mv2* and *mv3*).[9] Subject assignment for the derived predicate works in the same way as for the input predicate.

As pointed out above this proposal has the advantage of bringing out the specific status of the modals between full auxiliaries (the uses discussed in section 4, for which we proposed a treatment as predicate operators) and full verbs. It also accounts for the impossibility of pronominalizing the single argument of the epistemic modals and of the second argument with facultative and two-place deontic modals, which presented us with a difficulty in the treatment of these modals as predicates in their own right.

On the other hand it obscures the fact that for facultative modals and (although the case is less compelling there) certain deontic modals the constituent that turns up as Subject is indeed a separate argument in relation to the facultative or deontic modal.

All in all there seem to be good arguments for dealing with epistemic modals as instances of predicate formation, whereas facultative modals can best be argued on semantic grounds to be independent predicates. The deontic modals appear to hover in between. On the other hand it is clear that the syntactic arguments prove that all the English modals have become less central instances of independent predicates (if that is what one wants to consider them as).

7. Blends and shifts

To place the foregoing in a somewhat broader perspective I round off with a brief consideration of blends (in the sense of Halliday 1970) and shifts between the different modality types.

7.1. Blends

Instances like (34) may be a blend between a permission and a facultative reading:

(34)   Jack can't come

If we take the independent predicate position, (34) would have to be given the underlying predication (35):

$$(35) \quad \left\{ \begin{array}{l} \text{Neg Pres can}^2_{mv} \ (\text{come}_V \ (\text{Jack})_{Ag})_\emptyset \\ \text{Neg Pres can}^3_{mv} \ (x_1: \text{Jack} \ (x_1))_\emptyset \ (\text{come}_V (x_1)_{Ag})_\emptyset \end{array} \right\}$$

Subject assignment would result in identical linguistic expression, hence the blend.

In the derived predicate approach a double application of rule (33) would apply as is indicated in (36):

$$(36) \quad \left\{ \begin{array}{l} \text{come}_V (\text{Jack})_{Ag} \ \rightarrow \ \text{can}^2_{mv} \ \text{come}_V (\text{Jack})_{Ag} \\ \text{come}_V (\text{Jack})_{Ag} \ \rightarrow \ \text{can}^3_{mv} \ \text{come}_V (\text{Jack})_{Ag} \end{array} \right\}$$

again yielding a single structure after Subject assignment, as required.

Blends of this type would come out less neatly, however, if we decide on different solutions for the different modality types (e.g. predicate formation for the deontic versus independent predicate for the facultative modal).

7.2. *Shifts*

An important feature if one wants to understand the diachronic development of
the modals is their susceptibility to shifts. In the two approaches considered
the transition from deontic to epistemic modals would come out as a shift in the
state of affairs (especially from *event* to *situation*). The relation can also be
demonstrated synchronically as existing between a pair like (37) and (38):

(37)   Jill must travel up the hill (*travel* is an event; deontic)

(38)   Jill must be travelling up the hill (*be travelling* is *Progr*, hence a
         situation; epistemic)

At this point there would seem to be no principled objection to viewing the
shift as one from independent predicate (the deontic instance) to one that results from predicate formation (the epistemic example).

8. *Conclusion*

In this paper I have argued that in dealing with the English modals within FG a
first distinction should be made between, on the one hand, the basic modality
types and, on the other, the other grammaticalized uses as in the future or conditional tenses or in certain types of subclause.

The latter can be taken care of in terms of predicate operators. As regards
the former two solutions offer themselves: predicate formation or predicates in
their own right. Syntactic arguments seem to plead for predicate formation, but
there appear to be semantic arguments in favour of an independent predicate approach for facultative and (less outspokenly) for certain deontic modals. Which-
ever solution we approach, a distinction like that between *situations* and *events*
with further refinements is essential to differentiate between *epistemic* (which
typically requires combination with situations) and *deontic/facultative* modality
(where as a rule we get *events*). The distinction also deepens our insight into
certain shifts exhibited by the English modals.

As regards the necessity to expand FG so that it may cope more adequately
with a far-reaching phenomenon like the modals and modality, it was found that
a number of refinements are in order. In the first place further research into
the classification of states of affairs appears to be necessary, secondly additions will have to be made to the set of predicate operators, thirdly FG should
try to integrate additional pragmatic dimensions like speaker-orientation and
discourse-orientation. Finally, a general clarification of the demarcation

between predicate operators, predicate formation and independent predicate status deserves fuller investigation.

Obviously most if not all of my suggestions will have to be reviewed in the light of such further research.

NOTES

*   I wish to express my thanks to the editors of this volume (especially Machtelt Bolkestein) and to Co Vet for their critical remarks on earlier versions of this paper. Also to R. Gebruers for drawing my attention to Steedman (1977).

1   This is at least the case in most European languages. Samplings for Thai, Chinese and Arabic point in the same direction. To what extent it is a near-universal remains to be investigated. Such an investigation would have to ascertain, first, whether a given language (family) has the category modal verb, secondly, which modality dimensions are realized by individual modal verbs.

2   See in this respect Goossens (1982).

3   For a survey of the alternative ways of expression, see Halliday (1970).

4   Obviously this needs further elaboration. Inspiration can be taken from Givón (1979) and Lehmann (1982).

5   'Mood' refers to the opposition indicative: subjunctive: imperative (etc.).

6   For recent work on the classification of states of affairs within FG we refer to De Groot (this volume), R. Gebruers (work in progress) and Vester (1983).

7   I owe this observation to Co Vet (personal communication)

8   Palmer points out that *can* with a capacity-reading is not 'voice-neutral', which is his way of saying that the facultative meaning is not preserved in the combination with a passive.

9   This is only a first approximation, as pointed out in sections 5.1 and 5.2.

Chapter 12

The predicative relatives of French perception verbs

Johan van der Auwera
TEW Department, University of Antwerp

*0. Introduction**

Perception verbs express a relation between a perceiver (Experiencer) and something perceived (Goal). In French, as in many (most?) other languages, the Goal
may be expressed by a clause. French then uses the general subordinator *que*
'that':

(1)   J'ai   vu   *que* Paul fumait
        I have seen that Paul smoked
        'I have seen that Paul smoked'

The two-place frame of *voir* 'see' instantiated in (1) can be formalized as (2)
(cf. Dik 1981b: 32-33):

(2) $voir_V$ $(x_1)_{Exp}$ $(x_2: [\ldots] (x_2))_{Go}$

It is customary to call a clausal Goal a 'complement (clause)' and the subordinator used to introduce a complement (clause) can be called a 'complementizer'.[1]

   Voir has a second complement predicate frame, in which it opens three places
(cf. Dik 1981b: 32-33).

(3)   J'ai   vu Paul fumer
        I have seen Paul smoke
        'I have seen Paul smoke'

(4) $voir_V$ $(x_1)_{Exp}$ $(x_2)_{Go}$ $(x_3: [\ldots (x_2)_{Subj} \ldots] (x_3))_{Go}$

The formalization in (4) is only a first approximation. For one thing, perhaps
the (x_3) should not be considered to be a Goal (cf. Dik 1981b: 38).[2] For another
thing, as it stands, (4) formalizes only one of the selection restrictions of
the three-place predication, viz. the one requiring the subject of (x_3) to be
identical to (x_2). But there are more restrictions: the (x_3) predication must
refer to an observable process and there are also tense and aspect restrictions
(cf. Declerck 1981b).

What concerns me in this paper is yet a third pattern. Consider (5):

(5)   J'ai   vu   Paul *qui fumait*
        I have seen Paul who smoked
        'I have seen Paul smoking'

In (5) the Goal is followed by a relative clause and yet the meaning of (5) is close to that of (1) and closer still to that of (3). In other words, it seems that a relative clause is functioning as a complement clause. How is this possible? Perhaps because *qui fumait* really IS a complement clause rather than a relative clause, and *qui* a complementizer rather than a relative pronoun. In this view, things are not what they appear to be: complementizers and complement clauses are 'mas-*que*-rading' as relative pronouns and relative clauses. In this paper, I will argue the opposite point of view: things are what they appear to be. I do not deny that (5) has a complement clause meaning, but I will claim that the complement clause in (5) is not *qui fumait* but *Paul qui fumait*. Of course, I will have to make clear how a relative clause can combine with what seems to be its antecedent and yield a complement clause, but here I can rely on a century of French scholarship saying that there are relative clauses that are not restrictive, nor appositive, nor free, but predicative. I will also claim that the fact that *voir* can have a complement clause that contains a relative clause must be honored with a separate predicate-frame, in which *voir* is neither simply two-place nor three-place, but something in between.

In section 1, I will put the problem of (5) in a broader context and point to some related structures in other languages. In section 2, it will be shown how (5) is puzzling in at least 10 ways. In section 3, I will give my analysis.

1. Some related issues

1.1. Complementizers and relative pronouns

In part the problem of (5) concerns the relation between complementizers and relative pronouns. A minimal claim is that they are often homophonous. This is the case with English *that* and French *que*:

(6) a.   I believe *that* John has seen me
    b.   The book *that* I have written ...
(7) a.   Je crois   *que* Jean m' a   vu
          I believe that John me has seen

    b.   Le livre *que* j'ai   écrit ...
          the book that I have written

A stronger claim, first made by Jespersen (1885) for *that* and still found in
both TG and FG (cf. Van der Auwera 1984d) is that this homophony is indicative
of an identity: both *that*'s and *que*'s would be complementizers.

At first sight, the complementizer thesis on relative *que* is weaker than that
on relative *that*. In the paradigm of English relativizers, *that* would be a morphological isolate, and unlike the WH-forms (*who, whom, what, whose, which,
where*, ...), it does not have any interrogative use:

(8)   *Who/Whom/What/Which/Whose/Where/*That* did you eat?

Que, on the other hand, seems to form a morphological object-subject paradigm
with *qui*, and both allow an interrogative use:

(9) a. Le livre *que*   / *qui*   j' ai   lu ...
        the book which$_{acc}$ which$_{nom}$ I have read

     b. La femme *qui* / *que*   m' a   vu ...
        the woman who$_{nom}$ whom$_{acc}$ me has seen

(10) a. *Que* voulez-vous?
        what want   you

     b. *Qui* a   dit cela?
        who has said that

Thus the very existence of this *qui-que* alternation provides prima facie counter-
evidence to the complementizer view on relative *que*. Of course, prima facie
observations may deceive. The point about the *qui-que* alternation disappears if
one has *independent* reasons for thinking that even relative *qui* is a complementizer. This view is found in TG and the locus classicus is Kayne (1976): in his
view, *qui* is the variant of *que* that appears - roughly - when the latter is
immediately followed by a tensed verb. This variation is handled by a *que* → *qui*
rule.

Diachronically speaking, the claim that relative *qui* is a complementizer is
most implausible (cf. Harris 1978: 204-218; Jokinen 1978). Synchronically
speaking, simple relatives like those in (9) do not lend any obvious support to
the complementizer view on relative *qui* either. Yet French does have two types
of constructions in which relative *qui* seems to introduce complement clauses. It
is here, of course, that the *qui fumait* of (5) comes in again:

(5)   J'ai vu Paul *qui fumait*

Paul qui fumait does not distinguish one Paul from another, which is what one would expect if it involved a relative clause. Just like a complement clause, it says what it was that the speaker saw. So perhaps the *qui* of (5) is a complement-izer. Besides, the structure 'perceived entity - complementizer - tensed clause with the perceived entity as subject' is clearly documented in other languages, e.g. Rumanian ((11), Suñer 1984: 269) and Serbo-Croatian ((12), Gvozdanović 1981: 137):

(11)   Am   auzit-o   *că*   spunea   prostii
         have heard-her that   was talking nonsense
         'I have heard her talking nonsense'

(12)   Ivan   vidi PETAR / Petra   *da*   svira sonatu
         John$_{nom}$ sees Peter$_{nom}$ Peter$_{acc}$ that plays sonata$_{acc}$
                      contrastive
                      stress
         'John sees Peter play a sonata'

Romanian *că* and Serbo-Croatian *da* are unmistakable complementizers.

The second special *qui* construction is illustrated in (13):

(13)   L' homme que je crois   *qui* vient ...
         the man that I believe   comes
         'the man that I believe is coming ...'

Here, too, the *qui* clause does not in any obvious way restrict the reference of an antecedent; it rather seems to constitute a complement to the verb *croire* 'believe'.

As mentioned in section 1, this paper will focus on *J'ai vu Paul qui fumait* sentences, but at least I have shown how this problem bears on the *general* issue of the categorial status of *qui* and even that of *que*. My point of view on the '*que-qui* cascade' in (13) is hinted at in Van der Auwera (1984a) and further developed in Van der Auwera (1984c).

1.2. Other languages

It is good to signal that the phenomenon in (5) is by no means an exclusive property of French. It exists in Italian ((14), Radford 1977: 155) and in Spanish ((15), Suñer 1978: 107):[3]

(14)   Giorgio vide Maria *che* piangeva
         Giorgio saw Maria   was crying
         'Giorgio saw Maria crying'

(15)   Oigo   a Maria *que* toca   la guitarra
         I-hear   Maria   is playing the guitar
         'I hear Maria playing the guitar'

Note that the complementizer and complement clause theorist will have an easier
time with Spanish and Italian than with French: the former lack a *qui-que* contrast and they are both PRO-DROP languages, i.e. their *che/que* clauses could be
argued to have a covert subject.

   The case of English is more interesting. First, Declerck (1981a, 1981b: 105-
109, 1982: 4-11) has pointed out that the phenomenon marginally exists for
finite relative clauses. Though it is difficult with explicit perception verbs,
it is easier when the perception is understood:[4]

(16) a. ?? I hear Jim *who's falling down the stairs*

     b. - (Jane, on hearing a noise in the corridor) What is that?

        - (John, looking into the corridor) It's John *who's falling down the*
           stairs!

Dutch seems to be similar in this respect (cf. Van Langendonck 1983: 448):[5]

(17) a. ?? Ik hoor Marie die zingt
           I hear Mary who sings

     b.   Wat hoor ik? Marie die zingt
           what hear I   Mary who sings
           'What do I hear? Mary singing'

Note that cases without an explicit perception verb are found in French, too (cf.
Schwarze 1974: 29; Rothenberg 1979: 362-392).

(18)   Il est là-bas *qui arrose*
         he is there   who celebrates
         'He's over there celebrating'

Here, too, the perception is implicit: *il est là-bas* means as much as *le voilà*
'look at him' (cf. Schwarze 1974: 29-30).

   Second, the phenomenon may be clearer with participial relatives:

(19) a. Passengers *leaving on flight 655* are requested to go to gate 7

    b. I saw the passengers *leaving on flight 655*

Of course, the status of the participle following a perception verb is much
contested (cf. Declerck 1981a, 1981b, 1982) and few linguists have analyzed the
participle in (19b) as relative. Note that I am suggesting that it is a very
peculiar type of relative, as peculiar as the *qui fumait* of (5). French actually
supplies some indirect support for this idea: instead of finite clause relatives
French perception verbs also allow participles and the two constructions are
nearly synonymous (cf. Hatcher 1944: 400-405):

(20) a. Je le vois *qui sourit*
        I him see who smiles
        'I see him smiling'

    b. Je le vois *souriant*
        I him see smiling

2. The data

Let us now have a detailed look at the French data. Abbreviating and simultaneously generalizing, I will henceforth call the *qui fumait* of (5) a 'P-*qui* clause'
- 'P' for 'perception'.

On the whole, previous investigators have agreed that P-*qui* clauses are
puzzling in at least ten ways. Points (i), (iv) and (ix) restate some of the
observations made in section 1.1 and 1.2.

(i) On the surface, a P-*qui* clause does not seem to be appositive, for it lacks
the latter's characteristic comma intonation. Yet, if it is restrictive, it is
not obvious how it restricts the potential reference of its antecedent (cf. De
Geest 1973a: 157, 1973b: 239-240; Grevisse 1980: 1325; Declerck 1981a: 142).

(ii) The 'antecedent' can be a proper name, which is impossible for a normal
restrictive relative (cf. Radford 1975: 36-37; Declerck 1981a: 142).

(iii) The 'antecedent' can be an atonic clitic pronoun, which is impossible for
normal relatives (cf. Schwarze 1974: 21; Radford 1975: 37; Rothenberg 1979:
363-365):

(21) a.*Je *le* connais qui a   écrit   ce livre
        I him know   who has written that book

    b. Je *le* connais, *celui* qui a   écrit   ce livre
        I him know   him   who has written that book
        'I know him, the one who has written that book'

(21b) still contains *le*, but it is the tonic Tail *celui* which is the antecedent.

(iv) The P-*qui* construction is restricted to a very specific set of main clause predicates, mostly verbs of perception and discovery (cf. Haas 1909: 261); Wagner-Pinchon 1962: 564; Schwarze 1974: 18-19, 22, 29; Härmä 1979: 84-85; Rothenberg 1979: 393-395; Grevisse 1980: 1325). Ordinary relative clauses are not subject to this restriction.

(v) The 'relativized' constituent must be the subject of its clause.

(22)   Je l' ai   vu   *que* Jean frappait
        I him have seen   John hit
        'I have seen John hit him'

Kayne (1975: 127), Radford (1975: 38), and Rothenberg (1979: 372) would give (22) a star, Schwarze (1974: 21) a question mark. The point is again that ordinary relatives are not restricted to subjects.

(vi) If the 'antecedent' is the subject of a passive verb, the P-*qui* clause must immediately follow the verb, i.e. it cannot immediately follow its 'antecedent', in contradistinction to normal relatives (cf. Kayne 1975: 127):

(23) a. Ton frère a   été vu   qui volait   son voisin
        your brother has been seen   was robbing his neighbor
        'Your brother has been seen robbing his neighbor'

     b.*Ton frère qui volait son voisin a été vu

(vii) Another special restriction is that the P-*qui* clause typically describes a directly perceivable process. It does not normally describe a state (cf. Schwarze 1974: 22-24; Radford 1975: 40; Rothenberg 1979: 372):

(24)   ? Je l' ai   vu   qui était petit
         I him have seen   was   small
         'I saw him being small'

And it cannot normally contain negation or modality (cf. Schwarze 1974: 22-24; Radford 1975: 40; Rothenberg 1979: 374-375):

(25) a. Je le regardais qui *ne* bougeait *pas*
        I him watched   not moved   (not)
        'I watched him not moving'

b.?Je le vois qui *n'* arrive   *pas*
  I him see   not arrives (not)
  'I see him not arriving'

c. Je le vois qui *veut* travailler
   I him see   wants work
   'I see him wanting to work'

d.?Je le vois qui *peut* travailler
   I him see   can work
   'I see him having the permission to work'

(25a) and (25c) are acceptable in a context in which the speaker perceived some-
body's attempts not to move or eagerness to work. It is much harder, though not
impossible, to consider not arriving (in (25b)) or being permitted to work (in
(25d)) as a process.

(viii) The perception is represented as taking place during the time the P-*qui*
clause process is taking place, and the P-*qui* clause verb must be imperfective
(cf. Hatcher 1944; Gross 1968: 125; Schwarze 1974: 22; Kayne 1975: 127; Radford
1975: 38-39; Declerck 1981a: 140). Thus (26a) is unacceptable because present
and past time processes cannot take place together; (26b) is out because the
'relative' clause verb has a 'passé simple', which is perfective.

(26) a.*Je le *vois* qui *courait* à toute vitesse
       I him see   ran   at full speed
       'I see him having run at full speed'

  b.*Je l' ai   vue qui *fit* la vaisselle
     I her have seen   did the dishes
     'I saw her doing the dishes'

No such tense or aspect constraints hold for ordinary relatives.

(ix) The meaning of the P-*qui* constellation is close to that of a *que* clause,
closer still to that of an infinitival complement, and closest to that of a
present participle (cf. Haas 1909: 261; Hatcher 1944; Wagner-Pinchon 1962: 564;
De Geest 1973b: 239-241; Schwarze 1974: 24; Kayne 1975: 128; Radford 1975: 36;
Rothenberg 1979: 379-391; Declerck 1981b).

(x) With respect to various pronominalization phenomena, the P-*qui* clause sides
with complement clauses instead of ordinary relative clauses (cf. Radford 1975:
43-46). For example, when an ordinary antecedent-relative clause constellation
is in Tail position, then the predication contains a pronoun agreeing in gender
and number with the antecedent. In (27a) the antecedent is feminine and singular
and so is the pronoun *la*. In (27b), however, we get neuter *ça*, the pronoun that
is typical for complement clauses (27c):

(27) a. Tout le monde *la* déteste, la femme qui habite ...
         whole the world her detests the woman who lives
         'Everyone detests her, the woman who lives ...'

     b. Je n' ai   jamais vu *ça* Marie qui joue du piano
         I not have ever seen that Maria   plays   piano
         'I have never seen that, Maria playing the piano'

     c. Vous ne m' avez jamais dit *ça,* que vous êtes communiste
         you not me have ever   said that that you are communist
         'You have never told me that, that you are a communist'

3. The analysis

3.1. Predicative relatives

Do the above points still allow us to hold on to the idea that P-*qui* is a relative pronoun and its clause a relative clause? I think so, but only if we en-
dorse the claim of classical French grammar (e.g. Tobler 1896; Sandfeld 1936:
146-149; Grevisse 1980: 1325) that there are relative clauses which are not
restrictive, not appositive, not free, but predicative, and that P-*qui* relatives
are predicative (for endorsements in Dependency Grammar, see Rothenberg 1972,
1979; Van Langendonck 1983).

The way to understand predicative relatives is to start from the idea that
relative clauses are essentially clauses that function as adjectives (cf.
Lehmann 1984: 145-252) and that one would therefore expect them to be able to do
whatever adjectives can do. Thus both adjectives and relative clauses can be
restrictive as well as appositive.

(28) a. the *clever* and *shrewd* linguists ...
     b. the linguists *that were clever and shrewd* ...
(29) a. the linguists, *clever and shrewd,* ...
     b. the linguists, *who were clever and shrewd,* ...

Adjectives can function as substantives; when a relative clause does this, we
call it a 'free relative'.

(30) a. The *Spanish* do it the Spanish way
     b. *Whatever is Spanish* should have something to do with Spain

A fourth use of adjectives is the predicative one. In French, predicative adjectives take a copula, but in what I may impressionistically call 'mini-clauses'
they can do without.

(31) a. Son bébé était *malade*
    her baby was   ill
    'Her baby was ill'

   b. Avec son bébé *malade*, elle ne peut quitter la maison
    with her baby ill   she not can leave   the house
    'With her baby being ill, she can't leave the house'

Relative clauses can be used predicatively, too, though it seems to be a highly restricted phenomenon (cf. Lehmann 1984: 310, 357). The French examples of copula-less predicative adjectives and relatives in (32) and (33) are due to Rothenberg (1979: 360, 356):

(32)   Je voyais ... les amis   de M, les uns   *célèbres*, les autres
       I saw   the friends of M the ones famous   the others

       qui allaient l'être
       who went   it be
       'I saw the friends of M, some famous, the others who were going to be famous'

(33) a. Il a   les cheveux *blonds*
    he has the hairs   blond
    'His hair is blond'

   b. Il a   les cheveux *qui*   *tombent*
    he has the hairs   which fall
    'His hair is falling out'

P-*qui* clauses, now, are yet another subtype of predicative relatives:

(34) a. Je l' ai   vu   *ivre*
    I him have seen drunk
    'I saw him drunk'

   b. Je l' ai   vu   *qui mourait*
    I him have seen who died
    'I saw him dying'

Let us make the claim that P-*qui* clauses are predicative relatives more explicit in the following subclaims:

   (i) in a sentence like (5) *Paul* is not really an antecedent but a subject;

  (ii) *qui fumait* in (5) is simultaneously a relative clause and a predicate;

 (iii) together *Paul* and *qui fumait* constitute a predication, more particularly, an embedded one;

  (iv) ordinary antecedents and subjects coupled with predicative relatives have in common that they govern the number of the relative clause predicates; to reflect this, I will call them both 'governors'.

(35) a. J' ai   vu   les élèves *qui   étaient dans ma classe*
        I have seen the pupils that were   in my class
        'I have seen the pupils that were in my class'

     b. J' ai   vu   les élèves *qui entraient*
        I have seen the pupils who came in
        'I have seen the pupils coming in'

> *étaient* and *entraient* are both plural; in both cases this is due to
> *élèves*, which is an antecedent for the restrictive relative in (35a), yet
> a subject for the predicative relative in (35b).

With these hypotheses in mind we can go back to the puzzles of section 2. We
can take care of four of them. First, we have explained point (i): *qui fumait* is
a relative clause, even though it is neither restrictive nor appositive. Second,
it does not matter that proper names cannot be antecedents of restrictive relatives (point (ii)), for *qui fumait* is not a restrictive relative, and *Paul* is
not an antecedent; we are dealing with an embedded predication and its subject.
Third and fourth, saying that *Paul qui fumait* forms an embedded predication is
another way of saying that it is a complement clause (point (ix)); hence it is
also pronominalized as one (point (x)).

3.2. A new predicate frame

In one way, a P-*qui* relative is more permissive than an ordinary restrictive or
appositive relative. Restating point (ii) of section 2, P-*qui* relatives can even
have atonic clitic pronouns as governors. In another way, however, a P-*qui* relative is less permissive. In ordinary relatives, the only higher clause constituent to impose any selection restrictions on the relative clause is the
governor. In a P-*qui* clause, the higher clause predicate exerts its influence,
too (section 2, points (iv), (vii), and (viii)). This complement-predicate dependency, it seems to me, must be honored in a special predicate frame.[6] To do this,
we must first find a way to represent predicative relatives.

A predicative relative is a relative clause. Thus I will represent it as a
predication enclosed in square brackets and I will further assume that I may
give the relativized term, i.e. the open place for the governor, an R operator
(cf. Rijksbaron 1981: 235-237):

(36) $[\ldots (Rx_1) \ldots]$

A predicative relative is also a predicate, more specifically, a non-verbal one (cf. Dik 1980a: 90-112). Predicates are surrounded by curly brackets. Thus an entire predication of the *Paul qui fumait* type comes out as follows:

(37) $\{[\ldots (Rx_i) \ldots]_{SUB}\} (x_i)_{\emptyset}$

Of course, in (5) the predication *Paul qui fumait* functions as a term and its semantic function is arguably that of Goal.

(38) $(x_j: [\{[\ldots (Rx_i) \ldots]_{SUB}\} (x_i)_{\emptyset}] (x_j))_{Go}$

This gives us the following first attempt to give *voir* its P-*qui* predicate frame:

(39) $voir_V (x_k)_{Exp} (x_j: [\{[\ldots (Rx_i) \ldots]_{SUB}\} (x_i)_{\emptyset}] (x_j))_{Go}$

I will now amend (39) in two ways. First, we know from section 2 (point (v)) that the governor must be the Subject of the relative.

(40) $voir_V (x_k)_{Exp} (x_j: [\{[\ldots (Rx_i)_{Subj} \ldots]_{SUB}\} (x_i)_{\emptyset}] (x_j))_{Go}$

Second, I propose to treat (x_3) both as a zero function argument with respect to the predicative relative and as a Goal with respect to *voir*.

(41) $voir_V (x_k)_{Exp} (x_j: [\{[\ldots (Rx_i)_{Subj} \ldots]_{SUB}\} (x_i)_{\emptyset Go}] (x_j))_{Go}$

Giving one term two semantic functions may well be new in FG, but there cannot be any principled objection to it, especially not when we see that FG already sanctions a term's having two syntactic functions (cf. Dik 1979a). Another strange feature is, of course, that P-*qui* allowing *voir* ('$voir_{P\text{-}qui}$') ends up with two Goals. Again, there cannot be any principled objection to a predication's containing two semantic functions of the same type (cf. Dik 1978: 38-39). And if the double Goal assignment for $voir_{P\text{-}qui}$ is problematic, it is not any *more* problematic than that of the *voir* that takes the infinitive ('$voir_{inf}$'), formalized in (4), repeated here:

(4) $voir_V (x_1)_{Exp} (x_2)_{Go} (x_3: [\ldots (x_2)_{Subj} \ldots] (x_3))_{Go}$

I would suggest that a dual Goal assignment is simply the best tool for representing that speakers of both (3) and (5) express that they have seen two things:
they have seen Paul and they have seen that Paul was smoking.[7] Further evidence
for giving the (x_3) of (41) Goal status is the fact that when it is pronominal,
it takes the clitic *le, la,* or *les,* which are clearly Object-forms (section 2,
point (iii)). Again, there is a problem here: the Goal function is indeed the
first candidate for Object assignment (cf. Dik 1978: 76), but (41) has two Goals.
The problem is identical for (4), however, and a plausible solution easily suggests itself: when there is both a clausal and a (pro)nominal Goal, only the
latter comes in for Object assignment. A third and final piece of support for
giving the (x_3) of (41) Goal status is that it seems to be able to function as a
passive Subject (section 2, point (vi)).

I should stress that (41) is tentative and incomplete. Like (4) it should but
doesn't yet express that the embedded predicate must refer to an observable process (section 2, point (vii)). Neither does (41) reflect any tense or aspect
restrictions (section 2, point (viii)), which are definitely similar, but maybe
not identical to the ones required to complete (4) (cf. Hatcher 1944; Declerck
1981b). However incomplete (41), (4) and even (2), the predicate frame of
'*voir*$_{que}$', may be, they do show how *voir*$_{P-qui}$ is a kind of intermediate case. Like
voir$_{que}$, *voir*$_{P-qui}$ could be said to open two places. This is evidenced by the
fact that *que Paul fumait* and *Paul qui fumait* behave as one constituent, and that
Paul fumer does not. Compare the following triplets - the P-*qui* sentences are due
to Radford (1975: 45) (cf. Van Langendonck 1983: 448):

(42) a. Qu' avez-vous vu? Que Marie faisait du ski?
        what have you seen that Mary made   ski
        'What have you seen? That Mary was skiing?'

   b. Qu'avez-vous vu? Marie qui faisait du ski?

   c.*Qu'avez-vous vu? Marie faire du ski?

(43) a. Ce   que j' ai   vu, c'est que Heath dirigeait l' orchestre
        that that I have seen it is that Heath conducted the orchestra
        'What I have seen is that Heath was conducting the orchestra'

   b. Ce que j'ai vu, c'est Heath qui dirigeait l'orchestre

   c.*Ce que j'ai vu, c'est Heath diriger l'orchestre

It is true that governor and predicative relative do not always behave as a
single constituent. When the perception verb is passivized, the predicative relative cannot immediately follow the governor (section 2, point (vi)). Similarly,
clitic governors must precede the verb - in conformity with the LIPOC principle

(Dik 1978: 192) - rather than the relative. Though we should not forget that governors and relatives can be separated even when the relative is restrictive (see (44)):

(44)   Aucune collection ne serait   complète qui   n'   aurait   pas Tosca
        no   collection not would be complete which not would have not Tosca
        'No collection would be complete which didn't have Tosca'

the ordering rule for clitic governors does make $voir_{P-qui}$ more like $voir_{inf}$.

There are more similarities: (i) both have two Goals, one of which is clausal; (ii) their (pro)nominal Goals are the subject of the predications in the clausal Goals; (iii) their topmost embedded predicates (*fumer* and *qui fumait*) are non-finite; and (iv) their lowest embedded predicates (*fumer*, *fumait*) must refer to a process and are subject to similar tense and aspect restrictions. I suppose that the dual Goal assignment makes $voir_{P-qui}$ a three-place predicate. Does this contradict the claim that it is two-place? Not necessarily. The trouble is, of course, that one place occurs within another. There is no short, clear, and conventional terminology for this. I propose to call $voir_{P-qui}$ a 'three-in-two-place' predicate.

Note, finally, that (41) or better, its future more sophisticated version, has two functions. It describes one use of *voir*, but it also describes the P-*qui* phenomenon itself. A relative clause is a P-*qui* relative just in case it obeys the selection restrictions contained in the predicate frame.

4. *General conclusion*

The verbs that allow P-*qui* clauses have this possibility honored in a predicate frame. In this frame, the verbs open three places, but the unusual feature is that one place is within another. Hence they are partially like two-place predicates and partially like three-place ones.

P-*qui* clauses are relatives, yet they are neither restrictive or appositive, nor free, but predicative. Together with their governors they build complement clauses. Hence the phenomenon as a whole resembles both ordinary restrictive relatives and ordinary complement clauses. Because the P-*qui* clause is relative, there is no reason to doubt that its *qui* is a relative pronoun.

NOTES

*   Thanks are due to Willy van Langendonck.

[1]   The term 'complementizer' is typical of TG and originated in it (Rosenbaum 1967), but it has sneaked into FG, too (e.g. Junger 1981b, Dik 1983d). At present, transformationalists tend to use it in a very wide sense, in which it is synonymous with 'subordinator'. I am using it in the original Rosenbaum sense.

[2]   Dik (1981b: 33) prefers the following predicate frame of English 'three-place' *see*

(i) $(see_V \ (x_1: \ anim(x_1))_{Exp} \ (x_2)_{Go} \ (x_3: [\ldots \ (x_2) \ \ldots]) \ (x_3))_{Compl}$

[3]   Interestingly, the phenomenon does not seem to exist in Latin, yet Latin perception verbs do allow an accusative plus participle construction (cf. Bolkestein 1976: 283-288):

(i) puerum   venientem audio
    child$_{acc}$ coming$_{acc}$ hear
    'I hear the child coming'

This participle is arguably a non-finite relative.

[4]   Declerck (1981a: 149) claims that the perception verb may be explicit, but none of his examples have the 'entity perceived' and the relative clause immediately behind the perception verb. In (i), for example, they occur in Theme position:

(i) The moon *that was rising over the mountain,* that's what you saw

I would rather say that the perception is implicit, as in (16b). In general, I think Declerck overestimates the extent to which relative clauses can appear with complement clause meaning or, in his terminology, the extent to which superficially relative clauses are 'pseudo-modifiers'. Many of his examples are like (ii):

(ii) A   What was that noise yesterday?
     B   It was those drums *that Jimmy was beating*

I regard *that Jimmy was beating*, in its intended non-cleft reading, as an ordinary relative clause. Of course, when the speaker heard the drums that Jimmy was beating, it is most probable that he heard that Jimmy was beating the drums, but this is no reason for denying relative clause status. With this strained notion of 'pseudo-modification', Declerck is able to claim that 'pseudo-modifiers' may have the outward appearance of appositives. (iii) is his example:

(iii)   We heard a loud noise in the kitchen. We opened the door, and what
         did we see? John, who was fighting with a dog!

Few investigators would follow Declerck here (cf. Rothenberg 1972: 18), not even Touratier (1980: 338), who holds that 'pseudo-modifiers' are appositives, yet still does not claim that they have the typically appositive comma intonation. I do not follow Declerck either, for I consider *who was fighting with a dog* to be an ordinary appositive relative. Declerck (1981a: 159) further disagrees with those who claim that 'pseudo-modification' is restricted to embedded subjects. His example is (ii).

5   According to De Geest (1979: 71; cf. also 1973a: 157, 1973b: 240) East-
     Flemish dialects do accept explicit perception verb relatives such as (17a).

6   I realize that a complement-predicate dependency need not be reflected in a
     predicate frame. The fact that *believe* allows both a *that* clause and a
     'pseudo-argument' plus infinitive construction, for example, is taken care
     of through syntactic function assignment rules (cf. Dik 1979a, but also
     Van der Auwera 1983). In Bolkestein et al. (1981) other 'pseudo-argument'
     constructions are analyzed in terms of pragmatics and expression rules. I
     believe it could be shown that such solutions are unsuitable for the P-*qui*
     phenomenon. Note also that the decision to reflect P-*qui* relatives in a
     predicate frame is independent of the question whether this predicate frame
     is basic or derived.

7   Compare a dual semantic function assignment with a dual syntactic function
     assignment as proposed for (i):

     (i)   John believes Fred to be sick

     Though *Fred* can be looked upon as an Object to *believe*, it is certainly not
     a Goal. John only believes one thing, viz. that Fred is sick.

Chapter 13

Morphological causatives in Modern Hebrew

Judith Junger
Institute for General Linguistics, University of Amsterdam

*0. Introduction**

Causatives are constructions dealt with in almost all recent linguistic theories. Their interest lies probably in the wide range of constructions, often in the same language, expressing causativity. Causativity is sometimes inherent in the meaning of the verb, such as with *kill*, *break* and others, and sometimes expressed by means of an auxiliary predicate whose only function is to express causativity, like *cause* and *make*. Syntactically, causativity is closely bound to the topic of transitivity and transitivization.

The analyses of causative constructions vary. Whereas early transformation-alists like Lees (1960) saw causativization in all cases as a purely syntactic transformation by which even sentences like *John broke the window* are derived from a deep structure [John CAUSE [break the window]], later ones, like Jackendoff (1975) and Bresnan (1978), include causativization in the lexicon. Thus according to Jackendoff (1975), *break* in *John broke the window* and in *The window broke* are two different verbs, each with a separate lexical entry. One of the form [NP1 break] and the other of the form [NP2 CAUSE [NP1 break]]. In addition to lexical causatives (i.e. with auxiliary verbs like *cause* or *make*) there are also what Comrie (1981a) calls 'morphological causatives', namely those expressing causativity through the morphology of the verb. This type of construction is to be found for example in Semitic languages like Hebrew and Arabic. This paper will deal with the morphological causatives in Modern Hebrew. Consider the following illustrations:

(1)   hithalti liršom et kol hadvarim   še-*heesiku*   oti
        began-1sg to-note GM[1] all the-things which-made-occupied me
        'I started to write down all the things which occupied me'

(2)   josi *hišmiʔa*   lerina et hataklit   hahadaš
        Josi made-hear to-Rina GM the-record the-new
        'Josi made Rina listen to his new record'

(3)   hašemeš *himema*   et hagagot
        the-sun made-warm GM the-roofs
        'The sun warmed the roofs'

In all these sentences the causativity is expressed by means of the verbal morphology: in (1)-(2) by means of the HIFIL pattern, and in (3) by means of the
PIEL pattern. Each of these two patterns can have other syntactic functions as
well: the HIFIL can also express 'active-transitive' or inchoativeness, and the
PIEL too can be also 'active-transitive'. (In fact in the majority of the cases
the PIEL has this latter function.)[2] When used to express causativity these two
patterns are in complementary distribution regarding the roots with which they
can occur. That is, the same root cannot express causativity by both the HIFIL
and the PIEL patterns, but only with one of them.

 There are also other ways of expressing causativity in Modern Hebrew, such as
using an inherently causative predicate, like *ilec* or *garam* 'force', as in (4)
and (5) below:

(4)   hagešem hapitomi   ilec   otanu lehafsik et hatiyul
         the-rain the-sudden forced us   to-stop GM the-trip
         'The sudden rain forced us to stop the trip'

(5)   hayediʔa ʔal recah   hanasi   garma zaʔazuʔa rav
         the-news of murder-of the-president caused shock   big
         'The news of the president's murder caused a big shock'

This paper, however, will discuss only the morphological causatives. The article
will proceed as follows: section 1 provides background information, briefly presenting the system of *binyanim* (patterns) and the definition of causativity on
which this analysis is based; section 2 will include a short survey of the morphological causatives in Modern Hebrew (henceforth MH), and describe the distribution of the two *binyanim* HIFIL and PIEL; section 3 will take a closer look at
the HIFIL causatives, of which there are two types, in particular at the semantic
function of the causee. Finally, section 4 will offer conclusions and discussion.

1. Theoretical background

1.1. The binyanim

The morphology of the Semitic languages, i.e. the various Arabic languages and
Hebrew, is entirely different from that of the Indo-European languages. This is
manifested by the fact that in Semitic a large part of the vocabulary consists
of three consonantal roots which are fitted into 'patterns' so as to form the
actual words. Thus for example, we have a root *k-t-b*, which has the general
meaning 'write', and from which the following words can be derived (in (a) verbal
patterns, in (b) nominal ones):

(6) a. *katav*   'wrote' 3sgmasc

      yixtov   'will write' 3sgmasc

      kotev   'write' 3sg masc

  b. *katav*   'journalist'

      katava   'news report'

      mixtav   'letter'

      ktovet   'address'

      maxteva   'desk'

      ktiv   'spelling'

      katvanut   'typing'

      katvanit   'typist' (fem.)

As we see, all the words listed in (6) are morphologically and semantically related. The root is the semantic basis for a whole family of words, and as such is in Matthews' (1974) terms a 'lexeme', and the 'patterns' give a further modification and specification, as well as syntactic features of category, voice and aspect. The patterns are classified into two groups: the verbal ones called *binyanim* and the nominal ones called *misqalim*. Classical Arabic has 15 verbal patterns; Modern Hebrew has the following 7:

(7)   *binyan*   syntactic functions:

    PAAL (B1)   active, transitive, intransitive

    NIFAL (B2)   passive, inchoative, reflexive

    PIEL (B3)   active-transitive, causative

    PUAL (B4)   passive

    HIFIL (B5)   causative, active-transitive, inchoative

    HUFAL (B6)   passive, de-actualized

    HITPAEL (B7)   middle, reflexive, reciprocal, inchoative

According to Schwarzwald (1981) only about 23% of all the roots occur in all these patterns. The gaps in the system are partially accidental, and partially due to semantic or syntactic reasons. Sentences (8)-(12) below illustrate some of the uses of these *binyanim*:

(8) a. hu rašam   et kol hapritim barešima   (Active)
       he noted (B1) GM all the-items in-the-list
       'He noted all the items on the list'

    b. kol hapritim niršemu   barešima   (Passive)
       all the-items were-noted (B2) in-the-list
       'All the items were noted on the list'

(9) a. josi šilem   et hahešbon   (Active)
      Josi paid (B3) GM the-bill
      'Josi paid the bill'

    b. hahešbon kvar   šulam   (Passive)
       the-bill already paid (B4)
       'The bill was/has been already paid'

(10) a. reuven axal   tapuah   (Active)
      Reuven ate (B1) apple
      'Reuven ate an apple'

    b. dan heexil   et reuven et hatapuah   (Causative)
       Dan made-eat (B5) GM Reuven GM the-apple
       'Dan made Reuven eat the apple'

(11) a. horav   heviu   oto hena kšehaya   tinok   (Causative)
      parents-his brought him here when-he-was baby
      'His parents brought him here when he was a baby'

    b. hu huva   hena kšehaya   tinok   (Passive)
       he was-brought (B6) here when-he-was baby
       'He was brought here when he was a baby'

(12) a. josi mitgaleah kol   yom   (Reflexive)
      Josi shave (B7) every day
      'Josi shaves every day'

    b. hakvuca mitamenet paʔam bešavuʔa   (Middle)
       the-team train (B7) once in-week
       'The team trains once a week'

    c. hem hitkatvu   bemešex šanim   (Reciprocal)
       they write-each-other (B7) during years
       'They wrote to each other for years'

    d. haoxel   hitkarer   (Inchoative)
       the-food got-cold (B7)
       'The food got cold'

(8) and (9) illustrate the opposition Active:Passive with the PAAL:NIFAL (8a-b)
and the PIEL:PUAL (9a-b) respectively, (10a-b) the opposition Active:Causative
with PAAL:HIFIL, (11a-b) the opposition Causative:Passive with HIFIL:HUFAL, and
(12a-d) the various functions of the HITPAEL: Reflexive, Middle, Reciprocal and
Inchoative.

1.2. Causativity: a working definition

The term causativity is usually used with reference to a state of affairs in
which there is a causer and a causee, and the causer brings it about that the
causee performs an action, undergoes a process (or experience) or is in a state.
The causer may be a human Agent, as in (1) and (2) or a Force, as in (3). The

causee too may be human, as in (1) and (2), or a non-human entity as in (3). The
definition of the causative construction may focus on the situation, as does the
definition in Comrie (1981a), on matters of logic and truth value, as in
Shibatani (1976), on syntactic features and syntactic derivation, as in Cole
(1976) and Berman (1979), or on the syntactic process and the semantic changes
affecting the participants, as in Saad & Bolozky (1980).

In Dik (1980a: ch. 3) causativity is treated as a process of predicate formation by which the predicate frame of an active predicate undergoes an increase
in the number of arguments, and a change in meaning. A causative predicate has
the following meaning definition:

(13)   a causer x_0 brings it about that a causee x_1 perform the act or
        be in the state designated by the predicate.

The definition of causative constructions used in this paper is based on (13),
but is somewhat more general, because (13) refers only to one of the Dutch
causative constructions, those with the verb *laten*, whereas the Hebrew causatives
treated in this paper are semantically and syntactically of a wider range. The
working definition of causative constructions in this paper is as follows:

(14)   a causative construction is a construction which designates a state
        of affairs A in which a causer x_0 brings it about that a causee x_1
        performs an act or is in the state designated by the predicate.

When considering causative constructions, the following distinction will be made:
a distinction between two predicates involved, i.e. (i) the input predicate vs.
(ii) the output predicate; and a distinction between three states of affairs
involved, i.e.: (i) the state of affairs designated by a predication in which
the input predicate figures; vs. (ii) the state of affairs designated by the
predication in which the output predicate figures; vs. (iii) the state of affairs
which is brought about as a result of the causation, and which can be designated
by a predication with the causee as the first argument of the predicate. For
example, in sentence (15):

(15)   John strengthened the foot of the table by gluing it

the input predicate is *strong*, the output predicate is *strengthen*; the state of
affairs designated by the input predicate, or the 'pre-causative' state of

affairs is usually not made explicit in the causative predication itself, but it can be deduced from it. In the case of sentence (15) this would be something like *The foot of the table was wobbly (not very strong)*; it is, however, only implicit. The state of affairs designated by the predication in which the output predicate figures is sentence (15), i.e. John's action; and the state of affairs which is brought about is 'the leg of the table is stronger', a State. These distinctions will be used in the next section, when discussing the distribution of the two types of causative patterns in Hebrew.

2. *The HIFIL and PIEL causatives*

The following sentences exemplify causative constructions with the HIFIL and the PIEL patterns:

(16) a. hamefaked   *hic²id*   et haḥayalim
     the-commander made-march (B5) GM the-solders
     'The commander marched the soldiers'

   b. josi *heexil*   et dan et ha²uga
     Josi made-eat (B5) GM Dan GM the-cake
     'Josi made Dan eat the cake'

   c. haruaḥ   *hir²ida*   et ha²alim
     the-wind made-tremble (B5) GM the-leaves
     'The wind made the leaves tremble'

   d. hasapar   *hošiv*   et hayeled   ²al hakise
     the-barber made-sit (B5) GM the-child on the-chair
     'The barber made the child sit on the chair'

   e. hara²aš   *hirqiz*   oti
     the-noise made-angry (B5) me
     'The noise annoyed me'

(17) a. josi *hizek*   et hagader be²ezrat   kama krašim
     Josi made-strong (B3) GM the-fence with-help-of some planks
     'Josi strengthened the fence with some planks'

   b. haḥom   *yibeš*   et kol hacmaḥim
     the-heat made-dry (B3) GM all the-plants
     'The heat dried all the plants'

   c. dan *²icben*   et kulam
     Dan made-angry (B3) GM everyone
     'Dan annoyed everyone'

The underlying predications of e.g. (16a-b) and (17) are:

(16')   V-B5 $(x_0)_{Ag/Fo(causer)}$ $(x_1)_{causee}$ $(x_2)_{Go}$

(17')   V-B3 $(x_0)_{Ag/Fo(causer)}$ $(x_1)_{causee}$

Note the following points:

(i) x_0 is the causer. In MH it is never marked by any particle, i.e. is the equivalent of the nominative case of languages which have a case system.

(ii) x_1 is the causee. Its semantic function has been left unspecified for the time being; I will treat this in detail in section 3. The causee in the HIFIL (B5) constructions is always preceded by the particles *et* or *le*, and in the PIEL (B3) causatives by the particle *et*. Traditionally these are seen as the accusative and dative markers respectively.

(iii) Only HIFIL causatives can have a transitive (two-place) predicate as input; PIEL causatives always have a one-place predicate as input. (As we shall see this may not be a verbal predicate.) As a result, only HIFIL causative predicates can have three arguments; the PIEL causative predicates have two arguments.

2.1. *The distribution of HIFIL and PIEL*

As mentioned already, the HIFIL and PIEL patterns are in complementary distribution in the sense that the same root cannot form its causative with both of them, nor is the choice of one pattern or another free.[3]

Quantitatively the HIFIL is much more frequent than the PIEL. In all traditional grammars of Hebrew, only the HIFIL is mentioned as serving to express causativity, although, as demonstrated in (17), the PIEL can do so too. The regularity in the distribution of the two patterns can be (a) formulated in terms of syntactic or semantic features of the verbs in each group, or (b) formulated in terms of the input and output predicates and predications, following the distinctions made in the previous section (after the working definition of causativity). Let us consider possibilities (a) and (b) in turn.

(a) A study of all the roots in the frequency list of the commonest 200,000 words in Modern Hebrew, compiled by Balgur (1968), as well as all the verbs listed in the HIFIL in the New Hebrew Dictionary of Even Shoshan (1967), leads to the following observations:

(i)   the HIFIL is used as causative pattern for both transitive and intransitive verbs;

(ii) the HIFIL is used only with verbs which form their active in the PAAL (B1), as in (18). Otherwise, causativity is expressed by means of a separate causative predicate like *hixriah* or *ilec* 'force', as in (19):

(18) a. hasefer *nafal*   mehašulḥan
        the-book fell (B1) from-the-table
        'The book fell off the table'

   b. hahatul *hepil*   et hasefer mehašulḥan
        the-cat made-fall (B5) GM the-book from-the-table
        'The cat made the book fall off the table'

(19) a. josi *šilem*   et haḥešbon
        Josi paid (B3) GM the-bill
        'Josi paid the bill'

   b.*hamelcar   *hišlim*   et josi et haḥešbon
        the-waiter made-pay (B5) GM Josi GM the-bill

   c. hamelcar   *ilec*   et josi *lešalem* et haḥešbon
        the-waiter forced GM Josi to-pay GM the-bill
        'The waiter forced Josi to pay the bill'

(iii) The PIEL as causative is derived directly from an adjective or noun, i.e.
it is a denominal or deadjectival verb. In most cases such denominal or
deadjectival verbs occur further only in the PUAL and HITPAEL patterns.
The PIEL is then active-causative, the PUAL passive and the HITPAEL inchoative or middle. Some examples are given in (20):

(20) adjective	PIEL	PUAL	HITPAEL
ḥam	*ḥimem*	*ḥumam*	*hitḥamem*
'hot'	'heated'	'was-heated'	'got hot'
kar	*kerer*	*kurar*	*hitkarer*
'cold'	'cooled'	'was-cooled'	'got cold'
sameaḥ	*simeaḥ*		
'glad'	'made glad'		

As we see not all deadjectival verbs also occur in the PUAL and HITPAEL; the
exact nature of the gaps is, however, outside the scope of this study.
(b) When we take into consideration the distinction between input and output
predicates, and look at the resultant state of affairs, this yields some more
information. In FG each predication designates a certain state of affairs. States
of affairs may be divided into 4 types (Dik 1978) as in (21):

(21)   +Dynamic   -Dynamic

        +Control   Action   Position

        -Control   Process   State

When applying this typology of states of affairs to causative constructions we
find the following distribution: (i) In terms of the input predicate HIFIL and
PIEL differ: with HIFIL causatives the input predicate can be one- or two-place
and can occur in all four types of predications. It must belong to the category
V. With PIEL causatives the input predicate can be only an adjectival or nominal
predicate, and therefore a one-place predicate occurring only in State predications; (ii) In terms of the output predicate, HIFIL and PIEL do not differ:
the output predicate designates the causative situation, and can be only of the
types Action or Process, because causativity inherently involves change, i.e. is
+Dynamic. If the causer is Ag, the causative construction is Action, and if the
causer is Force the causative construction is Process; (iii) In terms of the
resultant predication ('caused state of affairs') the following difference arises:
the predication which results from the causative construction, the so-called
'caused state of affairs' can be an Action, Process or Position with a HIFIL
causative (i.e. an output predicate in the HIFIL) or, in the case of a few verbs
of perception and cognition, State. With a PIEL causative (i.e. an output predicate in the PIEL) the 'caused state of affairs' is always a State.

   We can now formulate the distribution of the HIFIL and PIEL causatives as
follows:

> If the input predicate is verbal, the output causative predicate will be
> in the HIFIL and the 'caused state of affairs' will be an Action,
> Process or Position (except for a few verbs of perception and cognition
> where the 'caused state of affairs' is a State);
> If the input predicate is nominal or adjectival, the output causative
> predicate will be in the PIEL, and the 'caused state of affairs' is
> always a State.

2.2. Derivation of the morphological causatives

In Dik (1980a: ch. 3) causativity in Dutch is treated as a predicate formation
operation. Specifically, the causatives formed by means of the auxiliary *laten*
'let' are derived by means of a predicate formation rule from any active predicate (except one denoting a State). Central to Dik's treatment of causative
constructions with the auxiliary *laten* is the notion of 'productivity'. Productivity, as defined in Dik (1981c), characterizes any process that can be described in general terms, i.e. as a rule applying to an open class. Such a rule
does not contain a list of items, which reflects the psychological reality of
the process. That is, it can be assumed that speakers know the rule, do not learn

all the cases to which it applies as separate items, and can apply it to new, not yet encountered cases which fulfil its input requirements. Thus, any speaker of Dutch knows that any active predicate which does not designate a State can be turned into a causative predicate by the addition of the auxiliary verb *laten*. The predicate formation rule suggested by Dik (1980a: 78-79) is the following:

(22)   CAUSATIVE PREDICATE FORMATION

input: any predicate frame $\varphi(x_1) \ldots (x_n)$ where (x_1) does not have
$\emptyset$ function (that is, the predicate-frame does not designate
a State)

output: $laten_V \varphi(x_0)_{Ag} (x_1) \ldots (x_n)$

meaning: 'x_0 brings it about that the state of affairs designated by
the input predicate-frame takes place'.

Let us see if this analysis is applicable to the HIFIL and PIEL causatives. The first condition which will have to be met is that of productivity. In the earlier mentioned frequency list of MH compiled by Balgur (1968) there are 276 roots which can occur in the HIFIL pattern. Of these 149 are causative,[4] 31 are active-transitive and 2 are inchoative. Despite its considerable frequency there are also verbs which do not occur at all in the HIFIL, although there is no morpho-logical or semantic reason for this. For example:

(23)   *šavar* 'break' 3sgmasc   –   **hišbir* 'cause to break' 3sgmasc
šaaf 'wish' 3sgmasc   –   **hišif* 'cause to wish' 3sgmasc
natan 'give' 3sgmasc   –   **hintin* 'cause to give' 3sgmasc

Verbs like those in (23) form the causatives analytically, i.e. by means of an auxiliary causative predicate. However, the group of verbs which do not have HIFIL is smaller than those which do, and they seem to form an accidental gap (I could not detect any semantic or syntactic common denominator in them). That the HIFIL pattern as causative is productive is supported by the fact that we can find innovative use of it, such as *hitrim* 'cause to donate' (3sgmasc) from the PAAL *taram* 'donated' (3sgmasc), or children's acceptance of the non standard *heehiv* 'caused to love' (3sgmasc) derived from *ahav* 'loved', found by Walden (1982). The HIFIL pattern can therefore be derived by means of a predicate formation rule similar to (22), given in (24):

(24)   CAUSATIVE HIFIL FORMATION

      input: $C.C.C._{V-B1}$ $(x_1) \ldots (x_n)$

      output: $C.C.C._{V-B5}$ $(x_0)_{Ag/Fo}$ $(x_1) \ldots (x_n)$

      meaning: 'the causer x_0 brings it about that causee x_1 is involved
                 in the state of affairs designated by the input predicate'.

Note the following points:

(i) The input predicate in (24) has to be a root whose active form is in the
PAAL pattern. *Binyanim* which form their active in e.g. the PIEL do not form
their causatives with the HIFIL, cf. (25):

(25)   *šilem* 'paid' 3sgmasc   -   **hišlim* 'made to pay' 3sgmasc

       ciyer 'drew' 3sgmasc   -   **hicyir* 'made to draw' 3sgmasc

       siper 'told' 3sgmasc   -   **hispir* 'made to tell' 3sgmasc

(ii) There is nothing in rule (24) to exclude its application to verbs which do
not occur in the HIFIL at all, such as those in (23). These verbs seem to form
an accidental gap, and should be marked in the lexicon as not occurring in the
HIFIL pattern.[5] For the rest, all the rules whose basic active pattern is in the
PAAL can be an input to rule (24), and the output will be a causative predicate.

The other causative pattern, as illustrated in (17a-c) and repeated here, is the
PIEL:

(17) a. josi hizek   et hagader   be?ezrat kama krašim
        Josi made-strong (B3) GM the-fence with   some planks
        'Josi strengthened the fence with some planks'

   b. hahom   yibeš   et kol hacmahim
        the-heat made-dry (B3) GM all the-plants
        'The heat dried all the plants'

   c. dan ?icben   et kulam
        Dan made-angry (B3) GM everyone
        'Dan annoyed everyone'

The PIEL predicates are all derived from a non-verbal predicate. It is, however,
hard to say whether they are denominal or deadjectival, because the same roots
occur both as nouns and as adjectives, and there is no independent criterion for
deciding which is basic, cf. (26):

(26)   *hazak*   'strong' / *hozek*   'strength' - *hizek* 'strengthened'

      yaveš   'dry' / *yoveš*   'drought' - *yibeš* 'made dry'

      ʔacbani 'angry' / *ʔacbanut* 'anger'   - *ʔicben* 'made angry'

There is another group of denominal verbs in the PIEL, innovations like the ones in (27):

(27)   *tafkid* 'task'   *tifked* 'functioned' 3sgmasc

      kaftor 'button' *kifter* 'buttoned'   3sgmasc

      ʔet   'time'   *ʔiyet* 'timed'   3sgmasc

Such PIEL predicates are denominal because the roots in question do not have an adjectival form at all. These verbs, however, are active-transitive and not causative.

    Thus, all we can say about the derivational regularity of the PIEL as denominal is the following: if it is derived from a root which has only nominal forms it will be active-transitive and not causative; if it is derived from a root which occurs both in nominal and adjectival patterns it will be causative. However, in this system too, there are gaps,[6] because not all the roots which occur in nominal and adjectival forms have a PIEL. This is the case with the forms in (28):

(28)   *adom* 'red'   / *odem* 'redness'   - **idem* 'made red'

      lavan 'white' / *loben* 'whiteness' - **liben* 'made white'

      raʔev 'hungry' / *raʔav* 'hunger'   - **riʔev* 'made hungry'

The PIEL is very productive in contemporary Hebrew as a denominal verb-form expressing active-transitive. As causative, however, it is neither very frequent, nor used innovatively by speakers. Therefore, the PIEL causative predicate will not be derived by a predicate formation rule similar to (24), but will be noted in the lexicon.

3. The semantic function of the causee

Let us again consider several causative constructions; those in (29) show the PIEL and those in (30)-(31) the HIFIL:

(29) a. josi *hizek*   et hagader
        Josi made-strong (B3) GM the-fence
        'Josi strengthened the fence'

   b. hašemeš *himema*   et hagagot
        the-sun made-warm (B3) GM the-roofs
        'The sun warmed the roofs'

(30) a. reuven *heexil*   et hayeled   et haaruḥa
        Reuven made-eat (B5) GM the-child GM the-meal
        'Reuven made the child eat the meal'

   b. haem   *hilbiša*   et hayeled   et hameʔil
        the-mother made-dress (B5) GM the-child GM the-coat
        'The mother made the child wear the coat'

   c. hašofet   *hišbiʔa*   et haʔed   et hašvuʔa
        the-judge made-swear (B5) GM the-witness GM the-oath
        'The judge made the witness take the oath'

(31) a. *hizkarti*   le-josi et havataḥato
        reminded-1sg (B5) to-Josi GM promise-his
        'I reminded Josi about his promise'

   b. dan *hišmiʔa*   le-josi et taklito   hahadaš
        Dan made-listen (B5) to-Josi GM record-his the-new
        'Dan made Josi listen to his new record'

   c. hasar   *hodiʔa*   laʔitonaim   et hahadašot
        the-minister made-know (B5) to-the-reporters GM the-news
        'The minister announced the news to the reporters'

In (29)-(30) the causee is preceded by the particle *et* and in (31) by the particle *le*. If the causative predicate is in the PIEL pattern the causee is always
preceded by the particle *et*. The particle *le* precedes the causee only in some of
the constructions with the causative predicate in the HIFIL. In the next section
I will go into more detail about the two types of HIFIL causative - those with
the particle *et* and those with the particle *le* - and try to answer the following
two questions:

(i) what are the particles *et* and *le*?

(ii) when they precede the causee, which semantic function does each of them
     mark?

3.1. The particles et and le

3.1.1. et

The following constructions illustrate the function of the particle *et*:

(32) a. V. Woolf katva   *et* hasefer   haze
        V. Woolf wrote-3sgfem (B1) GM the-book the-this
        'V. Woolf wrote this book'

b. ʔadayin lo raiti   *et* haseret haze
   yet   not saw-1sg (B1) GM the-film the-this
   'I haven't seen this film yet'

The underlying predications of these sentences are:

(32) a' Past katav (B1) (d1x$_i$: V.W. (x$_i$))$_{Ag}$ (d1x$_j$: sefer (x$_j$))$_{Go}$

   b' Neg Past raa (B1) (d1x$_i$: ani (x$_i$))$_{Ag}$ (d1x$_j$: seret (x$_j$))$_{Go}$

                                   (d1x$_k$: ʔadayin (x$_k$))$_{Temp}$

The particle *et* marks the Go. A typical feature of Go in FG is accessibility to
the assignment of Subj function, which then results in a passive construction.
In (32a) this is grammatically possible (though very rarely used), cf. (32c),
but not in (32b), as is shown by (32d):

(32) c. hasefer haze   nixtav   ʔal-yedei V. Woolf
        the-book the-this was-written (B2) by   V. Woolf
        'This book was written by V. Woolf'

    d.*haseret haze   ʔadayin lo nira   ʔal yadi
       the-film the-this yet   not was-seen (B2) by me

Inaccessibility of the Go to Subj function is quite frequent in Hebrew. In (32d)
it may be due to some peculiarity of the verb *raa* 'see', which is one of the
verbs of perception, and these have some idiosyncratic characteristics (on the
passive of verbs of perception and cognition see Junger 1983). However, the verb
katav 'wrote' in (32c) is a common transitive verb, yet the Go of many such
verbs cannot be assigned Subj either. Although the possibility of Subj assignment is one sign that an argument is a Go, inaccessibility to Subj assignment
may not necessarily mean that that argument is not Go. In Hebrew passive constructions are very rare, so that accessibility of the Go to Subj assignment is
very limited. For this reason, and because *sefer* 'book' is semantically the Go
of the verb in (32c), I think that the semantic function Go certainly does exist
in Hebrew, and that the particle *et* is the Goal Marker (GM). It only occurs
before a definite, singular Goal.[7]

3.1.2. le

The particle *le*, unlike *et*, can precede constituents which have several different
semantic functions. These are illustrated in (33)-(36):

(33) a. josi natan   *le*-dan   matana
        Josi gave-3sgmasc (B1) to-Dan_{Rec} present

        'Josi gave Dan a present'

(34) a. kaniti   et hasefer *le*-rina
        bought-1sg (B1) GM the-book for-Rina_{Ben}

        'I bought the book for Rina'

(35) a. yeš   *le*xa   et hasefer haze?
        there-is to-you_{Poss} GM the-book the-this

        'Do you have this book?'

(36) a. kar *li*
        cold to-me_{Exp}

        'I am cold'

In these constructions *le* marks Recipient, Beneficiary, Possessor and Experiencer.
In Hebrew none of these semantic functions is accessible to Subj assignment, and
indeed none of sentences (33)-(36) can be passivized:

(33) b.*dan nitan   et hamatana   al yedei josi
       Dan was-given (B2) GM the-present by   Josi

(34) b.*le-rina nikna   hasefer al yadi
       to-Rina was-bought (B2) the-book by me

(35) b.*hasefer haze   yešno   al yadxa?
       the-book the-this there-is by you

Sentence (36) is intransitive and has no passive anyway. The particle *le*, like
ʔal and *be*, can also sometimes occur as the obligatory preposition accompanying
a verb. In these cases it does not mark any semantic function. This is the case
with the verbs given in (37):

(37)   *šamʔa*   'heard'   3sgmasc   *šamʔa le*   'obeyed'   3sgmasc

       hicbiʔa 'voted'   3sgmasc   *hicbiʔa ʔal* 'pointed out' 3sgmasc

       kibed   'respected' 3sgmasc   *kibed be*   'offered'   3sgmasc

Such matters lie outside the scope of this paper.

3.2. The particles et and le and the semantic function of the causee

3.2.1. et

In causative constructions with the HIFIL both particles *et* and *le* can mark the
causee. With PIEL-causative predicates it is always *et*, and with HIFIL-causative

predicates it may be either. In the latter type of construction, in addition to
the *et* marking the causee, there is sometimes a second *et*, which marks the Go.
This depends on whether the input predicate was a one-place predicate, or a two-
place predicate. In the former case we get a causer and a causee in the output,
with only one *et*, and in the latter case we get a causer, a causee and a Go in
the output, with two *et*'s. There are several syntactic differences between these
two constituents marked by *et*. Cole (1976) has noted the following two main syntactic differences:

(i) Only the causee can be cliticized onto the verb. In the sentences below, (a)
is the full sentence, in (b) the causee is cliticized onto the verb, and in (c)
the Go is cliticized:

(38) a. hirkadeti   et hatalmidim   et harikud   haze
        made-dance-1sg (B5) GM the-students GM the-dance the-this
        'I made the students dance this dance'

    b. hirkadetim   et harikud   haze
        made-dance-1sg-them (B5) GM the-dance the-this
        'I made them dance this dance'

    c.*hirkadetim   et hatalmidim
        made-dance-1sg-it (B5) GM the-students

(39) a. hišbʔati   et haʔed   et hašvuʔa hazot
        made-swear-1sg (B5) GM the-witness GM the-oath the-this
        'I made the witness take this oath'

    b. hišbaʔativ   et hašvuʔa hazot
        made-swear-1sg-him (B5) GM the-oath the-this
        'I made him take this oath'

    c.*hišbaʔativ   et haʔed
        made-swear-1sg-it (B5) GM the-witness

Note that in plain active constructions the Go can be cliticized onto the verb:

(40) a. kaniti   et hasefer etmol
        bought-1sg (B1) GM the-book yesterday
        'I bought the book yesterday'

    b. kanitiv   etmol
        bought-1sg-it (B1) yesterday
        'I bought it yesterday'

(ii) Causative constructions in Hebrew occur rather seldom in the passive, but
when they do so, only the causee is accessible to the assignment of Subj function,
never the Go (unlike for example in Sanskrit - V. Bubenik p.c.):

(38) d. hatalmidim   hurkedu   et harikud   haḥadaš
     the-students were-made-to-dance-3plmasc (B6) GM the-dance the-new
     'The students were made to dance the new dance'

    e.*harikud   haḥadaš hurkad   et hatalmidim
     the-dance the-new was-made-to-dance-3sgmasc (B6) GM the-students

(39) d. haʔed   hušbʔa   et hašvuʔa hazot
     the-witness was-made-to-swear-3sgmasc (B6) GM the-oath the-this
     'The witness was made to take this oath'

    e.*hašvuʔa hazot   hušbeʔa   et haʔed
     the-oath the-this was-made-to-swear-3sgfem (B6) GM the-witness

The above sentences show that there are syntactic differences between the causee
and the x_2 Go. The behaviour of the causee is, however, identical to that of a
Go in a plain active sentence, as far as cliticizability is concerned.

It has been noted above that causative constructions cannot generally be
passivized. In the rare cases where they can, there is a strong tendency to leave
the Ag unspecified, and to leave the $(x_2)_{Go}$ always unspecified. In the following
sentences (a) is acceptable, (b) much less so, and (c) is completely ungrammatical:

(41) a. dan huaxal
     Dan was-made-to-eat-3sgmasc (B6)
     'Dan was made to eat'

    b.?dan huaxal   al yedei reuven
     Dan was-made-to-eat-3sgmasc (B6) by   Reuven
     'Dan was made to eat by Reuven'

    c.*dan huaxal   tapuah al yedei reuven
     Dan was-made-to-eat-3sgmasc (B6) apple by   Reuven
     'Dan was made to eat an apple by Reuven'

(42) a. haʔed   hušbʔa
     the-witness was-made-to-swear-3sgmasc (B6)
     'The witness was made to take the oath'

    b.?haʔed   hušbʔa   al yedei hašofet
     the-witness was-made-to-swear-3sgmasc (B6) by   the-judge

    c.*haʔed   hušbʔa   et hašvuʔa al yedei hašofet
     the-witness was-made-to-swear-3sgmasc (B6) GM the-oath by   the-judge

Of the 164 productive causative HIFIL verbs listed in Balgur (1968) only 29 can
occur in the HUFAL passive constructions. 108 of these roots do occur in the
HUFAL, but not as passive constructions. However, since passivizability is very
limited in the case of plain active transitive constructions the causee also resembles the Go in simplex sentences in this respect. This too could be evidence
in support of assigning the causee Go function. Possible counter-evidence is
furnished by constructions like (43):

(43)   dan hirgiz   et josi
        Dan made-angry-3sgmasc (B5) GM Josi
        'Dan made Josi angry'

Since *hirgiz* 'made angry' is a verb of emotion, the semantic function of Josi
might be Experiencer, Processed or $\emptyset$, rather than Go, despite the presence of
the particle *et*. Here we have to return to the distinctions made in 1.2. above
between the state of affairs designated by the causative output predicate and
the resultant 'caused state of affairs'. The 'caused state of affairs' is represented in (44):

(44)   josi hitragez
        Josi annoyed
        'Josi was/got annoyed'

In (44) Josi is either Experiencer, or Processed or $\emptyset$. But (43) does not designate the 'caused state of affairs', but the whole causative state of affairs.
In that state of affairs there is an Agent Dan, who committed an act of annoying
someone; Josi is the Go with respect to that act.

    Therefore, although there is no positive evidence that *et*-marked entities are
always Go, in the constructions which have been studied here there is no real
counter-evidence either; moreover, there is a similarity between the behaviour
of the causee and that of the Go in plain active-transitive sentences as regards
cliticizability and passivizability. Consequently I suggest that when the causee
is preceded by *et* it will be assigned Go function. The underlying predication of
HIFIL causatives will then be as in (45):

(45) $C.C.C._{V-B5}\ (x_0)_{Ag/Fo}\ (x_1)_{Go(causee)}\ (x_2)_{Go}{}^8$

3.2.2. le

The particle *le* is at first sight somewhat more problematic. As we have seen in
(33)-(36), it can mark several semantic functions. In causative constructions *le*
occurs with a fairly limited number of verbs. A list of the HIFIL causative
verbs which take *le* before the causee is given below:

(46)   *hodiʔa* 'made know', *hixtiv* 'made write', 'dictated',
       hišmiʔa 'made hear', *hera* 'made see', *hikna*
       'made acquire' (only in the context of acquiring knowledge),
       hizkir 'reminded', *hinhil* 'bequested', *hiskir*
       'rented', *hilbiš* 'made dress', *horiš* 'made inherit',
       hinʔim 'made pleasant', *hixiv* 'caused to feel pain'

These verbs are not homogeneous semantically: *hodiʔa* 'made know', *hišmiʔa* 'made
hear', *hera* 'made see', *hizkir* 'reminded' *hinʔim* 'made pleasant', and *hikna*
'made acquire (knowledge)' are verbs of perception and cognition, whereas the
rest, *horiš* 'made inherit', *hiskir* 'rented', *hixtiv* 'made write', *hinhil*
'bequested' and *hilbiš* 'made dress', are plain transitive verbs. All the verbs
form their active in the PAAL pattern, and all of them take the particle *et* in
the PAAL pattern. The first argument in active constructions is, however, for
the majority of these verbs not Ag but Positioner or Experiencer:

(47)   et hataklit   haze   kvar   šamʔati (Exp)
       GM the-record the-this already heard-1sg (B1)
       'I have already heard this record'

(48)   šaul (Pos) yaraš   et haoto haze   medodo
       Saul   inherit-3sg (B1) GM the-car the-this from-his-uncle
       'Saul inherited this car from his uncle'

(49)   naʔam   li (Exp) lišmoʔa et kol   chokam   šel hayeladim
       pleasant to-me   to-hear GM voice laughter of the-children
       'I liked hearing the sound of the children's laughter'

Exceptions where the first argument is Ag are the verbs *katav* 'wrote', *kana*
'bought' and *saxar* 'rented'.

   Causativization may in fact be viewed as a process of transitivization. If the
input verb is intransitive, an extra argument is added, the causer (who brings it
about that the predication designated by the input predicate takes place). In the
case of predicates with *et* causee, the argument which is Ag in the input predicate becomes Go in the output predicate. In the case of predicates which take *le*
causee it seems that no such change takes place in the semantic function of the
argument, and the causee remains Experiencer or Processed (or Ø). There are,
however, two verbs of emotion, *hirgiz* 'made angry' and *heʔeciv* 'made sad' which
mark the causee by *et*; moreover causative verbs of emotion formed in the PIEL
always take *et*. Here too, we would view the causee rather as Experiencer than as
Goal. There are two possible explanations for this phenomenon: either (i) there

is a certain inconsistency in the predicate frames of the verbs of perception, cognition and emotion such that some have Exp as second argument and some have Go. In this way the particle *et* remains a consistent Go marker; or (ii) the particle *et* in active constructions always marks the Go, but in causative constructions with verbs of perception, cognition and emotion it can also mark Exp (or Proc or $\emptyset$). The latter explanation seems preferable, because it retains the consistency within the group of verbs of perception and cognition, a consistency for which there is independent evidence (cf. Junger 1983). As a consequence we have to modify the claim made in 3.2.1. regarding the semantic function of the causee in the following way: 'A causee preceded by *et* is Go, except for verbs of emotion, where it is sometimes Exp (or Proc, or $\emptyset$)'. Thus there is a difference between *et* causee and *le* causee; the former is generally Go (except with some verbs of emotion) and the latter is always Exp (or Proc or $\emptyset$). A difference correlating with the two construction types is that with Go-causee the x_2 is optional, but with an Exp-causee it is obligatory. Thus in (30a-c) (x_2) can be left unspecified, but in (31a-c) it cannot. This holds for all the verbs listed in (46).

We can sum up by assigning the following predicate frames to the two types of HIFIL causatives (where [ ] means optional):

$$(50) \quad \text{C.C.C.}_{V-B5} \left\langle \begin{array}{l} (x_0)_{Ag/Fo} \ (x_1)_{Go(causee)} \ [(x_2)_{Go}] \\[2ex] (x_0)_{Ag/Fo} \ (x_1)_{Exp(causee)} \ (x_2)_{Go} \end{array} \right.$$

4. Conclusion and discussion

In this paper we have taken a close look at the morphological causative construction in Modern Hebrew, specifically at the following aspects:
1. the distribution of the HIFIL and the PIEL patterns
2. the particles marking the causee and the semantic function of the causee.

As for the first point, we saw that the distribution of the HIFIL and of the PIEL can be stated in terms of the input predicate (if verbal, the causative pattern is HIFIL, if denominal, the causative pattern is PIEL) and in terms of the 'caused state of affairs'. When the caused state of affairs is an Action, Process or Position, the HIFIL is used. When the 'caused state of affairs' is a State, the PIEL is usually used; the HIFIL occurs only with a few verbs of perception and cognition. Furthermore, only the HIFIL is productive as causative pattern, the PIEL is not. Therefore, only the HIFIL is derived by means of a predicate formation rule, and the PIEL, when causative, is marked in the lexicon.

As for the causee, we have seen that in the majority of the HIFIL and PIEL causatives, it is preceded by the particle *et* and has the semantic function Go. There is a limited group of verbs in the HIFIL where the causee has the semantic function Experiencer (or Processed or ∅) and is preceded by the particle *le*. Sometimes there is also an (x_2), which is always Go. This x_2 is optional in constructions where the causee is Go, and obligatory in constructions where the causee is Experiencer.

This paper has left some questions open which deserve separate research. Thus there is no answer to the question whether the HIFIL is derived directly from the roots in question, or from the PAAL form, i.e. from a concrete word. (As we have seen, an important restriction on the occurrence of the HIFIL as causative is that the root in question should form its active in the PAAL and no other pattern.) The answer to this question depends on what the final form in which the roots will be represented in the lexicon will be. The lexicon will also have to solve the problem of the application of rule (24) to roots which do occur in the PAAL in their active form, but nevertheless do not have a HIFIL causative (some of these are listed in (23)). The same holds for the actual form of representation of the non-productive regularities, such as the causative function of the PIEL. The occurrence of the PIEL has been described in terms of properties of the 'caused state of affairs' and of the category of the input predicate. The latter factor is part of the lexicon (unlike types of states of affairs); the problem remains that not all the nominal or adjectival predicates can form a causative verb with the PIEL.

NOTES

*   This research was supported by the Foundation for Linguistic Research, which is founded by the Netherlands Organization for the Advancement of Pure Research. I wish to thank A.M. Bolkestein, S.C. Dik, C. de Groot, J.L. Mackenzie and Y. Tobin for their remarks on a previous version of this article.

1   GM = Goal Marker. The particle *et* is in all traditional and modern grammars glossed as 'accusative'. However, since in most of the cases dealt with here it marks the Goal, and since there are good reasons not to assume that Hebrew has a case system, it is referred to here as Goal Marker.

2   Examples of the HIFIL as active and inchoative and of the PIEL as active are:

(i)   hu hizkin   meod beʔikvot hamaḥala
      he got-old-3sgmasc (B5) very following the-illness
      'He grew very old as a result of the illness'

(ii) mi himci   et hatelefon?
      who invented-3sgmasc (B5) GM the-telephone
      'Who invented the telephone?'

(iii) hu šilem   et haḥešbon
      he paid-3sgmasc (B3) GM the-bill
      'He paid the bill'

[3]

According to Saad & Bolozky (1980) the following verbs can occur both in the
HIFIL and in the PIEL as causatives, without any difference in meaning:

(iv) hirva, rivva 'saturate', hehya, hiyya 'revived',
      himʔit, miʔet 'decreased', hoviš (literary), yibeš 'dried',
      hiškir (rare), šikker 'made drunk', hogiʔa, yigeʔa 'tired
      out', hitbil, tibbel (literary), 'immersed', hinpik, nippek
      'issued', and higriv, gerrev 'drew close'

However, I disagree with viewing all these pairs as synonymous. In some cases
Saad & Bolozky themselves mention that one of the pair is literary or rare
(actually these are hardly ever used). In addition, also hiyya 'revive' and
yigeʔa 'tired out' are very rare, and higriv actually means 'sacrificed'; it
is used in the sense of 'draw close' only by children or in highly sub-
standard usage. The only pairs where both forms are interchangeable are
hinpik, nippek 'issued', hirva, rivva 'saturated' and himʔit, miʔet
'decreased'. To the best of my knowledge these three pairs form an exception
to the rule of complementary distribution between the HIFIL and PIEL. I do
not consider their existence as a sufficient reason to invalidate the general
statement regarding the distribution of the two patterns.

[4]

Verbs in the HIFIL pattern which occur also in the PAAL are historically the
causatives of the roots in question, the PAAL being the basic active form.
In Modern Hebrew, however, this causative nature is not always obvious. In
the following examples the same verb hevi 'brought' has a decreasing degree
of causativeness in (a)-(c):

(v) a. hašaliaḥ   hevi   oti hena
       the-messenger brought-3sg (B5) me here
       'The messenger brought me here'
    b. hamatos   šehimceti   hevi   oti hena
       the-plane that-invented-1sg brought (B5) me here
       'The plane which I invented made me come here'
    c. hamatos   hevi   oti hena
       the-plane brought (B5) me here
       'The plane brought me here'

In (a) the messenger is obviously the causer of 'my coming'; in (b) the plane
is less obviously the causer, but it is still the cause of 'my coming'; in
(c) 'the plane' is more the instrument by which the coming took place, i.e.
the verb hevi has no causative function. Thus whether the verb hevi is causative or not depends on the context. In my view, if we classify the verb itself, this should be done on the grounds of its derivational history - i.e.
as causative. The only clearly non-causative verbs in HIFIL are the denominal
innovations like in (vi):

(vi) hišpric 'sprinkled', hišvic 'bragged' etc.

[5]

Each root in the lexicon should carry at least the following information: the
semantic field to which it refers, the basic active binyan and a list of
patterns in which it can occur.

6   These gaps cannot be described in terms of the semantic groups of the roots in question.

7   A restriction on the occurrence of *et* is that the Go has to be +definite. With a -definite Go we get no marker:

(vii) josi kana   oto hadaš
      Josi bought-3sgmasc car new
      'Josi bought a new car'

8   The verbs which can take an optional $(x_2)_{Go}$ are (according to Cole 1976):

(viii) *heexil* 'made eat', *hifšit* 'caused to undress', *hirkid*
      'made dance', *hišbiʔa* 'made to take an oath', *hiška*
      'caused to drink', and *hilbiš* 'caused to dress'.

References

AFMAN, L.
 1983   *Les constructions pronominales en français dans la grammaire fonction-elle*. MA-thesis, Department of French, University of Amsterdam.

AISSEN, J.
 1982   'Valence and coreference'. In: P.J. Hopper & S.A. Thompson (eds.) *Syntax and Semantics 15: Studies in transitivity*, 7-35. London/New York: Academic Press.

ALLERTON, D.J.
 1982   *Valency and the English verb*. London/New York: Academic Press.

ALLIN, T.R.
 1976   *A grammar of Resígaro*. High Wycombe: Summer Institute of Linguistics.

ANCEAUX, J.C.
 1952   *The Wolio language: Outline of grammatical description and texts*. The Hague: De Nederlandse Boek- en Steendrukkerij.

ANDERSON, S.R.
 1974   *The organization of phonology*. London/New York: Academic Press.

 1975   'On the interaction of phonological rules of various types'. *Journal of Linguistics* 11, 39-62.

 1982   'Where's morphology?'. *Linguistic Inquiry* 13, 571-612.

ANDERSON, S.R. & P. KIPARSKY eds.
 1973   *A Festschrift for Morris Halle*. New York: Holt, Rinehart and Winston.

ARONOFF, M.
 1976   'Word formation in generative grammar'. *Linguistic Inquiry Monograph 1*. Cambridge, MA: MIT Press.

AROTÇARENA, C.
 1951   *Grammaire basque (Dialectes Navarro-Labourdins)*. Tours: Maison Mame.

ASHER, R.E.
 1982   *Tamil*. Lingua Descriptive Studies 7. Amsterdam: North-Holland.

AUWERA, J. van der
 1983   'Predication and expression in Functional Grammar' (Review article of Bolkestein et al. (1981)). *Journal of Pragmatics* 7, 433-442.

 1984a 'Subject vs. non-subject asymmetries in the relativization of embedded NP's'. In: W. de Geest & Y. Putseys (eds.) *Sentential Complementation*, 257-269. Dordrecht: Foris.

 1984b *Language and logic. A speculative and condition-theoretic study*. Amsterdam: Benjamins.

 1984c 'More predicative relatives in French: the "l'homme que je dis ressemble à un chat" construction'. In: J. Nuyts (ed.) *Antwerp studies in Functional Grammar*. Antwerpen: Universitaire Instelling Antwerpen (to appear).

 1984d 'Relative *that* - a centennial dispute'. *Journal of Linguistics* (to appear).

BALGUR, R.
 1968   *Resimat milot yesod lebeyt hasefer*. Jerusalem: Ocar Hamore.

BARKALI, Sh.
 1980   *Luax hapealim hašalem*. Jerusalem: Rutsin Mas.

BELL, A.
 1978   'Language samples'. In: J.H. Greenberg (ed.) *Universals of Human Language*,
         vol. I, 123-156. Stanford, CA: Stanford University Press.

BENNIS, H. & W.U.S. van LESSEN KLOEKE eds.
 1983   *Linguistics in the Netherlands 1983*. Dordrecht: Foris.

BERGSLAND, K.
 1969   'A problem of transformation in Aleut'. *Word* 25, 24-38.

 1976   'Some questions of subordination in Aleut and Eskimo'. In: E.P. Hamp (ed.)
         Papers in Eskimo and Aleut Linguistics, 11-21. Chicago: University of
         Chicago Press.

BERGSLAND, K. & W. DIRKS
 1981   *Atkan Aleut School Grammar*. Anchorage: National Bilingual Materials
         Development Center.

BERMAN (ARONSON), R.
 1979   'Lexical decomposition and lexical unity in the expression of derived
         verbal categories in Modern Hebrew'. *Afroasiatic Linguistics* 6/3.

BIRD, C.
 1966   'Relative clauses in Bambara'. *Journal of West African Languages* 5, 35-47.

BLOOMFIELD, L.
 1957   *Eastern Ojibwa*. Ann Arbor, MI: University of Michigan.

BOLKESTEIN, A.M.
 1976   'AcI- and *ut*-clauses with verba dicendi in Latin'. *Glotta* 54, 263-291.

 1980   *Problems in the description of modal verbs; an investigation of Latin*.
         Assen: Van Gorcum.

 1983   'Genitive and dative possessors in Latin'. In: Dik ed. (1983), 55-91.

BOLKESTEIN, A.M., H.A. COMBÉ, S.C. DIK, C. de GROOT, J. GVOZDANOVIĆ,
A. RIJKSBARON & C. VET
 1981   *Predication and expression in Functional Grammar*. London/New York:
         Academic Press.

BOLLENBACHER, J.
 1977   'The Basque passive'. In: W.A. Douglas, R.W. Etulain & W.H. Jacobsen jr.
         (eds.) *Anglo-American contributions to Basque studies: essays in honor of
         Jon Bilbao*, 181-192. Reno: University of Nevada Desert Research Institute.

BOLOZKY, Sh.
 1978   'Word formation strategies in the Hebrew verb system: denominative verb'.
         Afroasiatic Linguistics 5/3.

BOOMER, D.S.
 1965   'Hesitation and grammatical encoding'. *Language and Speech* 8, 118-158.

BOUDA, K.
 1973   'Berichtigungen zu einer Abhandlung über baskische Syntax'. *Fontes
         Linguae Vasconum* 15, 21-36.

BRETTSCHNEIDER, G.
 1979   'Typological characteristics of Basque'. In: F. Plank (ed.) *Ergativity:*
        Towards a theory of grammatical relations, 371-384. London/New York:
        Academic Press.

BRIGDEN, N.
 1984   'Towards a Functional Grammar of aspect in Finnish'. In: De Groot &
        Tommola eds. (1984), 179-198.

BUBENIK, V.
 1983   'Impersonal constructions in Functional Grammar'. In: Dik ed. (1983),
        183-204.

BUNT, H.
 1976   'The formal semantics of mass terms'. In: F. Karlsson (ed.) *Papers from*
        the Third Scandinavian Conference of Linguistics, 81-94. Turku: Academy
        of Finland.

CHAO, Y.
 1961   *Mandarin primer*. Cambridge, MA: Harvard University Press.

CHOMSKY, N.
 1970   'Remarks on nominalization'. In: R. Jacobs & P.S. Rosenbaum (eds.)
        Readings in English Transformational Grammar, 184-221. Waltham, MA: Ginn.

 1973   'Conditions on transformations'. In: Anderson & Kiparsky eds. (1973),
        232-286.

 1980   'On binding'. *Linguistic Inquiry* 11, 1-46.

CHUNG, S.
 1973   'The syntax of nominalizations in Polynesian'. *Oceanic Linguistics* 12,
        641-686.

COLE, P.
 1976   'A causative construction in Modern Hebrew: theoretical implications'.
        In: P. Cole (ed.) *Studies in Modern Hebrew syntax and semantics,* 99-128.
        Amsterdam: North-Holland.

 1982   *Imbabura Quechua*. Lingua Descriptive Studies 5. Amsterdam: North-Holland.

 1983   'The grammatical role of the Causee in Universal Grammar'. *IJAL* 49,
        115-133.

COMRIE, B.
 1975   'Causatives and universal grammar'. *Transactions of the Philological*
        Society 1974, 1-32.

 1976a 'The syntax of causative constructions: cross-language similarities and
        divergences'. In: Shibatani ed. (1976), 261-312.

 1976b 'The syntax of action nominals: a cross-language study'. *Lingua* 40,
        177-201.

 1976c *Aspect*. Cambridge: Cambridge University Press.

 1977   'In defense of spontaneous demotion: the impersonal passive'. In: P. Cole
        & J.M. Sadock (eds.) *Syntax and Semantics 8: Grammatical Relations*, 47-
        58. London/New York: Academic Press.

 1981a *Language universals and linguistic typology*. Oxford: Blackwell.

 1981b 'Aspect and voice: some reflections on perfect and passive'. In:
        Tedeschi & Zaenen eds. (1981), 65-78.

 1981c *The language of the Soviet Union*. Cambridge: Cambridge University Press.

COOK, W.A.
1969   *Introduction to tagmemic analysis*. New York: Holt, Rinehart and Winston.

CORUM, C. et al. eds.
1973   *You take the high node and I'll take the low node*. Chicago: Chicago Linguistic Society.

CRAIG, C.G.
1977   *The structure of Jacaltec*. Austin, TX: Texas University Press.

DAHL, Ö.
1981   'On the definition of the telic-atelic, (bounded-unbounded) distinction'. In: Tedeschi & Zaenen eds. (1981), 79-90.

DAVIES, J.
1981   *Kobon*. Lingua Descriptive Studies 3. Amsterdam: North-Holland.

DECLERCK, R.
1979   'Aspect, and the bounded/unbounded (telic/atelic) distinction'. *Linguistics* 17, 761-794.

1981a   'Pseudo-modifiers'. *Lingua* 54, 135-163.

1981b   'On the role of progressive aspect in non-finite perception verb complements'. *Glossa* 15, 83-114.

1982   'The triple origin of participial perception verb complements'. *Linguistic Analysis* 10, 1-26.

DERBYSHIRE, D.C.
1979   *Hixkaryana*. Lingua Descriptive Studies 1. Amsterdam: North-Holland.

DIK, S.C.
1975   *Universal quantifiers in Dutch*. Lisse: Peter de Ridder.

1978   *Functional Grammar*. North-Holland Linguistic Series 37. Amsterdam: North-Holland (3rd printing, Dordrecht: Foris).

1979a   'Raising in a Functional Grammar'. *Lingua* 47, 119-140.

1979b   'Funktionele morfologie'. In: T. Hoekstra & H. van der Hulst (eds.) *Morfologie in Nederland,* 72-100. Leiden: Glot-special.

1980a   *Studies in Functional Grammar*. London/New York: Academic Press.

1980b   'Seventeen sentences: basic principles and application of Functional Grammar'. In: E. Moravcsik & J.R. Wirth (eds.) *Syntax and Semantics 13: Current approaches to syntax,* 45-75. London/New York: Academic Press.

1981a   'Predication and expression: the problem and the theoretical framework'. In: Bolkestein et al. (1981), 1-17.

1981b   'Discrepancies between predication and expression in natural languages'. In: Bolkestein et al. (1981), 19-39.

1983a   'On the status of verbal reflexives'. *Communication and Cognition* 16, 39-63.

1983b   'Basic principles of Functional Grammar'. In: Dik ed. (1983), 3-28.

1983c   'Auxiliary and copula BE in a functional grammar of English'. In: F. Heny & B. Richards (eds.) *Linguistic categories: auxiliaries and related puzzles,* vol. II, 121-143. Dordrecht: Reidel.

1983d   'Two constraints on relators and what they can do for us'. In: Dik ed. (1983), 267-298.

forth-   'Nominalisaties in het Nederlands'
coming

DIK, S.C. ed.
1983   *Advances in Functional Grammar*. Dordrecht: Foris.

DIK, S.C. & J. GVOZDANOVIĆ
1981   'Subject and Object in Serbo-Croatian'. In: T. Hoekstra et al. eds.
       (1981), 21-39.

DIK, S.C. et al.
(in   'The typology of embedded predications'
prep.)

DIMMENDAAL, G.J.
1983   *The Turkana language*. Dordrecht: Foris.

DONALDSON, T.
1979   *Ngiyambaa, the language of Wangaaybuwan*. Cambridge: Cambridge University
       Press.

DOWTY, T.R.
1979   *Word meaning and Montague Grammar*. Dordrecht: Reidel.

DUIJKEREN-HRABOVÁ, M. van & A. de JONG-STUNOVÁ
1984   'De 'se-constructies' in het Tsjechisch'. Term paper, Institute for
       General Linguistics, University of Amsterdam.

EGUZKITZA, A.
1981   'On the so-called passive in Basque'. *Fontes Linguae Vasconum* 37, 233-253.

EVEN SHOSHAN, A.
1967   *New dictionary (of Hebrew)*. Jerusalem: Kiryat Sepher.

FIENGO, R.
1980   *Surface structure: the interface of autonomous components*. Cambridge,
       MA/London: Harvard University Press.

FIRBAS, J.
1966   'On defining the Theme in Functional Sentence Analysis'. *Travaux
       Linguistiques de Prague* 1, 267-286.

FORTESCUE, M.
1980   *A discourse production model of twenty questions*. Pragmatics and Beyond 2.
       Amsterdam: Benjamins.

1984   *Some problems concerning the correlation and reconstruction of Eskimo
       and Aleut mood markers*. Institut for Eskimologis skriftrække 12,
       Copenhagen.

FULLER, J.W.
1981   'Theme, rheme and word order in Ojibwa'. In: R.V. Miranda (ed.) *Minnesota
       Working Papers in Linguistics and Philosophy of Language* 7, 123-148.

GARY, J.O. & S. GAMAL-ELDIN
1982   *Cairene Egyptian Colloquial Arabic*. Lingua Descriptive Studies 6.
       Amsterdam: North-Holland.

GEEST, W.P.F. de
1973a *Complementaire constructies bij verba sentienda in het Nederlands*.
       Utrecht: HES.

1973b 'Recent advances in the theory of complementations and their relevance
       for contrastive linguistics'. In: A.P. ten Cate & P. Jordans (eds.)
       Linguistische Perspektiven, 230-241. Tübingen: Niemeyer.

1979   'Naar een beter begrip voor "Kale Infinitiefconstructies"'. *Handelingen
       Koninklijke Zuidnederlandse Maatschappij voor Taal- en Letterkunde en
       Geschiedenis* 33, 53-72.

GIVÓN, T.
1976a   'Some constraints on Bantu causativization'. In: Shibatani ed. (1976),
        325-351.

1976b   'Topic, pronouns and grammatical agreement'. In: Li ed. (1976), 149-188.

1979   On understanding grammar. London/New York: Academic Press.

1982   'Typology and functional domains'. Preprints of the Plenary Session
        Papers, XIIIth International Congress of Linguists, 4-34, Tokyo.

GOENAGA, P.
1978   Grammatika bideetan. San Sebastián: Erein.

GOOSSENS, L.
1982   'On the development of the modals and of the epistemic function in
        English'. In: A. Ahlqvist (ed.) Papers from the 5th International Con-
        ference on Historical Linguistics, 74-84. Amsterdam/Philadelphia:
        Benjamins.

GREENBERG, J.H.
1963   'Some universals of grammar with particular reference to the order of
        meaningful elements'. In: J.H. Greenberg (ed.) Universals of language,
        58-91. Cambridge, MA: MIT Press.

GREGORES, E. & J.A. SUÁREZ
1967   A description of colloquial Guaraní. The Hague: Mouton.

GREVISSE, M.
1980   Le bon usage. Paris/Gembloux: Duculot.

GRICE, H.P.
1975   'Logic and conversation'. In: P. Cole & J.L. Morgan (eds.) Syntax and
        Semantics 3: Speech acts, 41-58. London/New York: Academic Press.

GROOT, C. de
1981   'Sentence-intertwining in Hungarian'. In: Bolkestein et al. (1981),
        41-62.

1983a   'Typology of states of affairs'. In: Bennis & Van Lessen Kloeke eds.
        (1983), 73-81.

1983b   'On non-verbal predicates in Functional Grammar: the case of possessives
        in Hungarian'. In: Dik ed. (1983), 93-122.

1984   'Totally affected. Aspect and three-place predicates in Hungarian'. In:
        De Groot & Tommola eds. (1984), 133-151.

GROOT, C. de & M.J. LIMBURG
(in   'Pronominal affixes: diachrony, typology and formalisation in Functional
prep.) Grammar'.

GROOT, C. de & H. TOMMOLA eds.
1984   Aspect Bound: A voyage into the realm of Germanic, Slavonic and Finno-
        Ugrian aspectology. Dordrecht: Foris.

GROOT, W. de
1982   De SJA-werkwoorden in het Russisch. MA-Thesis, Slavic Department,
        University of Amsterdam.

GROSS, M.
1968   Grammaire transformationelle du français: Syntaxe du verbe. Paris:
        Larousse.

GVOZDANOVIĆ, J.
1981   'Word order and displacement in Serbo-Croatian'. In: Bolkestein et al.
        (1981), 125-141.

HAAS, J.
1909   *Neufranzösische Syntax*. Halle a.S.: Niemeyer.

HAGMAN, R.S.
1973   *Nama Hottentot Grammar*. Ann Arbor, MI: University Microfilms Inter-
        national.

HAIMAN, J.
1980   *Hua: a Papuan language of the Eastern Highlands of New Guinea*. Amsterdam:
        Benjamins.

HALLIDAY, M.A.K.
1970   'Functional diversity in language as seen from a consideration of
        modality and mood in English'. *Foundations of Language* 6, 322-361.

HARRIS, M.
1978   *The evolution of French syntax*. London/New York: Longman.

HATCHER, A.G.
1944   'Je le vois sourire; Je le vois qui sourit; Je le vois souriant'.
        Modern Language Quarterly 5, 275-301, 387-405.

HÄRMÄ, J.
1979   *Recherches sur les constructions imbriquées relatives et interrogatives
        en français*. Helsinki: Suomalainen Tudekatemia.

HAWKINS, J.A.
1983   *Word order universals*. London/New York: Academic Press.

HETZRON, R.
1969   'Des compléments obligatoires en hongrois'. *Word* 25, 3, 140-154.

1976   'On the Hungarian causative verb and its syntax'. In: Shibatani ed.
        (1976), 371-398.

HEWITT, B.G.
1979   *Abkhaz*. Lingua Descriptive Studies 2. Amsterdam: North-Holland.

HEIJN PAPOUSEK, A.
1983   'Subject en Object in het Spaans'. Term paper, Institute for General
        Linguistics, University of Amsterdam.

HOCKETT, C.F.
1958   *A course in modern linguistics*. New York: Macmillan.

HOEKSTRA, T., H. van der HULST & M. MOORTGAT eds.
1981   *Perspectives on Functional Grammar*. Dordrecht: Foris.

HOPE, E.R.
1974   *The deep syntax of Lisu sentences: a transformational case grammar*.
        Canberra: The Australian National University, Pacific Linguistics,
        Series B 34.

HOPPER, P. & S.A. THOMPSON
1980   'Transitivity in grammar and discourse'. *Language* 56, 251-299.

HORN, G.M.
1983   'Argument reduction'. *Linguistic Analysis* 12, 339-378.

HUDDLESTON, R.D.
1976   'Some theoretical issues in the description of the English verb'. *Lingua*
        40, 331-383.

JACKENDOFF, R.S.
1975   'Morphological and semantic regularities in the lexicon'. *Language* 51, 639-671.

1977   *X' Syntax: a study of phrase structure*. Cambridge, MA: MIT Press.

JESPERSEN, O.
1885   *Kortfattet Engelsk Grammatik for Tale- og Skriftsproget*. Copenhagen: Carl Larsens Forlag.

JOKINEN, U.
1978   *Les relatifs en moyen français*. Helsinki: Suomalainen Tudekatemia.

JONES, M. & A.R. THOMAS
1977   *The Welsh language: studies in its syntax and semantics*. Cardiff: The University of Wales Press.

JUNGER, J.
1981a   'Copula constructions in Modern Hebrew'. In: Hoekstra et al. eds. (1981), 117-134.

1981b   'The resumptive particle in Modern Hebrew relatives'. In: S. Daalder & M. Gerritsen (eds.) *Linguistics in the Netherlands 1981*, 169-179. Amsterdam: North-Holland.

1983   'The problem of the passive in constructions of perception and cognition in Modern Hebrew'. In: Bennis & Van Lessen Kloeke eds. (1983), 115-123.

KAHREL, P.
1984   *Some aspects of derived intransitivity*. MA-Thesis, Institute for General Linguistics, University of Amsterdam.

KAYNE, R.S.
1975   *French syntax*. Cambridge, MA/London: MIT Press.

1976   'French Relative 'que''. In: M. Luján & F. Hensey (eds.) *Current Studies in Romance Linguistics*, 225-299. Washington D.C.: Georgetown University Press.

KEENAN, E.L.
1975   'Logical expressive power and syntactic variation in natural language'. In: E.L. Keenan (ed.) *Formal semantics of natural language*, 407-421. Cambridge: Cambridge University Press.

1984   'Passive in Universal Grammar'. Paper read at NIAS, Wassenaar, May 1984.

KEENAN, E.L. & R.D. HULL
1973   'The logical syntax of direct and indirect questions'. In: Corum et al. eds. (1973), 348-371.

KEENAN, E.L. & B. COMRIE
1977   'Noun phrase accessibility and universal grammar'. *Linguistic Inquiry* 8, 63-99.

KIEFER, F.
1982   'The aspectual system of Hungarian'. In: F. Kiefer (ed.) *Hungarian Linguistics*, 293-329. Amsterdam: Benjamins.

KIPARSKY, P.
1973   '"Elsewhere" in phonology'. In: Anderson & Kiparsky eds. (1973), 93-106.

KRAUS, M.
1976   'Eskimo-Aleut'. In: T.A. Sebeok (ed.) *Native Languages of the Americas*, 175-281. New York: Plenum.

KUIPERS, A.H.
 1967   *The Squamish language*. The Hague: Mouton.

KUNO, S.
 1972   'Functional Sentence Perspective: a case study from Japanese and English'.
         Linguistic Inquiry 3, 269-320.

LAFITTE, P.
 1962   *Grammaire basque (navarro-labourdin littéraire)*. Bayonne: Elkar et Ikas.

LANGACKER, R.W.
 1977   *Uto-Aztecan Grammar*. Summer Institute of Linguistics 56. Arlington,
         TX: University of Texas at Austin.

 1979   *Studies in Uto-Aztecan Grammar, vol. 2: Modern Aztec grammatical
         sketches*. Dallas, TX: Summer Institute of Linguistics.

LANGENDONCK, W. van
 1983   'Remarques sur les constructions "verbe de perception + complément de
         perception directe" en français et en néerlandais'. In: C. Angelet et al.
         (eds.) *Langage, dialecte, littérature*, 439-454. Leuven: Leuven University
         Press.

LARSEN, T.W.
 1981   'Functional correlates of ergativity in Aguacatec'. *Berkeley Linguistics
         Society* 7, 136-153.

LAYCOCK, D.C.
 1965   *The Ndu language family (Sepik District, New Guinea)*. Canberra: The
         Australian National University.

LEES, R.B.
 1960   *The grammar of English nominalizations*. Bloomington: Indiana University
         Press.

LEHMANN, Chr.
 1982a   'Nominalisierung: Typisierung von Propositionen'. In: H. Seiler & Chr.
         Lehmann (eds.) *Apprehension: das sprachliche Erfassen von Gegenständen
         (Teil I: Bereich und Ordnung der Phänomene)*, 66-83. Tübingen: Narr.

 1982b   *Thoughts on grammaticalization*. Cologne: Acup (Kölner Universalienprojekt).

 1984   *Der Relativsatz*. Tübingen: Narr.

LI, C.N. ed.
 1976   *Subject and topic*. London/New York: Academic Press.

LI, C.N. & S.A. THOMPSON
 1976   'Subject and topic: a new typology of language'. In: Li ed. (1976),
         457-489.

 1978   'An exploration of Mandarin Chinese'. In: W.P. Lehmann (ed.) *Syntactic
         typology*, 223-266. Sussex: Harvester.

 1981   *Mandarin Chinese. A functional reference grammar*. Berkeley, CA: Univer-
         sity of California Press.

LIMBURG, M.J.
 1983   'The parameter preposition/postposition in word order typology'. In:
         Bennis & Van Lessen Kloeke eds. (1983), 149-159.

LINCOLN, P.C.
 1976   *Describing Banoni: an Austronesian language of Southwest Bougainville*.
         London: University Microfilms International.

LINDSTEDT, J.
 1984   'Nested aspects'. In: De Groot & Tommola eds. (1984), 23-38.

LINELL, P.
1979   *Psychological reality in phonology*. Cambridge: Cambridge University Press.

LONGACRE, R.E.
1964   *Grammar discovery procedures: a field manual*. The Hague: Mouton.

LORD, C.
1976   'Evidence for syntactic reanalysis: from verb to complementiser in Kwa'. In: S. Steever, C. Walker & S. Nufwene (eds.) *Papers from the parasession on Diachronic Syntax*, 179-191. Chicago: Chicago Linguistic Society.

LYONS, J.
1968   *Introduction to theoretical linguistics*. Cambridge: Cambridge University Press.

1977   *Semantics*. Cambridge: Cambridge University Press.

1979   'Knowledge and truth: a localistic approach'. In: D.J. Allerton, E. Carney & D. Holdcroft (eds.) *Function and context in linguistic analysis: a Festschrift for William Haas*, 111-141. Cambridge: Cambridge University Press.

McARTHUR, H. & L. McARTHUR
1966   'Aguacatec'. In: M.K. Myers (ed.) *Languages of Guatemala*, 140-165. The Hague: Mouton.

McCAWLEY, J.D.
1981   *Everything that linguists have always wanted to know about logic*. Chicago: University of Chicago Press.

MACKENZIE, J.L.
1981   'Functions and cases'. In: Hoekstra et al. eds. (1981), 299-318.

1983   'Nominal predicates in a Functional Grammar of English'. In: Dik ed. (1983), 31-51.

1984a 'Communicative functions of subordination'. In: J.L. Mackenzie & H. Wekker (eds.) *English language research: the Dutch contribution I*, 67-84. Amsterdam: Free University Press.

1984b 'Genominaliseer'. Paper, Free University of Amsterdam.

MACKENZIE, J.L. & M. HANNAY
1982   'Prepositional predicates and Focus constructions in a Functional Grammar of English'. *Lingua* 56, 43-57.

MALLINSON, G. & B.J. BLAKE
1981   *Language typology*. Amsterdam: North-Holland.

MARION, R.J.
1981   'A unified temporal theory of tense and aspect'. In: Tedeschi & Zaenen eds. (1981), 145-175.

MATTHEWS, P.H.
1974   *Morphology: an introduction to the theory of word structure*. Cambridge: Cambridge University Press.

MATTHIESSEN, Chr.
1983   'Primary tense in English'. *Studies in Language* 7, 369-429.

MERLAN, F.
1982   *Mangarayi*. Lingua Descriptive Studies 4. Amsterdam: North-Holland.

MURANE, E.
1974   *Doga grammar: from morpheme to discourse*. Norman, OK: Summer Institute of Linguistics of the University of Oklahoma.

NIDA, E.A.
1949   *Morphology: a descriptive analysis of words*. Ann Arbor: University of
        Michigan Press.

OGUNBQWALE, P.O.
1970   *The essentials of the Yoruba language*. London: University of London Press.

PALMER, F.R.
1979   *Modality and the English modals*. London/New York: Longman.

PERLMUTTER, D. & P.M. POSTAL
1977   'Toward a universal characterization of passive'. *Berkeley Linguistics
        Society* 3, 394-417.

PINKSTER, H.
1983   'Tempus, Aspect and Aktionsart in Latin (Recent trends 1961-1981)'. In:
        H. Temporini & W. Haase (eds.) *Aufstieg und Niedergang der Römischen
        Welt*, II, 29, 1, 270-319. Berlin: De Gruyter.

QUIRK, R., S. GREENBAUM, G. LEECH & J. SVARTVIK
1972   *A Grammar of Contemporary English*. London: Longman.

RADFORD, A.
1975   'Pseudo-relatives and the unity of subject-raising'. *Archivum Linguis-
        ticum* 6, 32-64.

1977   *Italian syntax*. Cambridge: Cambridge University Press.

REBUSCHI, G.
1982   *Structure de l'énoncé en Basque*. Paris: Université de Paris 7, Labora-
        toire de Linguistique Formelle, ERA 642.

RIJK, R.P.G. de
1978   'Topic fronting, Focus positioning and the nature of the verb phrases in
        Basque'. In: F. Jansen (ed.) *Studies in Fronting*, 81-112. Lisse:
        Peter de Ridder.

RIJKSBARON, A.
1981   'Relative clause formation in Ancient Greek'. In: Bolkestein et al.
        (1981), 235-259.

ROBINS, R.H.
1967   *A short history of linguistics*. Bloomington/London: Indiana University
        Press.

ROSENBAUM, P.S.
1967   *The grammar of English predicate complement constructions*. Cambridge,
        MA: MIT Press.

ROSS, J.R.
1973a   'Nouniness'. In: O. Fujimura (ed.) *Three dimensions of linguistic
        theory*, 137-257. Tokyo: TEC.

1973b   'The penthouse principle and the order of constituents'. In: Corum et al.
        eds. (1973), 397-422.

ROTHENBERG, M.
1972   'Les propositions relatives adjointe en français'. *Bulletin de la
        Société de Linguistique de Paris* 67, 175-213.

1979   'Les propositions relatives prédicatives et attributives: problème de
        linguistique française'. *Bulletin de la Société de Linguistique de Paris*
        74, 351-395.

RUWET, N.
1972   *Théorie syntaxique et syntaxe du français*. Paris: Seuil.

SAAD, N.G. & S. BOLOZKY
1980   'Theoretical implications of morphological causativization in Arabic
        and Hebrew'. Paper, University of Massachusetts.

SANDFIELD, K.
1936   *Syntaxe du français contemporain, II: Les propositions subordonnées.*
        Paris: Droz.

SAPIR, E. & M. SWADESH
1939   *Nootka Texts.* Philadelphia, PA: University of Pennsylvania.

SCHAAIK, G. van
1983   *A functional analysis of aspects of Turkish grammar.* MA-Thesis, Institute
        for General Linguistics, University of Amsterdam.

SCHACHTER, P. & Fe.T. OTANES
1972   *Tagalog reference grammar.* Berkeley, CA: University of California Press.

SCHUTTER, G. de
1983   'Modaliteit en andere modificaties in de Nederlandse grammatica'. In:
        F. Daems & L. Goossens (eds.) *Een Spyeghel voor G. Jo Steenbergen,*
        277-291. Leuven: Acco.

SCHUTTER, G. de & J. NUYTS
1983   'Towards an integrated model of a Functional Grammar'. In: Dik ed.
        (1983), 387-404.

SCHWARZE, C.
1974   'Les constructions du type "Je le vois qui arrive"'. In: C. Rohrer & N.
        Ruwet (eds.) *Actes du Colloque Franco-Allemand de Grammaire Transforma-*
        tionelle, I, 18-30. Tübingen-Niemeyer.

SCHWARZWALD, O.
1981   'Frequency factors as determinance of the Binyanim meaning'. *Hebrew*
        Studies 22, 131-137.

SEILER, H.
1977   *Cahuilla grammar.* Banning, CA: Malki Museum Press.

1983   *Possession as an operational dimension of language.* Tübingen: Narr.

SHIBATANI, M.
1976   'The grammar of causative constructions: a conspectus'. In: Shibatani
        ed. (1976), 1-40.

SHIBATANI, M. ed.
1976   *Syntax and Semantics 6: the grammar of causative constructions.* London/
        New York: Academic Press.

SHIRATSUKI, N.
1982   *On ergativity in Basque.* MA-Thesis, Kyoto University.

SMITH, L.R.
1981   'Propositional nominalization in Labrador Inuttut (Eskimo)'. *Linguistics*
        19, 63-99.

STEEDMAN, M.J.
1977   'Verbs, time and modality'. *Cognitive Science* 1, 216-234.

SUÑER, M.
1978   'Perception verb complements in Spanish: same or different?' *Canadian*
        Journal of Linguistics 23, 107-127.

1984   'Controlled *Pro*'. In: P. Baldi (ed.) *Papers from the XIIth Linguistic*
        Symposium on Romance Languages, 253-273. Amsterdam/Philadelphia:
        Benjamins.

TEDESCHI, Ph.J. & A. ZAENEN eds.
 1981   *Syntax and Semantics 14: Tense and aspect*. London/New York: Academic
        Press.

THOMAS, D.D.
 1971   *Chrau grammar*. Honolulu, Hawaii: Hawaii University Press.

THOMAS-FLINDERS, T. ed.
 1981   *Inflectional morphology: Introduction to the extended word-and-paradigm
        theory*. UCLA Working Papers 4: Working Papers in Morphology.

THORNE, J.P., R. BRATLEY & H. DEWAR
 1968   'The syntactic analysis of English by machine'. *Machine Intelligence*
        3, 281-309.

TOBLER, A.
 1896   'Relativsatz als prädikative Bestimmung'. *Zeitschrift für romanische
        Philologie* 20, 55-58.

TOMLIN, R. & R. RHODES
 1979   'An introduction to information distribution in Ojibwa'. In: P.R. Clyne,
        W.F. Hanks & C.L. Hofbauer (eds.) *Papers from the 15th Meeting of the
        Chicago Linguistic Society*, 307-320. Chicago: Linguistic Society.

TOURATIER, Chr.
 1980   *La relative*. Paris: Klincksieck.

TRITHART, M.L.
 1979   *Relational Grammar and Chichewa subjectivisation rules*. Bloomington,
        IN: Indiana University Linguistics Club.

TRYON, D.T.
 1970   *An introduction to Maranungku (Northern Australia)*. Canberra: The
        Australian National University, Pacific Linguistics, Series B 15.

VAN VALIN, R.B.
 1977   *Aspects of Lakhota Syntax*. Ann Arbor, MI: University of Michigan Press.

VENDLER, Z.
 1967   'Verbs and times'. In: *Linguistics in Philosophy*, 97-121. Ithaca:
        Cornell University Press.

VERKUYL, H.J.
 1972   *On the compositional nature of the aspects*. Dordrecht: Reidel.

VESTER, E.
 1983   *Instrument and manner expressions in Latin*. Assen: Van Gorcum.

VET, C.
 1981a 'Subject assignment in the impersonal constructions of French'. In:
        Bolkestein et al. (1981), 143-163.

 1981b 'Les constructions impersonnelles en français: une approche dans le
        cadre de la Grammaire Fonctionelle de S.C. Dik'. *Travaux de Linguistique
        (Gand)* 8, 49-64.

 1983   'Possessive constructions in French'. In: Dik ed. (1983), 123-140.

VILLASANTE, Fr. L.
 1980   *Sintaxis de la oración simple*. Oñate: Editorial Franciscana Aranzazu.

VOEGELIN, C.F. & F.M. VOEGELIN
 1977   *Classification and index of the world's languages*. New York: Elsevier.

WAGNER, R.L. & J. PINCHON
 1962   *Grammaire du français classique et moderne*. Paris: Hachette.

WALDEN (PERES), Z.
 1982   *The root of roots: children's construction on word formation processes*.
        Ph.D. dissertation, Harvard University.

WATTERS, J.R.
 1981   *A phonology and morphology of Ejagham - with notes on dialect variation*.
        Doctoral dissertation, University of California, Los Angeles, California.

WELLS, M.A.
 1979   *Siroi grammar*. Canberra: The Australian National University, Pacific
        Linguistics, Series B 51.

WELMERS, Wm.E.
 1973   *African language structures*. Berkeley, CA: University of California Press.

 1976   *A grammar of Vai*. Berkeley, CA: University of California Press.

WILBUR, T.H.
 1979   *Prolegomena to a grammar of Basque*. Current issues in linguistic theory
        8. Amsterdam: Benjamins.

ZIMMER, K.E.
 1976   'Some constraints on Turkish causativization'. In: Shibatani ed. (1976),
        399-412.

Index of authors

Index of languages and language-families

Index of subjects